T0330784

ROUTLEDGE LIBRARY EDITIONS:
SCOTLAND

Volume 4

THE WORKING CLASS IN GLASGOW

THE WORKING CLASS IN GLASGOW
1750–1914

Edited by
R. A. CAGE

Routledge
Taylor & Francis Group

LONDON AND NEW YORK

First published in 1987 by Croom Helm Ltd

This edition first published in 2022
by Routledge
2 Park Square, Milton Park, Abingdon, Oxon OX14 4RN

and by Routledge
605 Third Avenue, New York, NY 10158

Routledge is an imprint of the Taylor & Francis Group, an informa business

British Library Cataloguing in Publication Data
A catalogue record for this book is available from the British Library

ISBN: 978-1-03-206184-9 (Set)
ISBN: 978-1-00-321338-3 (Set) (ebk)
ISBN: 978-1-03-206938-8 (Volume 4) (hbk)
ISBN: 978-1-03-206940-1 (Volume 4) (pbk)
ISBN: 978-1-00-320464-0 (Volume 4) (ebk)

DOI: 10.4324/9781003204640

Publisher's Note
The publisher has gone to great lengths to ensure the quality of this reprint but
points out that some imperfections in the original copies may be apparent.

Disclaimer
The publisher has made every effort to trace copyright holders and would welcome
correspondence from those they have been unable to trace.

THE WORKING CLASS IN GLASGOW 1750-1914

Edited by R.A. CAGE

CROOM HELM
London • Sydney • Wolfeboro, New Hampshire

© 1987 R.A. Cage
Croom Helm Ltd, Provident House, Burrell Row,
Beckenham, Kent, BR3 1AT
Croom Helm Australia, 44-50 Waterloo Road,
North Ryde, 2113, New South Wales
Croom Helm, 27 South Main Street, Wolfeboro,
New Hampshire 03894-2069

British Library Cataloguing in Publication Data

The Working class in Glasgow 1750–1914.
  1. Labor and laboring classes — Scotland
  — Glasgow (Strathclyde) — History
  2. Glasgow (Strathclyde) — Social
  conditions
  I. Title
  305.5′62′0941443   HD8400.G57
  ISBN 0-7099-3415-7

Library of Congress Cataloging-in-Publication Data

Cage, R.A.
  The working class in Glasgow, 1750-1914.

  Bibliography: p.
  Includes index.
  1. Labor and laboring classes — Scotland — Glasgow
(Strathclyde) — History. 2. Glasgow (Strathclyde) —
Economic conditions. I. Title.
HD8400.G57C34 1987 305.5′62′0941443   86-24059
ISBN 0-7099-3415-7

Printed and bound in Great Britain by
Biddles Ltd, Guildford and King's Lynn

TO

Mrs. Mary Manchester

former Librarian, The Bailies Institute

Those who came into contact with Mary's
devotion to Glasgow's history also caught
the fever. To her we will always be grateful.

CONTENTS

Introduction

THE STANDARD OF LIVING DEBATE

R. A. Cage

I: The Standard of Living Debate, a Review

The standard of living debate has been with us for some time, indeed, in one form or other, since the firm establishment of industrialisation. The central issue has been whether or not workers benefited from the industrialisation process. Some of the early participants were Chadwick, Mill, Engels, Marx, the Webbs, Rowntree, Booth, Clapham and the Hammonds. The latter two are viewed as being the originators of the current approach. Clapham was representative of the optimistic viewpoint; the Hammonds were stalwarts of the pessimistic school. Two major contemporary flag-bearers are R. M. Hartwell and E. J. Hobsbawm, respectively. Both sides at various times have examined three major issues: 1) level of real wages, 2) changing patterns of consumption, and 3) the size and distribution of national income. The course of the debate up to 1975 is extremely well documented by A. J. Taylor in his introduction to *The Standard of Living in Britain in the Industrial Revolution*. As Taylor points out, there is still general disagreement on the major issues because of '1) disagreement and confusion about definitions and terms of reference; 2) limitations of, and disagreements about, the validity of evidence; and 3) differences of interpretation'.[1]

In general terms the debate has been an emotionally charged issue. It has been couched in both qualitative and quantitative terms. The qualitative arguments have centred around the question as to whether or not the quality of the working-class lifestyle improved during the years of rapid industrialisation; evidence is presented using such factors as housing conditions, diets, mortality rates and working conditions. Quantitative measurements have concentrated on developing and improving a real wage index. Both approaches have relied mainly on national data, which is heavily weighted by data for London. This spurious practice has been defended largely on the basis that some information is better than none. However, this practice is especially questionable with respect to the real wage indices which have been constructed—all are based on sketchy wage rate information (instead of earnings) and for a few occupations, and price series for different assumed baskets of goods. The main redeeming feature of the various indices is that they all tend to move in the same direction, though it is questionable as to which is the most important, trends or cycles.[2]

Hartwell claims that the historian can answer two questions about the Industrial Revolution in Britain: 'whether or not the worker's 'bundle' of goods increased; whether or not the worker willingly gave up a rural, pre-industrial way of life for the way of life of an urban industrial society'.[3] He asks that since there was substantial rural-urban migration, why should the debate continue, as workers must have at least thought they were better off. Unfortunately, the solution is not that simple, as it fails to explain fully the reasons for migration; not all migrants left rural areas because of an attraction to urban areas; some were pushed out of rural areas. Moreover, Hartwell's argument does not take into account an analysis of urban workers' real wages over a period of time. In a similar fashion, any argument for improvement based upon increasing per capita figures must be qualified, as per capita information casts no light upon the important question of income distribution. Thus, it still is not possible to state with certainty that the bundle of goods increased for the working classes.

Hartwell argues that the major reasons for a dichotomy (or, indeed, the debate) are the ideologies and prejudices of historians. That those with socialist or Marxian overtones view the industrialisation process as a destructive social element, a catastrophic experience; whereas, those with *laissez-faire* ideals view the process as one allowing growth, thus leading to more individual freedom.

> The catastrophic theory pictures the destruction of a valued way of life and its replacement by an inferior and degraded way of life, along with a deterioration in the standard of living; the growth theory sees the industrial revolution as economic growth through industrialization, with the replacement of an urban for a rural way of life, with the growing independence of the working classes, and with a gradual but sustained improvement in the standard of living for the masses.[4]

Such analysis belittles the debate and the participants, for it fails in itself to address the crucial issue of the debate, that is, did the level of living of the British urban industrial labour force improve with industrialisation, and if so, at what stage. In not addressing himself to this question, Hartwell is guilty of perpetuating the emotive arguments he claims to abhor in his opponents. Hartwell continues,

> in order to prove the catastrophic theory of the industrial revolution, it is necessary to devise a model of the English economy of the period, which will fit the facts of history, but in which there was sustained growth of output over a long period of time without raising general living standards. The exponents of catastrophe, however, have not thought of the historical problem explicitly as that of explaining how a particular example of sustained growth, the industrial revolution, resulted in falling living standards over a long period, when the expectations of common sense, economic theory and later examples of growth suggest the opposite.[5]

How can we expect historians to agree, when economists disagree on theoretical grounds as to what happens to income distribution during an industrial revolution. It has been suggested, for example, that '. . . wages must fall during the early stages of industrialism, to provide the necessary investment, profit incentive and low labour costs'.[6] Hartwell's statement is based upon empirical evidence for stable societies which have completed the social upheaval of industrialisation. His statement also assumes a homogenous working class, which is, of course, utter nonsense, as the experience of the unskilled workers was entirely different from that of the skilled, as was the case also between factory operatives and domestic servants. Even if we ignore this point, at least some of the evidence indicates that income distribution changed in such a way as to benefit the rich; 'The number of servants increased faster than population. . . a clear indication that the rich could afford to buy more of the labour of the poor, and so of the widening gap in income distribution'.[7] In support of his arguments, Hartwell never provides empirical evidence, he only asserts his case, as for example, 'In any case, income distribution could have been biased against the worker increasingly, and their real incomes could still have risen if the rate of growth of output had been sufficiently great; and during the great war against France, this is probably what happened'.[8]

Hartwell concludes by asserting that,

> the historical facts were: average per capita real incomes increased; there was no trend in distribution against the workers; the terms of trade were not so unfavourable as to seriously affect living standards; after 1815 prices fell more than money wages; per capita consumption of food and other consumer goods increased; capital accumulation did not make excessive demands on total income; government increasingly intervened to protect and raise the living standards of the poor.[9]

This statement was made in 1970; his views are essentially the same today, that is those of an optimist, in spite of mounting empirical evidence of a differing nature.

Hobsbawm rejects the optimist's arguments based upon price and wage data. His reasons are straight-forward; we cannot hope to obtain an accurate reflection of actual earnings when we know little about unemployment and when our money-wage statistics are based mainly on time-rates for skilled artisans. Thus, we know almost nothing about the vast bulk of the industrial labour force, the unskilled. Hobsbawm, therefore, centres his arguments around 1) mortality and health, 2) unemployment, and 3) consumption. He considers that the evidence in these areas supports the pessimistic view.[10] For Britain as a whole, mortality rates increased between 1811-1841, and, as we will see, for some places, like Glasgow, there was a dramatic increase. In the sphere of unemployment, Hobsbawm admits that the information is too sketchy to form firm conclusions, but he asserts that the available data indicate both higher levels and greater cyclical unemployment than would be admitted by the optimists. Thus, putting to question the statements that industrial workers enjoyed greater job security; this conclusion is supported in the recent article by D. J. Oddy on the Lancashire cotton famine.[11] In terms of consumption, Hobsbawm states, 'There is no evidence of a major rise in the *per capita* consumption of several foodstuffs, and in some instances evidence of a temporary fall which had not yet been completely made good by the middle 1840s'.[12] This, Hobsbawm suggests, represents a deterioration in the living standards of the average working-class individual. This argument is strengthened when taken in conjunction with the fact that the widespread alteration of food in the nineteenth century decreased its nutritional value.[13] In conclusion, Hobsbawm is of the opinion that deterioration occurred whether evaluated in quantitative or qualitative terms.

Within the past decade there has been an increase in the number of articles based upon the quantitative approach. The first was by M. W. Flinn, in which he reconsidered the London-based price series, coming to the conclusion that real wage gains were largely confined to the period 1813 to 1825.[14] Flinn's methodology and conclusions were questioned by T. R. Gourvish, who called for more regional information, more distinction of occupational groups, and the need to achieve a blend of retail prices and earnings.[15] A follow-up article then appeared by G. N. Von Tunzelmann. He concluded that the various general indices of prices behave in a similar fashion, though the patterns of real wages between 1750 and 1850 could have increased anywhere from no increase to one of 150 per cent. However, he makes one further extremely important point: short-term gains from increases in real wages can quickly be lost by sudden decreases in real wages.[16] Viewed in these terms, whether or not *individual* workers benefited, depends upon the point in a business cycle that they entered the labour force.

Quantitative work now appears to be dominated by two Americans, P. H. Lindert and J. G. Williamson. Williamson states that inequality in earnings of wage-earners rose sharply between the 1820s and the 1850s, after which the trend reversed, though the inequality in 1901 was still greater than in 1827. In other words the skilled benefited more from industrialisation than the unskilled, for despite the introduction of machinery there was still a high demand for skilled labour. Williamson then hedges when he claims that his results still do not answer the crucial question at the heart of the debate: 'How much of British inequality experience was due to inherent aspects of industrial development, how much to demographic forces, and how much to chance?'.[17]

Williamson and Lindert have combined forces and joined the debate, claiming that the net gain in the standard of life was over 86 per cent for blue-collar workers and over 140 per cent for all workers in the period 1781-1851,[18] presumably in spite of inequalities. With this article Lindert and Williamson become the undisputed kings of the data dazzlers.

In their article Lindert and Williamson claim to have mined an expanding data base. Furthermore,

> While optimists and pessimists can both draw support from the enterprise, the pessimists' case emerges with the greater need for redirection and repair. The evidence suggests that material gains were even bigger after 1820 than optimists had previously claimed, even if the concept of material well-being is expanded to include health and environmental factors. Although the pessimists can still find deplorable trends in the collective environment after 1820, particularly rising inequality and social disorder, this article suggests that their case must be shifted to the period 1750-1820 to retain its central relevance.[19]

In their efforts they readily admit to sketchy data on the number of days or weeks worked per year, and indeed on daily or weekly wage rates (even though they do not clearly admit it, some apprehension is expressed about the nature of wage rates). The authors attempt to improve an existing earnings series by utilising five employee classes: farm labour, middle group (largely unskilled or low skills), artisans, blue-collar workers (the aggregate of the first three), and white-collar workers. Eighteen different occupations are represented, though no attempt is made to indicate their relative importance within the labour force, and a significant group, weavers, is left out. At this stage it is interesting to note that for most of the occupations, nominal annual earnings fell between 1810 and 1851, a fact that raises problems, weakening their argument that workers moved to urban areas because they knew they would be better off. Furthermore, it should also be noted that very little new wage rate information has been incorporated into their series.

In order to obtain their ultimate goal of determining the course of real wages, Lindert and Williamson need to construct a cost of living index. Here again they use mainly existing information; however, they have made some important changes in household budgets by eliminating irrelevant industrial raw materials and including household rents. The latter was determined from a rent series based on a few dozen cottages in Trentham, Staffordshire; they claim this housing stock was of unchanging quality! These cottages were on a rural estate, thus not representative of urban working-class housing conditions. At any rate, on this basis they come up with a cost of living index which shows rising costs in the 1820s, a levelling off in the 1830s, and a slight downward adjustment in the 1840s. Overall, the downward adjustment is not sufficient to produce the doubling of real earnings which they argued occurred, especially when it is realised that their series for each group is determined on a non-weighted average basis.

Finally, their most magical work is done in terms of estimating unemployment. Using unemployment statistics for engineering, metals and shipbuilding (all skilled occupations) for the years 1851-1892 and regression analysis, they estimate unemployment levels for the 1830s and 1840s. Their conclusion is that the level of unemployment was substantially lower than all previous estimates. They fail, even, to realise that the experience of the unskilled was probably completely different than for the skilled. During periods of business downturns, employers attempted to maintain their skilled labour force, firing only the low and unskilled. Moreover, they take no account of substantial structural changes in the economy, as these three industrial groups were significantly more important after 1850 than before.

Ironically, the conclusions of these 'empirical' studies have not been questioned with any vigour, in spite of the fact that a number of regional studies negate their findings. The first serious regional study was undertaken by R. S. Neale, who examined Bath.[20] His study is important for several reasons: 1) it supplied an answer to T. S. Ashton's pleas for more than one index, as Neale compares the experience of non-agricultural labourers in Bath for two time periods, 2) it extended the time period of the debate, recognising the importance of making comparisons between the pre- and post-Napoleonic Wars period, 3) it was the first detailed regional study, and 4) it was the first study to compute a retail price index and an earnings index. As such it offered conclusions which were different from the traditional, national approach. To date, Neale is the only author to consider the age-cohort approach to determine the wage and life experience of workers. Other regional studies undertaken by T.R. Gourvish,[21] L.D. Schwarz[22] and myself[23] support Neale's general conclusions about regional differences and, indeed, the general pattern of real wage movements. These case studies, taken collectively, must put to question the value of conclusions based upon nationalised trends.

II: The Standard of Living, Some Relevant Questions

In spite of nearly 150 years of controversy, we are still far from agreement as to the actual impact of industrialisation on the standard of living of the working classes. I have already indicated some of the major reasons for the lack of agreement, such as the persistent use of sketchy, national data, with some regional modifications. But perhaps the major failure of the debate has been the inability to establish common parameters. Some suggestions for correcting this situation will be made in this section.

Most participants of the debate agree with the need to construct a real wage index for the working classes. This in itself has problems and limitations. First, a single index fails to take into consideration the fact that the working class is not a unified group, but rather a collection of numerous occupations with different skill levels, different expectations, and different experiences. Moreover, rates of pay were different for males, females and children. Ideally, therefore, we need an index to cope with these issues. This, of course, is probably aiming for the impossible. However, without such detail it is not possible for the optimists to claim that, without doubt, the standard of living of the working class improved. Second, even if a series of real wage indices could be constructed, their usefulness would still be limited, as real wages provide no indication of workers' real income. In order to determine the latter it is necessary to obtain detailed information on employment patterns for all groups. All real earnings series constructed to date have a major drawback, for they only include male workers, ignoring females and children. Thus, for a more accurate picture it is necessary to reconstruct family real incomes, adjusted over time to account for changing participation rates, as women and children were forced to leave the labour force. If family real incomes were to remain constant, it would be necessary for the male's real income to increase at fairly substantial rates. It is also important to adjust family earnings by changing age structures and by the age and date of entry into the work force. Finally, real wage indices do not cast any light on income distribution. It is possible for real wages to increase, yet at the same time for the gap between low and high income earners to widen. In such a situation there would be a deterioration in the standard of living for the lower income earners. It is indeed unfortunate that given our present state of knowledge, it is doubtful if we will ever be able to reconstruct accurately income trends.

It is necessary to extend the time bounds of the debate, rather than deal in isolation with the generally accepted period of initial industrialisation. We should study the experiences of various groups within society before, during and after the Industrial Revolution, treating each group separately. At the same time we should narrow the time period, as individuals did not live through the whole period. It is individuals we are interested in, not an average mass. It is irrelevant to people if future generations enjoy more benefits. The central issue in the debate should be whether or not most people were able to enjoy a better standard of living within their own life time. By both extending the time period and breaking it up into shorter periods for analysis, it should then be possible to determine if and when improvements occurred for the various groups within society.

In a similar vein many more regional studies are necessary. We already have enough case studies, indicating sometimes extreme variation, to challenge seriously the practice of extending to a national level conclusions derived from local information. Yet, this practice continues. We know that different areas experienced industrialisation at different times and with varying degrees of intensity, yielding different consequences. Only by piecing together numerous local/regional studies will it ever be possible to construct a comprehensive picture of the British industrialisation process.

The pre-twentieth century characteristics of the debate were centred around the quality of life components. Within the past fifteen years there has been a swing back to these factors, largely on the basis that they yield the most complete information and because of the upsurge in social research. Thus far mortality, housing, working-class diets, and working-class political movements have received prime emphasis. Besides these, it also seems necessary to evaluate a number of others: education, leisure activities, sanitary conditions, morbidity and poor relief. Even the traditional four need amplification. For example in most discussions mortality rates have been for selected areas, on average for the whole population, for the years 1800-1850. Surprisingly different results can be obtained by extending the time period, by looking at age-specific groups, especially infant mortality, the sexes, and by breaking the rates up into broad occupational levels, such as skilled, unskilled, professional. Thus mortality rates could readily lend themselves to greater quantification. The same could be said for housing. It is not enough to state that the quality of housing improved or deteriorated. We need to know over a longer time scale the number of houses constructed and how they were financed, the density per house, and the level of rents for each type. Finally, working-class political movements could serve as a barometer for working-class feelings and attitudes. For instance it would be nice to know the extent of their protests—what were the issues, the frequency, the results, the reasons for protest, and even the reasons for a lack of protest?

The five proposed new areas where much more detailed study is called for also have the potential to yield more than emotive, descriptive material, as each to a degree is quantifiable. In terms of education we should examine the period of establishment and number of public and private schools, their respective number of students and their backgrounds, number of teachers, methods of finance, level of fees, and finally, the curriculum. It is important to know the point in time in which working-class people in general received the benefits of education. It is also important to know if there were losses associated with education. Unfortunately, a detailed study of education in Glasgow has yet to be undertaken. Before the second half of the nineteenth century, very little is known about how the working classes utilised their non-working hours. Some light could be cast on this by determining the number of public houses at any point in time, by the establishment of parks, by the development of spectator sports and by examining the course of attendance records at such activities. Changes in sanitary conditions, or at least those in the public sphere, are easy enough to trace, and can be measured by such factors as the extension of provision for water, the rate of extension of sewage facilities, determining for both the neighbourhoods of most extensive development. Morbidity rates can also cast light on the quality of life issue, for from hospital records it should be possible to determine the types of disease and their incidence, allowing us to draw some conclusions about class propensities with respect to disease. Poor relief information should enable us to estimate the incidence of poverty over time, and society's willingness to care for the destitute.

The above suggestions for expanding the nature of the debate are perhaps idealistic. Yet, this would merely be a reflection of the debate as a whole. The major impact of the debate has not been who is right and who is wrong. Rather, the most important aspect has been the amount of research into primary source material that has resulted from the desire to prove one's 'rightness'.

In what follows, no pretension is made about providing the final answers. We are expanding the parameters of the debate. We are analysing in a microcosm the experiences of the working class in its various components. We are looking at the experience of one major British industrial centre.

III: A Summary of the Findings

In a 1983 article I argue that average real wages for workers in 19 occupational groups fell after 1815 until at least 1839.[24] Unfortunately, wage rate data after 1840 for Glasgow simply is too sparse to enable the construction of a real wage index for the later part of the nineteenth century. Even if it were possible to construct such an index, it would not cast all that much light on the actual experiences of members of the working class. It would still not be possible to state with certainty that their living standards had changed significantly in any direction as a result of the industrialisation process. We just do not know enough about income distribution. In the same article I concluded, after examining a number of other factors such as housing, mortality rates, consumption patterns, that the conditions of the skilled members of the work force improved, while those of the unskilled realised no improvements. To a large extent, I feel that the chapters in this volume tend to support that conclusion.

Chapter One indicates that as the nineteenth century progressed, the economic activity of Glasgow shifted from being centred around cotton textiles to an emphasis upon engineering and machinery, industries requiring more skilled labour. However, it is not possible to determine the relative composition of the labour force in terms of the skilled and the unskilled. In spite of an increase in industrial employment, in relative terms this sector fell compared to the commercial and transportation sectors, areas of the economy which possibly had lower wages. Even if there were an increase in wages, family incomes probably were lower after 1861, as a result of the percentage of women in the labour force decreasing and because of a drop in the percentage of males under the age of 20 in the labour force. Thus, unless there was a significant increase in real wages, family incomes had to fall. The limited available evidence does not demonstrate such a massive wage increase. This conclusion is supported by the fact that the population in the suburbs grew at a faster rate than in the city, and that the average age of the population of the city increased as the century progressed, as a result of those in the younger age groups moving out:

John Butt in Chapter Two examines the experience with respect to housing. In particular he looks at the number and type of houses being constructed, and who was responsible for the construction. Most of the housing was built by individuals and partnerships on a small scale, utilising little capital. As population increased, it was not possible for the available housing stock and the small annual additions to keep pace. For this reason housing was sub-divided, and the notorious practice of having lodgers developed. The scale was such that for every two householders there was one lodger. Thus, serious overcrowding occurred. Professor Butt further argues that low incomes and irregular work ensured that adequate housing could not be obtained for large numbers of the working class. Moreover, many families were forced to live in 'single-ends', or a one-room dwelling within the tenements. It was in this environment that the town council stepped in to help try to provide more adequate housing. Under the Improvement Trust model lodging houses were constructed and operated, houses were ticketed for lodgers, and a little over 2,000 houses were constructed. Thus, by the end of the century some of the problems of overcrowding had been reduced, though there was still a persistent problem.

In Chapter Three I examine the state of health in nineteenth century Glasgow. A major feature was the emergence of health crises beginning in the 1820s and lasting until the 1870s. These crises were the result of typhus and cholera epidemics. Such periods of crises had not been experienced in Glasgow since the late-seventeenth/early-eighteenth centuries. The deterioration of the mortality rate was not the result exclusively of infant mortality rates, but for all age groups, and especially the 20-40 age bracket. The cause was a combination of a number of factors: a lack of adequate sanitary facilities, overcrowding, and poor nutrition resulting from low incomes and insecure employment. Improvements came with the introduction of a pure water supply, a decrease in overcrowding, and other sanitary improvements resulting from the establishment of the Health Department. By 1900 mortality rates were back to the level they were at the beginning of the nineteenth century.

In Chapter Four I examine the state of poor relief and provision for the unemployed. I argue that the lot of the poor and the unemployed worsened during the century. Provision for both groups was not increased, and indeed, for the unemployed after 1852 they were no longer eligible for relief from the public funds. The attitude of the administrators hardened. Glasgow was no longer a leader in poor relief reform, but rather a follower.

Dr Hutchison examines in Chapter Five the impact of the working classes on Glasgow politics. The basic conclusion is that their involvement was minor, and that Glasgow's shift toward the Labour Party occurred after the First World War. Indeed, working-class involvement in politics was probably greater in the first quarter of the nineteenth century than later. There was considerable merging of the working class with middle class endeavours for change, yet the working classes should not be viewed as having been subservient to middle-class ideals. Nonetheless, a clear working-class political philosophy or identity did not emerge in Glasgow until the twentieth century.

Elspeth King's chapter on leisure activities provides an indication that the working classes did enjoy some benefits from industrialisation. However, even here some caution must be expressed. At the beginning of the nineteenth century most leisure activities were pursued on an individual basis, with little regulation. As the century progressed, activities became more organised and regulated; value judgements were imposed on the moral worth of the various types of leisure activities, resulting in severe restrictions being placed on some. Hence, even in their non-working hours, the lives of the workers were overseen by their masters.

IV: Acknowledgements

The job of an editor is a varied one. A team must be assembled, the various authors charged with the responsibility of fitting their contribution into the central theme. The editor's task can be either pleasant or a nightmare, especially as deadlines approach. My task has largely been a pleasure.

I first lived in Glasgow in the early 1970s, and have made numerous return trips since. The more I learn about the city, the more I am intrigued. To me, heaven is contained within Glasgow and its people. Special thanks are extended to Marlene, Alison, Anne, Sandie, Shiela, Blythe, Tony, Dennis, Charles, Iain, Tom, David, Frank, Gerry, Danny, Stewart, and John for helping to make Glasgow so fantastic.

This book is important to me for another reason: I typeset it utilising TEX and a laser printer. Difficult problems were solved by members of the University of New England Computer Centre, especially Julian Creedy. So, in the true sense of the meaning, all errors in presentation are my responsibility.

Notes

1. A. J. Taylor, ed., *The Standard of Living in Britain in the Industrial Revolution* (Methuen & Co., Ltd., London, 1975), p. xviii.
2. See G. N. Von Tunzelmann, 'Trends in Real Wages, 1750-1850, Revisited', *Economic History Review*, second series, XXXII (February 1979), pp. 33-49.
3. R. M Hartwell, 'The Standard of Living Controversy', in Hartwell, ed., *The Industrial Revolution* (Blackwell, Oxford, 1970), p. 170.
4. *Ibid.*, pp. 172-3.

5. *Ibid.*, p. 173.
6. Harold Perkin, *The Origins of Modern English Society, 1780-1880* (Routledge & Kegan Paul, London, 1969), p. 138.
7. *Ibid.*, p. 143.
8. Hartwell, 'The Standard of Living Controversy', p. 176.
9. *Ibid.*, pp. 177-8.
10. E. J. Hobsbawm, 'The British Standard of Living, 1790-1850', A. J. Taylor, *The Standard of Living*, p. 66.
11. D. J. Oddy, 'Urban Famine in Nineteenth-Century Britain: The Effect of the Lancashire Cotton Famine on Working-Class Diet and Health', *Economic History Review*, second series, XXVI (February 1983), pp. 68-86.
12. Hobsbawm, 'The British Standard of Living', p. 76.
13. See John Burnett, *Plenty and Want* (Scolar Press, London, 1979).
14. M. W. Flinn, 'Trends in Real Wages, 1750-1850', *Economic History Review*, second series, XXVII (August 1974), pp. 395-413.
15. T. R. Gourvish, 'M. W. Flinn and Real Wage Trends in Britain, 1750-1850: A Comment', *Economic History Review*, second series, XXIX (February 1976), pp. 136-42.
16. G. N. Von Tunzelmann, 'Trends in Real Wages', pp. 33-49.
17. J. G. Williamson, 'Earnings Inequality in Nineteenth-Century Britain', *Journal of Economic History* 3 (September 1980), pp. 457-75.
18. Peter H. Lindert and Jeffery G. Williamson, 'English Workers' Living Standard during the Industrial Revolution: A New Look', *Economic History Review*, second series, XXVI (February 1983), pp. 1-25.
19. *Ibid.*, pp. 1-2.
20. R. S. Neale, 'The Standard of Living, 1780-1844: A Regional and Class Study', *Economic History Review*, second series, XIX (August 1966), pp. 590-606. See also R.S. Neale, *Writing Marxist History* (Blackwell, Oxford, 1985), pp. 109-41.
21. T. R. Gourvish, 'The Cost of Living in Glasgow in the Early Nineteenth Century', *Economic History Review*, second series, XXV (February 1972), pp. 65-80.
22. L.D. Schwarz, 'The Standard of Living in the Long Run: London, 1700-1860', *Economic History Review*, second series, XXXVIII (February 1985), pp. 24-41.
23. R. A. Cage, 'The Standard of Living Debate: Glasgow, 1800-1850', *Journal of Economic History* XLIII (March 1983), pp. 175-82.
24. *Ibid.*, p. 178.

Chapter One

POPULATION AND EMPLOYMENT CHARACTERISTICS

R. A. Cage

I: The Development of Glasgow, a General Outline

Glasgow was a working-class city. The Industrial Revolution did not alter this reality. In 1841 nearly 94 per cent of the individuals enumerated in the occupational census were classified as working class; by 1901 the corresponding figure was reduced slightly, to 91 per cent. During this period, however, Glasgow underwent a major metamorphosis, reflecting a period of rapid industrialisation, one causing dramatic structural changes within the economy.

Numerous excellent histories of Glasgow have been written. From these, and especially those by Andrew Gibb,[1] W. Forsyth[2] (especially useful for spatial distribution of firms and industries) and S.G. Checkland[3], it is possible to describe the course of the economic, social and geographical development of Glasgow. In fact, for the urban historian, Glasgow provides an excellent case study of rapid growth, a plateau of prosperity and reform, and then decline. During its heyday Glasgow was a familiar name in every corner of the world. Clyde-built engines drove the world's machinery; Clyde-built steamers commanded the seas; the machinery-engineering industries of Glasgow were the centre piece of the industrial showcase.

In general terms the story is well-known. The sleepy little cathedral and university town on the River Clyde came alive with the expansion of tobacco production in colonial America. By 1750 over half of the British tobacco trade was controlled by Glasgow merchants. They accomplished this by establishing a series of internal warehouses and stores in the tobacco-growing areas, thus stream-lining the production and distribution process. Moreover, the Clyde ports were located considerably closer to Virginia than were the English ports. This geographical advantage combined with new commercial techniques allowed the Glasgow merchants to control the market. The result was the accumulation of massive fortunes. A portion of their new-found wealth was used for conspicuous consumption—building their mansion houses and creating the first major expansion of the medieval city. The remaining wealth was ploughed back into investment opportunities. It was these tobacco lords who quickly recognised the significance of mechanisation within the cotton textile industry. They were able to utilise both their wealth and established networks in the Americas to exploit to full advantage the potential offered by the industrialisation of textiles. By 1755 the Industrial Revolution had made its mark on Glasgow; besides the tobacco trade Glasgow's citizens were also active in the manufacture of woollen, cotton and linen cloth, leather goods, furniture, pottery, glass, rope, and wrought iron. Partly as a result of the activities of the tobacco merchants, Glasgow developed a commercial infrastructure, including banks, port facilities, and warehouses. These activities were essential for the continued development of the city.

The tobacco trade suffered a decline with the American War of Independence. This, however, did not prove to be detrimental to Glasgow's development, mainly because the major economic activity of the city was focused increasingly upon textiles. Glasgow during the third quarter of the eighteenth century was a major British centre for the linen industry. The city's spinners and weavers were noted for their highly developed skills, indeed, it has been argued that, 'Until about 1780, the skill of the local hand-spinners was better employed in producing fine linen yarns than in working up the finer cotton yarns on spinning jennies, since this yarn was weak and suited only for the weft in cloths of mixed fibres'.[4] Only in 1779 was the problem overcome when Samuel Crompton introduced his spinning mule. From that date there was a shift into cotton textiles and for the next three-quarters of a century the economic livelihood of Glasgow depended upon cotton textiles and related industries, such as chemicals, machinery and steam engines. The city's cotton manufacturing was concentrated in three broad categories: a) large-scale spinning and power loom weaving firms, b) handloom weavers, and c) sewed muslin makers.

The spinning-cum-weaving mills frequently were large scale, most employing between 1,000 and 2,000 people. Power looms were first installed in the larger spinning mills, as these establishments were the only ones capable of gathering together sufficient amounts of capital.

> The cotton spinning industry had been mechanised before the weaving branch and was firmly established in the city in the 1830's. Originally the purpose of the mills was to supply cotton yarns to the handloom weavers but later many firms expanded by adding power-loom sections

and also began to supply yarns to independent weaving concerns. In 1840 there were 44 cotton spinners in Glasgow alone, and this number further increased to over 50 in 1861 when this branch of the industry reached its peak. It was estimated that out of the formidable total of 1,915,000 cotton spindles employed in Scotland, Glasgow possessed about 1,200,000.

    The first power-loom factory in the Glasgow district was established by John Monteith in Pollokshaws at the dawn of the nineteenth century. It contained 200 looms. From that date the weaving establishments multiplied until in 1861 they reached the figure of about 60. Some were quite large, employing frequently from 1,500 to 2,000 workers, and they contained in all about 20,000 looms served by up to 12,000 employees. The largest proportion was occupied in the manufacture of plain goods which gave rise to the development of the bleaching, dyeing and printing industries where another army of workers, only slightly less numerous was employed.[5]

After 1860 both spinning and weaving decreased significantly in importance. Though, in comparison to spinning, weaving did not suffer so complete a fall. With the introduction of the power loom, the fate of the handloom weaver was sealed.

> When it is considered that about four handloom weavers are required to equal the output of one power loom, and that only one female weaver is required to operate four power looms of the non-automatic type, it becomes increasingly clear that the hand process cannot compete successfully with the mechanised operation. . . the decline in handloom weavers' wages [coincided] with the increase in the number of power looms in the Glasgow area.
>
>   In spite of the disastrous fall in wages, there were still about 37,000 cotton handloom weavers in the West of Scotland in 1830 and 10,000 managed to survive until 1872. It may be suspected, however, that most of them were women and children working at home in their spare time whilst the chief bread-winner had another occupation, since it appears that the wage rate was considerably below the subsistence minimum of a single person. After 1875 they virtually disappeared from the industrial life of the region, the last survivors being the Paisley Shawl weavers, but even their highly-specialised trade was already doomed.[6]

Even though sewed muslin makers comprised a major industry, they disappeared from the Glasgow industrial scene by 1900. This occupation was extremely labour intensive; at the peak of its activity the industry employed approximately 200,000 women in Glasgow. Trouble arose with the collapse in 1857 of the Western Bank, which had financed most of the firms in the industry.

> As a result of the collapse, vast stocks of merchandise came under the auctioneer's hammer and were unloaded on the market at ridiculously low prices which enabled the poorer classes to start buying and wearing these embroidered muslins. This immediately caused a loss of popularity

amongst the usual consumers and even when the markets became stabilised again, in 1860, the demand could not be found. In 1861 there were still 7,220 people employed in sewed muslins in Glasgow alone but the industry continued to decline. . . Its collapse was hastened by the development of embroidery machines in Switzerland with which the hand processing could not successfully compete even though it was considered more durable.[7]

The development and progress of the machinery industry was largely a response to other industrial developments. As the textile industry expanded, so did the engineering sector. In a sense its foundations can be traced to the development of the steam engine, with most being made for the expanding cotton textile industry. Indeed, some of the early machinery-producing firms originated as textile firms. Their evolution to engineering resulted from a need to design and build new and improved machines for their operations. As new industries came into existence, engineering firms changed their emphasis to cater for the new demands. For example the second major new development was the formation of locomotive machinery. As the railway age came into being, this branch of the engineering sector became an important component of the city's economic structure.

At first a number of general engineering firms experimented with the manufacture of the new locomotive, and some for a time combined marine and locomotive engineering. From the 1850's, however, locomotive engineering became a separate, specialised branch of the industry. The first to specialise solely in this branch of engineering was the firm of Neilson & Company of the Hyde Park Locomotive Works. The firm was founded as a general engineering concern in 1836 by a son of James Neilson, the inventor of the hot-blast, and first started the manufacture of locomotives about 1843.

.   At the same time the rapidly developing coal and iron industries of Lanarkshire were making their own special demands on the engineering industry. In addition, a new and important machine tools industry was growing up in the area. Indeed, the improvement and expansion of the iron industry was providing the basis for a growing number of engineering products. The position by the middle of the century was one in which the textile industry still held its own, but side by side with it there existed a rapidly expanding group of metal industries.

Early in the second half of the century the pattern was radically altered. For some time the cotton industry had just been holding its own with difficulty against increasing foreign competition. The financial crisis of 1857 seriously weakened the industry and depleted its ranks. The final blow came with the outbreak of the American Civil War, when the industry was cut off from its main sources of supply. Many suffered heavy losses and the industry fell into a decline from which it never recovered. The young, expanding metal industries, which had been steadily gaining on the cotton industry, now reigned supreme.

In the development of the heavy industries in the Glasgow region overseas trade played an important part from the outset, although it is almost impossible to determine its relative importance in their development or disentangle its influence from that of domestic factors. No doubt many branches of engineering, if not all, started originally to supply the needs of local industries. At the same time, the presence of plentiful supplies of coal and iron in the area provided the basis for an engineering industry on a scale too vast to meet only the requirements of the domestic market and thus enabled it to satisfy a growing foreign demand for metal goods.[8]

Perhaps the most important aspect for continued growth of the machinery industry centred around the utilisation of steam engines for ships. Even though the shipbuilding industry was located a short distance outwith Glasgow, the major engine works were situated within Glasgow. To some extent the growth of the marine engine and locomotive sectors enabled engineering firms in Glasgow to withstand the vicissitudes of the business cycles, particularly as these firms were also engaged in the essential international market.

A final important engineering activity to consider was the machine tool firms. They were highly specialised, producing mainly tools for the local heavy industries. They supplied the needs of shipbuilding, heavy machinery, and the iron and steel industries. Thus, Glasgow engineering firms catered for the whole spectrum of engineering activities.

In spite of the appearance of infinite variety and diversity, however, the industrial pattern which emerged from the nineteenth century was one of extreme specialisation in the heavy industries, and this was reflected in the structure of the city's engineering industry. According to the returns of the 1901 Census Report 53,382 or some 21 per cent of the occupied male population were engaged in the category of "metals, machines, implements and conveyances." Of these, 6,306 were engaged in the iron and steel industry, 3,010 on ships and boats and 34,757 in engineering and machine making. The latter was in fact predominantly of the heavy type, and these three together accounted for nearly 83 per cent of the total in this category. In addition, tool making in the area was geared to the heavy industries. The manufacture of vehicles accounted for just over 4 per cent, and of these the largest number were employed in the manufacture of coaches and carriages, while next in importance came railway coaches and waggons. Cycle and motor manufacture together employed only 350. The diversity comes under the heading "miscellaneous," in which group are listed seventeen different trades, but together these employed only 4,819 or 9 per cent of the total in the engineering and metal trades.[9]

The following lengthy quotation serves as an excellent summary of the general trend of development within Glasgow.

Glasgow's growth can be discerned in the growth of its built-up area, the changing structure of its employment and in the constantly changing locational interaction of its commercial, industrial and residential activities. Between 1775 and 1800 the city's built-up area nearly trebled whilst its population doubled. This growth was dominantly eastwards where a booming cotton industry was fast expanding on greenfield sites in the industrial villages of Calton, Mile-end and Bridgeton. Rapid growth was also occurring elsewhere, in the industrial, weaving and engineering suburbs of Anderston in the west, and Hutchesontown in the south, both of them with access to the Clyde; and in the north where the Forth and Clyde and Monkland Canals delivered grain, timber and coal for the brewing, distilling, milling, sawmilling and chemical industries at Port Dundas. Northwest of the old core, round the town cross, a residential west end began to emerge as the commercial élite exchanged the cramped tenements of the old city for more desirable ones on newly feued land south of George Square.

By 1825 the city's built-up area and its population had again doubled and its westward migration had begun. A clear division of spatial function had appeared, and distinct industrial, commercial and residential areas can be recognised. Existing industrial areas grew. But, like commerce and residence, industry also advanced westwards and northwards to new sites. The eastern edge of the city changed little despite the continuing development of cotton production. Northwest of Glasgow Cross residential expansion was underway as the civic élite moved from the desirable tenements of the 1790s and 1800s to the space and terraced respectability of a second west end on Blythswood Hill. But they moved only their homes. Their counting houses remained in the discarded residences of the earlier west end. Eastwards lay an area of obsolescent structures, low amenity, and jumbled activities which still retained remnants of its former centrality: the town Green, the Cross, the Exchange and the University. Into these cast-off buildings crowded warehouses, workshops and a growing stream of rural immigrants.

Expansion was most dynamic around 1850. Since 1825 the city's population had again doubled and was increasing by some 7,000 a year. And the growth of the built-up area was the largest of any of the time periods. Moreover the first major changes occurred in the city's political area. By 1850 the new parliamentary burgh was, at 20 square kilometres, treble the area of the old royalty in 1800. The built-up area continued its dominantly westward growth along the Clyde and the northern canals. But this hid an array of other changes. Much of the physical increase was due to the filling up of space in the industrial areas. Residential expansion was primarily in the west, where elegant terraces and circuses were being built for the high income groups. By 1850 the commercial and cultural élite, together with their solicitors, accountants and bankers, were living near the River Kelvin, 2-4 kilometres from the old core. In the old city little residential building had occurred for years. Yet this was the area which had long attracted immigrants. With heavy and uncontrolled immigration in the 1840s—the city's population rose by 70,000 in the decade—an old housing problem degenerated into an acute social crisis. By 1851 nearly 13 per cent of the city's people were paupers.

Grossly overcrowded and ravaged by epidemic diseases, the immigrant and the poor inhabited an x-shaped zone of decaying structures centred on Glasgow Cross.

Between these areas of patrician comfort and proletarian blight lay Glasgow's commercial core, whilst around them was the horseshoe of industrial sections which had appeared between 1775 and 1825. In them change was extensive. New industries had appeared. In Anderston, shipbuilding and marine engineering eclipsed the textile sector. And from Hutchesontown to Tradeston textile bleaching and finishing, shipbuilding and engineering all grew. For the riverside activities, the improvement of the harbour and the Clyde navigation was a major influence. Between 1825 and 1850 quayage quadrupled to one kilometre whilst the river's depth increased to 4.4 metres. But both they and the industries in the northern centres of St. Rollox and Port Dundas were also being affected by a new and most powerful influence on the city's subsequent growth: the railway.

Until 1850 Glasgow's growth was subject mainly to centripetal forces. The railway and later the tramway changed that. They reduced transport and time costs, increased the worker's mobility, the periphery's access to the centre and the city's links to the British market. By 1875 centrifugal forces were of increasing importance. The built-up area and population continued growing, but at half the rate of previous periods. And, after 1871, the city centre began to lose population, though this was due primarily to urban redevelopment, not to improved transport.

The third quarter of the century brought the suburban age to Glasgow. High-quality residential developments continued in the west. But they were now supplemented by new ones in other directions, beyond the horseshoe of the industrial areas which encircled the old city to the north, east and south.

By 1875 Glasgow's economic morphology was mature and stable. A full complement of functional areas existed. There was a sizeable central commercial and administrative area surrounded by the industrial horseshoe. Westwards, along the Clyde, was a ribbon of quays, shipyards and engineering works. And within and beyond these districts were distinct residential areas: the slums of the city centre, the cramped workers' tenements on the edge of the core and among the factories of the industrial neighbourhoods, and the superior tenements, terraces and villas. Although urban activity grew substantially in the last quarter of the century, the city's functional distributions altered in relatively minor ways. By 1900 Glasgow was a world metropolis. It had a powerful economy based on commerce and a range of heavy industries. Its built-up area and political extent covered about 50 square kilometres; but in fact it was only the largest node in an industrial, Clydeside conurbation stretching almost unbroken for over 30 kilometres. It was also the focus of an extensive local and long-distance transport network which was fundamental to the city's undoubted prosperity. Much had changed since 1800; but, as will be argued presently, much remained remarkably the same.[10]

II: Population and Employment Characteristics

The remainder of this chapter will mainly consist of an analysis of the statistical information obtained from the census reports of 1801 to 1901. In particular, an examination will be made of population movements, age distribution, male-female ratios, educational data, and employment patterns, with special emphasis on the changing nature of occupations.

Nineteenth century census data can be useful; they can also be fraught with difficulties. Thus, in order to put the conclusions in this chapter into proper perspective, it is necessary to discuss first the methodological approach I used for clustering the data.

The year 1801 was the beginning of Britain's regular decennial census. Each successive census year produced a refinement of techniques and the inclusion of additional information. Hence it is very important that researchers utilising the census material be aware of changing definitions and geographical boundaries if they wish to maintain consistency for analytical purposes. With respect to boundary changes, there were nine after 1800—1800, 1830, 1843, 1846, 1872, 1878, 1891, 1896, and 1912.

> In the first six Census Reports, 1801 to 1851, the area whose population was counted was one [*sic*] called at first 'The City and Town of Glasgow', later 'Glasgow City and Burgh', and later again 'Glasgow City and Suburbs'. The population of Glasgow, in this sense, was not again enumerated after 1851. . . The Report of the Census of 1841 published the result of an enumeration of the population of another 'Glasgow'. This was the Parliamentary Burgh created for electoral purposes under the Reform Act of 1832, and the population of Glasgow in this sense has been enumerated at every Census since then. . . By an Act of 1846 the boundaries of the municipal area had been made to coincide with those of the Parliamentary Burgh, and these areas remained unchanged and equal until the former was extended in 1872; so that in enumerating the population of the Parliamentary Burgh in 1851, 1861, and 1871, the Census was at the same time enumerating the population of the municipal area. In 1881 (i.e. at the first Census date after the extension of the municipal area in 1872) the Census began to enumerate separately the population of the Municipal Burgh, and it has continued to do so at each Census date up to 1951.[11]

For the population statistics I decided to use as my categories of classification Glasgow City and the suburbs, where Glasgow City is composed solely of the ten 'traditional' inner city parishes. For both the non-occupational and the occupational characteristics of the population, it is possible to obtain the data for the parliamentary burgh and for the municipal burgh; I chose to use the municipal burgh data, as they are more representative of the metropolitan area, hence approximating Glasgow City plus the suburbs. The major definitional problem concerned the classification of occupations. Simply stated, how does one deal with the disappearance and emergence of occupations over time? My solution to the problem was to use the classifications contained in the 1901 Census and reclassify all the others accordingly—the task was largely a time-consuming one, presenting few conceptual problems. Unfortunately, my approach can only be considered a 'best solution' approximation, producing a reflection of the actual experience in Glasgow.

A: Population Characteristics

The first year for which detailed census information is available was 1801. The data for this and subsequent census years are presented in Table 1.1. The information is divided into Glasgow City (consisting of the ten traditional parishes) and the suburbs. Percentage changes and male-female ratios are contained in Table 1.2. Census year 1901 has been excluded, as extensions in 1891, 1896 and 1899 included within the boundary of Glasgow City the former suburban areas of Govanhill, Crosshill, Pollokshields East, Pollokshields, Hillhead, Maryhill, Mount Florida, Langside, Shawlands, Possilpark, Springburn, Blackhill and Shawfield.

A number of important points can be gleaned from this information. Firstly, the rate of growth of the population was faster for the suburbs than for Glasgow City, though the 1821 Census was the first to record a total population in the suburbs exceeding that of Glasgow City (incidentally, this was also the case with respect to the number of males and females in each respective area). After 1851 the growth rates of Glasgow City fell considerably, from an average rate of growth of 25.87 per cent before 1851 to an average of 4.68 per cent afterwards. Even the suburbs experienced a slowing down in the rate of growth of population, from an average rate of 35.28 per cent before 1841 to an average of 22.48 per cent after 1841. The radical changes in the rates of growth for certain suburbs can generally be regarded as the result of boundary modifications, however some of the effect can be accounted for by the changing residential/industrial structure of the Glasgow metropolitan area. A detailed examination of Table 1.2 provides a better understanding of the shifting population patterns within the Glasgow metropolitan area. For every decade the suburbs grew at a faster rate than Glasgow City, though until the 1850s both areas had impressive rates of growth. Commencing with the 1861 Census, the rate of growth of Glasgow City was substantially lower than for previous decades and compared to the suburbs. Given that there was continued migration into the Glasgow area, most of the migrants were moving into

Table 1.1: Population, by Sex, Glasgow and Suburbs, for Census Years

	1801			1811			1821			1831		
	Male	Female	Total	Male	Female	Total	Male	Female	Total	Male	Female	Total
Glasgow City:												
St Pauls	2,364	2,889	5,253	2,699	3,460	6,159	3,282	3,916	7,198	4,230	4,907	9,137
St Enoch	2,803	3,601	6,404	3,394	4,321	7,715	3,156	3,882	7,038	3,572	4,349	7,921
St James	—	—	—	—	—	—	3,448	3,815	7,263	3,730	4,487	8,217
St Johns	—	—	—	—	—	—	3,752	4,213	7,965	5,482	6,264	11,746
St Andrews	1,878	2,460	4,338	2,363	2,887	5,250	2,555	3,176	5,731	2,705	3,218	5,923
St Mungo	3,595	4,494	8,089	5,001	6,158	11,159	4,010	4,813	8,823	4,834	5,461	10,295
St David	3,159	4,242	7,401	4,276	5,662	9,940	2,667	3,346	6,013	2,772	3,496	6,268
Blackfriars	2,093	2,808	4,901	2,657	3,101	5,758	2,876	3,390	6,266	3,452	4,117	7,569
St Mary's	2,920	3,674	6,594	3,536	4,627	8,163	3,095	3,770	6,865	3,481	4,048	7,529
St Georges	1,634	2,165	3,799	1,860	2,330	4,190	4,250	5,353	9,603	6,885	8,357	15,242
Total	20,446	26,333	46,779	25,786	32,546	58,334	33,091	39,674	72,765	41,143	48,704	89,847
Suburbs:												
Barony	12,717	13,993	26,710	17,125	20,091	37,216	24,628	27,292	51,919	36,230	41,155	77,385
Gorbals	3,914	3,645	7,559	6,282	6,956	13,238	10,400	11,959	22,359	16,351	18,843	35,194
Govan	1,207	1,831	3,038	1,556	1,986	3,542	2,099	2,226	4,325	2,722	2,955	5,677
Calton												
Maryhill												
Shettleston												
Springburn												
Total	17,838	19,469	37,307	24,933	29,033	53,996	37,127	41,476	78,603	55,303	62,953	118,256
Totals	38,284	45,802	84,086	50,719	61,579	112,330	70,218	81,150	151,368	96,446	111,657	208,103

Table 1.1: cont.

	1841 Male	1841 Female	1841 Total	1851 Male	1851 Female	1851 Total	1861 Male	1861 Female	1861 Total
Glasgow City:									
St Pauls	4,375	5,208	9,583	7,045	7,657	14,702	7,021	8,044	15,065
St Enoch	4,078	4,799	8,877	3,847	4,237	8,084	2,686	3,085	5,771
St James	5,377	5,839	11,216	6,033	6,714	12,747	5,699	6,616	12,315
St Johns	7,185	8,240	15,425	9,766	11,353	21,119	13,142	14,601	27,743
St Andrews	3,369	3,948	7,317	4,651	5,022	9,673	4,534	5,058	9,592
St Mungo	7,585	7,859	15,444	10,083	10,919	21,001	7,300	8,005	15,305
St David	4,598	5,166	9,764	4,810	5,735	10,545	5,312	6,013	11,325
Blackfriars	4,828	5,749	10,574	5,491	6,459	11,950	4,828	5,747	10,575
St Mary's	4,881	5,109	9,990	5,662	6,115	11,777	4,899	5,381	10,280
St Georges	9,528	10,842	20,370	12,448	13,524	25,972	14,458	15,182	29,640
Total	55,804	62,759	118,563	69,836	77,735	147,571	69,879	77,732	147,611
Suburbs:									
Barony	50,147	55,928	106,075	35,725	41,774	77,499	46,778	54,650	101,428
Gorbals	23,831	25,264	49,095	29,376	31,373	60,749	5,047	5,447	10,494
Govan	3,703	4,107	7,810	7,286	7,710	14,996	47,971	52,745	100,716
Calton				20,994	24,526	45,520	24,295	28,762	53,057
Maryhill				3,265	3,435	6,700	5,393	5,867	11,260
Shettleston				3,279	3,285	6,564	3,445	3,469	6,914
Springburn							7,391	7,571	14,962
Total	77,681	85,299	162,980	99,925	112,103	212,028	140,320	158,511	298,831
Totals	133,485	148,058	281,543	169,761	189,838	359,599	210,199	236,243	446,442

Table 1.1: cont.

	1871 Male	1871 Female	1871 Total	1881 Male	1881 Female	1881 Total	1891 Male	1891 Female	1891 Total
Glasgow City:									
St Pauls	6,851	7,478	14,329	—	—	—	—	—	—
St Enoch	2,019	2,267	4,286	—	—	—	—	—	—
St James	5,343	5,866	11,209	—	—	—	—	—	—
St Johns	17,524	18,370	35,894	—	—	—	—	—	—
St Andrews	4,652	4,691	9,343	—	—	—	—	—	—
St Mungo	8,760	9,024	17,784	—	—	—	—	—	—
St David	5,743	5,957	11,700	—	—	—	—	—	—
Blackfriars	4,803	5,172	10,002	—	—	—	·	—	—
St Mary's	4,191	4,280	8,471	—	—	—	—	—	—
St Georges	18,745	18,486	37,231	—	—	—	—	—	—
Total	78,658	81,591	160,249	82,315	83,813	166,128	89,224	87,600	176,824
Suburbs:									
Barony	62,546	68,223	130,769	127,082	137,427	264,509	150,614	159,198	309,812
Gorbals	5,009	5,153	10,162	2,906	2,661	5,567	3,159	2,847	6,006
Govan	74,840	76,562	151,402	113,647	119,249	232,896	135,627	144,648	280,275
Calton	31,089	36,132	67,221	—	—	—	—	—	—
Maryhill	8,370	8,737	17,107	—	—	—	—	—	—
Shettleston	3,670	3,847	7,517	—	—	—	—	—	—
Springburn	11,180	10,502	21,682	—	—	—	—	—	—
Total	196,704	209,156	405,860	243,635	259,337	502,972	289,400	306,693	596,093
Totals	275,362	290,747	566,109	325,950	343,150	669,100	378,624	394,293	772,917

Source: Computed from Census data.

Table 1.2: Male-Female Ratio, Percentage Increase by Sex, for Census Years

	1811				1821				1831			
	Male Female Ratio	Male % increase	Female % increase	Total % increase	Male Female Ratio	Male % increase	Female % increase	Total % increase	Male Female Ratio	Male % increase	Female % increase	Total % increase
Glasgow City:												
St Pauls	.780	14.17	19.76	17.25	.838	21.60	13.18	16.87	.862	28.88	27.32	26.94
St Enoch	.785	21.08	19.99	20.47	.813	-7.01	-10.16	-8.78	.821	13.18	12.03	12.55
St James	—	—	—	—	.904	—	—	—	.831	8.18	17.61	13.14
St Johns	—	—	—	—	.891	—	—	—	.875	46.11	48.68	47.47
St Andrews	.818	25.83	17.36	21.02	.804	8.13	10.01	9.16	.841	5.87	1.32	3.35
St Mungo	.812	39.11	37.03	37.95	.833	-19.82	-21.84	-20.93	.885	20.30	13.46	16.68
St David	.755	35.36	33.47	34.31	.797	-37.63	-40.90	-39.51	.793	3.94	4.48	4.24
Blackfriars	.857	26.95	10.43	17.49	.848	8.24	9.32	8.82	.838	20.03	21.45	20.79
St Mary's	.764	21.10	25.94	23.79	.821	-12.47	-18.52	-15.90	.860	12.48	7.37	9.67
St Georges	.798	13.83	7.62	10.29	.794	128.49	129.74	129.19	.824	62.00	56.12	58.72
Total	.792	26.12	23.59	24.70	.834	28.33	21.90	24.74	.845	42.33	22.75	23.48
Suburbs:												
Barony	.852	34.66	43.58	39.33	.902	43.81	35.84	39.51	.880	47.11	50.80	49.05
Gorbals	.903	60.50	90.84	75.13	.870	65.55	71.92	68.90	.868	57.22	57.56	57.40
Govan	.783	28.91	8.47	16.59	.943	34.90	12.08	22.11	.921	29.68	32.75	31.26
Calton	—	—	—	—	—	—	—	—	—	—	—	—
Maryhill	—	—	—	—	—	—	—	—	—	—	—	—
Shettleston	—	—	—	—	—	—	—	—	—	—	—	—
Springburn	—	—	—	—	—	—	—	—	—	—	—	—
Total	.859	39.77	49.12	44.73	.895	48.91	42.86	45.57	.878	48.96	51.78	50.45
Totals	.824	32.48	34.45	33.59	.865	38.45	31.78	34.75	.864	37.35	37.59	37.48

Table 1.2: cont.

	1841				1851				1861			
	Male Female Ratio	Male % increase	Female % increase	Total % increase	Male Female Ratio	Male % increase	Female % increase	Total % increase	Male Female Ratio	Male % increase	Female % increase	Total % increase
Glasgow City:												
St Pauls	.840	3.36	6.13	4.88	.920	61.03	47.02	53.42	.873	-0.34	5.05	2.47
St Enoch	.850	14.07	10.35	12.07	.908	-5.66	-11.71	-8.93	.871	-30.18	-27.19	-28.61
St James	.921	44.16	30.13	36.50	.899	12.20	14.99	13.65	.861	-5.54	-1.46	-3.39
St Johns	.872	31.07	31.55	31.22	.860	35.92	37.78	36.91	.900	34.57	28.61	31.37
St Andrews	.853	24.55	22.68	23.54	.926	38.05	27.20	32.30	.896	-2.52	0.72	-0.84
St Mungo	.965	56.91	45.11	50.01	.923	32.93	38.94	35.98	.912	-27.60	-26.69	-27.12
St David	.890	65.87	47.77	55.78	.839	4.61	11.01	8.00	.883	10.44	4.85	7.40
Blackfriars	.840	39.86	39.64	39.70	.850	13.73	12.35	13.01	.840	-12.07	-11.02	11.51
St Mary's	.955	40.22	26.21	32.69	.926	16.00	19.69	17.89	.910	-13.48	-12.00	-12.71
St Georges	.879	38.39	30.93	33.64	.920	30.65	24.74	27.50	.952	16.15	12.26	14.12
Total	.889	35.63	28.86	31.96	.898	25.15	23.86	24.47	.899	0.06	0.00	0.02
Suburbs:												
Barony	.897	38.41	35.90	37.07	.855	-28.76	-25.31	-26.94	.856	30.94	30.82	30.88
Gorbals	.943	45.75	34.08	39.50	.936	23.27	24.18	23.74	.927	-82.82	-82.64	-82.73
Govan	.902	36.04	38.90	30.57	.945	96.76	87.73	92.01	.909	558.40	584.11	571.62
Calton	—	—	—	—	.856	—	—	—	.845	15.72	17.27	16.56
Maryhill	—	—	—	—	.951	—	—	—	.919	65.18	70.80	68.06
Shettleston	—	—	—	—	.998	—	—	—	.993	5.06	5.60	5.33
Springburn	—	—	—	—	—	—	—	—	.976	—	—	—
Total	.911	40.46	35.50	37.82	.891	26.64	31.42	30.09	.885	40.43	41.40	40.94
Totals	.902	38.40	32.60	35.29	.894	27.18	28.22	27.72	.890	23.82	24.44	24.15

Table 1.2: cont.

	1871				1881				1891			
	Male Female Ratio	Male % increase	Female % increase	Total % increase	Male Female Ratio	Male % increase	Female % increase	Total % increase	Male Female Ratio	Male % increase	Female % increase	Total % increase
Glasgow City:												
St Pauls	.916	- 2.42	7.04	4.89	—	—	—	—	—	—	—	—
St Enoch	.891	-24.83	-25.52	-25.73	—	—	—	—	—	—	—	—
St James	.911	- 6.07	-11.34	- 8.98	—	—	—	—	—	—	—	—
St Johns	.954	33.34	25.81	29.38	—	—	—	—	—	—	—	—
St Andrews	.992	2.60	- 7.26	- 2.60	—	—	—	—	—	—	—	—
St Mungo	.971	20.00	12.73	16.20	—	—	—	—	—	—	—	—
St David	.964	8.11	- 0.93	3.31	—	—	—	—	—	—	—	—
Blackfriars	.934	0.00	-10.01	- 5.42	—	—	—	—	—	—	—	—
St Mary's	.979	-14.45	-20.46	-17.60	—	—	—	—	—	—	—	—
St Georges	1.014	29.65	21.76	25.61	—	—	—	—	—	—	—	—
Total	9.64	12.56	4.96	8.56	.982	4.65	2.72	3.67	1.019	8.39	4.52	6.44
Suburbs:												
Barony	.917	33.71	24.84	28.93	.925	103.18	101.44	102.27	.946	18.52	15.84	17.13
Gorbals	.972	- 0.75	- 5.40	- 3.16	1.092	-41.98	-48.36	-45.22	1.110	8.71	6.99	7.89
Govan	.978	56.01	45.16	50.33	.953	51.85	55.75	53.83	.938	19.34	21.30	20.34
Calton	.860	27.96	25.62	26.70	—	—	—	—	—	—	—	—
Maryhill	.958	55.20	48.92	51.93	—	—	—	—	—	—	—	—
Shettleston	.954	6.53	10.90	8.72	—	—	—	—	—	—	—	—
Springburn	1.065	51.27	38.71	44.91	—	—	—	—	—	—	—	—
Total	.940	40.18	31.95	35.82	.939	23.86	23.99	23.93	.944	18.78	18.26	18.51
Totals	.947	31.00	23.07	26.80	.950	18.37	18.02	18.19	.960	16.16	14.90	15.52

Source: Computed from Census data

the suburban districts. Within Glasgow City there was also considerable movement. The decreases recorded for four parishes in 1821 were the result of the formation of the parishes of St Johns and St James. From 1861 onwards, most Glasgow City parishes experienced losses of population. In general these parishes were the older ones, having the highest densities of population and poor quality housing. People were moving out of these parishes, whenever possible, into the newer districts. Furthermore, the destruction of housing associated with railway development and the slum clearance initiated by the Glasgow Improvement Trust accelerated this movement. Govan was the major benefactor. Moreover, women were leaving the central parishes at a higher rate than men, probably reflecting their employment possibilites as domestics.

Secondly, with the exception of the 1891 Census for Glasgow City, looking at the total figures for the two major subdivisions, it can be seen that the number of females was greater than the number of males. However, the rate of growth of the female population was generally less than that for the males, when examining the combined totals. However, this statement must be modified slightly if the totals are broken up; for Glasgow City the rate of increase for males was always higher, with the differences increasing over time; for the suburbs the female population increased at approximately the same rate as for males. For Glasgow City the average rate of growth for males throughout the century was 18.36 per cent; for females it was 14.80 per cent. For the suburbs the rate of growth for males was 36.44 per cent and for females it was 36.25 per cent. To some extent the differential growth rates can be explained by the high proportion of the female labour force in domestic service, and the shifting of the middle and upper classes to the suburbs.

Thirdly, because of the higher rate of increase for the male population, the male-female ratio approaches unity toward the end of the nineteenth century for the combined totals. The temporary peak for the male-female ratio in 1841 can best be explained when taken in conjunction with the age distribution statistics given in Table 1.3. It can be seen that nearly half of the population was under the age of twenty. Of this age group, the percentage of the male population under the age of 20 was slightly higher than the corresponding figure for females. For both groups the percentage declines as the century progresses. For the 20-40 age group, the percentage figure for females is higher than that for males, but by 1871 the situation was reversed. There was a decline in the percentage figures for both sexes throughout the century, though the decrease was greatest for females. The relative decline of the 20-40 age group can perhaps be accounted for by out-migration; members of this group would be the most

Table 1.3: Age Distribution of the City and Suburbs

	1841	1851	1861	1871	1881	1891	1901
Percentage of Males, by Age Group							
under 15	35.70	34.90	36.43	35.97	35.58	35.22	32.81
under 20	46.16	46.13	46.98	46.30	46.00	45.47	42.87
20-40	36.12	35.13	33.22	34.22	33.97	33.62	35.32
40-60	13.80	14.97	15.85	15.37	15.74	16.41	17.22
over 60	3.77	3.76	3.95	4.11	4.28	4.94	4.59
Percentage of Females, by Age Group							
under 15	32.58	30.86	31.59	33.56	33.63	33.31	31.58
under 20	44.33	42.25	41.97	43.56	43.76	43.56	41.63
20-40	37.13	37.09	35.84	33.62	32.47	32.96	35.01
40-60	13.77	15.65	16.70	16.90	17.53	17.19	17.14
over 60	4.63	5.01	5.49	5.92	6.24	6.30	6.21
Ratio of Females to Males							
under 20	105.88	106.90	101.08	100.49	100.74	101.20	100.91
over 20	114.04	119.93	123.84	112.27	110.32	109.33	106.17

Source: Computed from Census data.

likely to migrate as they would be more mobile, adventuresome, and possess less ties than the members of the other age groups. This makes sense, as a concerted effort was made to encourage females to migrate in an attempt to correct what was considered to be an excessive surplus of females in the population. Examining the statistics for those over the age of 40, as one would expect, the relative percentage for females was higher than for males. This coincides with standard demographic theory that after females pass the child-bearing years, their life expectancy is greater than that for males. Though it must be noted that the life expectancy for both males and females was increasing throughout the century, as there was a substantial increase in the percentage of the population over the age of 40. Overall, the population of Glasgow was getting older throughout the nineteenth century, with a higher percentage of females than males surviving into old age.

The conjugal condition of the population over the age of fifteen for the municipal burgh of Glasgow is given in Table 1.4. As can be seen, the male-female ratio for this age group increases, though less dramatically than for the population as a whole. The importance of the statistics can be seen in a clearer light, when it is pointed out that approximately 44 per cent of the total male population was between the ages of 15 and 40; the corresponding figure for females was approximately 43 per cent. Thus, three conclusions are readily apparent. First, males were less likely to marry than females. Second, the average age of marriage was surprisingly late, probably at about the age of thirty. Third, a high proportion of the population never married.

Table 1.4: Conjugal Condition of the Population over the Age of 15

	1861	1871	1881	1891	1901
Men					
Men 15+	117,960	147,904	160,000	207,358	250,985
Number of					
Bachelors	50,303	66,171	72,029	95,137	118,944
Husbands	61,877	74,467	79,785	102,061	119,528
Widowers	5,780	7,266	8,186	10,160	12,513
Percentage of Men above the Age of 15					
Bachelors	42.64	44.74	45.02	45.88	47.39
Husbands	52.46	50.35	49.87	49.22	47.62
Widowers	4.90	4.91	5.12	4.90	4.99
Women					
Women 15+	143,616	163,935	174,584	225,483	265,588
Number of					
Spinsters	59,097	63,762	67,487	92,433	112,684
Wives	64,466	76,489	82,089	104,962	122,188
Widows	20,053	23,684	25,008	28,088	30,716
Percentage of Women above the Age of 15					
Spinsters	41.15	38.90	38.66	40.99	42.43
Wives	44.89	46.66	47.02	46.55	46.01
Widows	13.96	14.45	14.32	12.46	11.57
Male-Female Ratio	.821	.902	.916	.920	.945

Source: Computed from Census data.

Table 1.5: Percentage of the Population of Glasgow by Place of Birth

	1851	1861	1871	1881	1891	1901
Glasgow	44.07	50.96	57.84	68.70	62.31	61.51
out of Glasgow	55.93	49.04	42.15	31.30	37.69	38.49
Scotland	78.75	81.00	81.91	82.83	85.24	85.72
England	2.45	2.60	2.99	3.07	3.58	3.62
Ireland	18.17	15.70	14.32	13.12	10.04	8.88
Wales	0.03	0.04	0.05	0.07	0.08	0.07
Channel Islands	0.03	0.03	0.03	0.04	0.03	0.03
British Colonies	0.28	0.29	0.30	0.34	0.40	1.31
At Sea	0.02	0.02	0.19	0.23	0.25	0.01
Foreigners	0.19	0.13	0.21	0.30	0.38	1.31

Source: Computed from Census data.

Table 1.5 contains information on the place of birth. It is clear that migration into Glasgow became less important as a source of population increase. In fact Glasgow lost its ability to attract people from outside the general area, and especially from other areas within Scotland. After 1871 Scots outwith Glasgow were more willing to migrate to other countries than to Glasgow in search of employment opportunities. Even the traditional Irish source of labour decreased significantly in importance.

Ironically, as the century progressed, there was a greater propensity for the English to move northwards.

Table 1.6: Educational Statistics

	1871	1881	1891	1901 burgh
Total Population	477,732	511,415	658,198	
Population at Three Groups of Ages				
under 5	65,202	70,061	83,472	75,609
5-15	100,691	106,770	141,885	114,895
above 15	311,839	334,584	432,841	75,179
Number of Persons in the Receipt of Education				
under 5	621	1,075	1,404	832
5-15	60,649	75,065	104,910	105,493
above 15	2,454	3,184	3,725	4,733
Percentage of Persons in the Receipt of Education to the Population of each Group of Ages				
under 5	0.95	1.53	1.68	1.10
5-15	60.23	70.31	73.94	91.82
above 15	0.79	0.95	0.86	6.30
Total	13.34	15.50	16.74	

Source: Computed from Census data.

In 1872 the Scottish system of education was altered, with the passage of the Education (Scotland) Act, which established elected school boards. Prior to this date the Established Church was mainly the body responsible for education. The Education Act sought to revise the curriculum and improve the facilities available to students, while at the same time seeking to reduce the fees charged. Thus, even though Scotland had long had in operation a parish school system, the Education Act of 1872 represents a serious attempt to provide a more universal education system. The results of these efforts are readily apparent from an examination of Table 1.6. The proportion of the population receiving an education jumped from 13.34 in 1871 to 15.5 in 1881 to 16.74 in 1891. The major gains were in the percentage of 5-15 year olds attending school, which went from 60.23 in 1871 to 70.31 per cent in 1881. The reason for the increase in the latter category was that school attendance was compulsory for those between the ages of 5 and 13. Clearly, education played a more important role in the average Glasgwegian's life.

B: Employment Characteristics

The first census to include information on the occupations of the population was that of 1841. This census lists in alphabetical order all the occupations enumerated; unfortunately, it was not a comprehensive listing; however, it was representational of all the major occupations. The 1851 Census was the first to organise the information by classes and sub-groups. Table 1.7 presents the number of people employed in each occupational group, by sex and age group (under and over the age of twenty), for census years 1841 to 1901. Table 1.8 shows each group as a percentage of total workers involved in productive occupations.

The statistics indicate a number of interesting structural changes within Glasgow's economy. As one would expect, the percentage of workers employed in agricultural-related occupations decreased throughout the century from a high of 3.01 per cent of the total productive labour force in 1841 to a low of 0.36 in 1901. Domestic service was another area which experienced a relative decline, except for a brief upturn in 1881 and 1891. The professional category improved slightly in its relative position.

The classification 'Industrial' was a major loser, falling from a peak of 77.87 per cent of the total productive labour force in 1871 to a low of 67.67 in 1891. Within this category there were several dramatic changes. The textile sector in particular decreased significantly in importance as an agent of employment, falling continuously from a high of 30.61 per cent of the labour force in 1841 to a low of 7.69 per cent in 1901. The big gainer within industrial occupations was machinery and implements. This category increased from 1.53 per cent in 1841 to 10.93 per cent in 1901. The bulk of the increase can be accounted for by employment in engine and machine workers, fitters, turners, and boiler makers. These statistics demonstrate the shift in economic activity within Glasgow from textiles to the heavy machinery goods industry. The small relative increase for ships and boats should not be too surprising, as the bulk of shipbuilding was based further down the Clyde.

As far as the major classifications are concerned, the commercial category enjoyed a substantial increase in relative employment from 7.53 per cent in 1841 to 19.05 per cent in 1901. Even though the commercial occupations themselves enjoyed a sizeable increase, the conveyance activities account for the largest proportion, rising from 4.10 per cent in 1841 to 11.80 per cent in 1901. This reflects the increasing importance of railways and shipping and the need to transport goods and people both within and outwith the city.

The male-female composition of the labour force was affected by shifts in the occupational structure. The percentage of female workers peaked in 1861 at 37.13 per cent, falling to 31.06 per cent by 1901. Most of this

Table 1.7: Number Employed by Occupation, Sex, Age Group, by Census Years

	1841						1851					
	Males under 20	Males over 20	Females under 20	Females over 20	Total under 20	Total over 20	Males under 20	Males over 20	Females under 20	Females over 20	Total under 20	Total over 20
CLASS I: Professional												
1. Government	4	724		5	4	729	12	1,245		4	12	1,249
2. Army & Navy	100	1,133			100	1,133	89	597			89	597
3. Other	138	1,531	75	804	213	2,335	471	2,433	74	585	545	3,018
Total	242	3,388	75	809	317	4,197	572	4,275	74	589	646	4,864
CLASS II: Domestic	347	1,001	4,386	8,162	4,733	9,163	251	572	5,241	11,291	5,492	11,863
CLASS III: Commercial												
1. Commercial	712	3,389	7	102	719	3,491	1,027	3,281	208	143	1,235	3,424
2. Conveyance	769	4,110	31	116	800	4,226	2,924	7,055			2,924	7,055
Total	1,481	7,499	38	218	1,519	7,717	3,951	10,336	208	143	4,159	10,479
CLASS IV: Agricultural												
1. Agriculture	389	3,180	9	63	398	3,243	173	1,878	22	216	195	2,094
2. About Animals	3	39		1	3	40	5	83			5	83
3. Fishermen	2	8			2	8		7				7
Total	394	3,227	9	64	403	3,291	178	1,968	22	216	200	2,184
CLASS V: Industrial												
1. Books, Maps	560	1,429	62	85	622	1,514	725	1,371	100	106	825	1,477
2. Machines & Implements	399	1,348	65	71	646	1,419	757	3,044	49	76	806	3,120
3. Houses, Furnishings	1,520	7,150	30	72	1,550	7,222	1,790	9,644	74	171	1,864	9,815
4. Carriages & Harness	105	370	1	6	106	376	122	504		4	122	508
5. Ships & Boats	110	264		1	110	265	75	382			75	382
6. Chemicals & Compounds	52	156	40	142	92	298	157	920	23	38	180	958
7. Tobacco & Pipes	256	233	4	18	260	251	130	217	26	52	156	269
8. Food & Lodging	806	4,192	33	1,387	839	5,579	1,900	6,673	161	2,379	2,061	9,052
9. Textile Fabrics	4,166	13,691	8,063	11,641	12,229	25,332	4,930	14,739	10,404	17,213	15,334	31,952
10. Dress	1,238	5,668	1,338	4,400	2,576	10,068	1,606	7,204	2,716	8,008	4,322	15,212
11. Animal Substances	155	508	7	34	162	542	149	618	10	56	159	674
12. Vegetable Substances	271	1,176	45	69	316	1,245	681	2,185	139	293	820	3,298
13. Mineral Substances	2,079	5,564	49	139	2,128	5,703	4,797	10,953	221	356	5,018	11,309
14. General or Unspecified	1,037	8,364	50	518	1,087	8,882	876	5,403	155	737	1,031	6,140
15. Refuse Matters	49	77	1	10	50	87	55	72	20	91	75	163
Total	12,803	50,190	9,788	18,593	22,591	68,783	18,750	63,929	14,098	29,580	32,848	93,509
CLASS VI: Unspecified	682	2,533	549	5,322	1,231	7,855	4	140	33	1,419	37	1,559
GRAND TOTAL	15,949	67,838	14,845	33,168	30,794	101,006	23,706	81,220	19,676	43,238	43,382	124,458

Table 1.7: cont.

	1861 Males		1861 Females		1861 Total		1871 Males		1871 Females		1871 Total	
	under 20	over 20	under 20	over 20	under 20	over 20	under 20	over 20	under 20	over 20	under 20	over 20
CLASS I:												
1.	37	1,451		27	37	1,478	182	1,718		23	182	1,741
2.	70	1,006			70	1,006	131	741			131	741
3.	728	2,872	200	698	928	3,570	787	3,124	307	888	1,094	4,012
Total.	835	5,329	200	725	1,035	6,054	1,100	5,583	307	911	1,407	6,494
CLASS II:	132	728	4,283	9,624	4,415	10,352	274	1,327	4,558	9,279	4,832	10,606
CLASS III:												
1.	1,362	4,473	153	975	1,515	5,448	2,110	5,962	130	286	2,240	6,248
2.	3,268	9,418	507	366	3,775	9,784	5,354	12,749	1,159	559	6,513	13,308
Total	4,630	13,891	660	1,341	5,290	15,232	7,464	18,711	1,289	845	8,753	19,556
CLASS IV:												
1.	99	1,044	38	363	137	1,407	48	585	9	114	57	699
2.	28	424		3	28	427	54	637		2	54	639
3.	3	17		1	3	18	1	12		3	1	15
Total	130	1,485	38	367	168	1,852	103	1,234	9	119	112	1,353
CLASS V:												
1.	975	1,742	350	212	1,325	1,954	1,054	2,114	597	328	1,651	2,442
2.	1,151	4,040	86	132	1,237	4,172	1,618	6,654	102	133	1,720	6,787
3.	2,151	10,609	37	594	2,188	11,203	3,101	15,275	60	261	3,161	15,536
4.	133	603	1	1	134	604	154	863	4	3	158	866
5.	276	1,260		1	276	1,261	484	2,370	1	3	485	2,373
6.	486	1,309	150	165	636	1,474	367	1,602	294	211	661	1,813
7.	349	279	12	64	361	343						
8.	1,971	7,734	344	3,202	2,315	10,936	2,512	8,924	5,093	11,037	7,605	19,961
9.	3,292	13,708	10,044	16,173	13,336	29,881	2,272	10,512	11,994	17,456	14,266	27,968
10.	1,955	8,020	2,941	14,685	4,896	22,705	1,334	7,980	3,744	13,577	5,078	21,557
11.	161	705	87	129	248	834	206	904	82	176	288	1,080
12.	1,032	2,656	477	659	1,509	3,315	895	3,337	805	736	1,700	4,073
13.	5,258	15,318	309	536	5,567	15,854	6,753	22,265	546	618	7,299	22,883
14.	1,104	7,315	1,502	2,486	2,606	9,801	1,566	11,419	495	1,958	2,061	13,377
15.	5	145			5	145						
Total	20,299	75,443	16,340	39,039	36,639	114,482	22,316	94,219	23,817	46,497	46,133	140,716
CLASS VI:	149	1,072	296	1,933	445	3,005	28	1,158	104	3,972	132	5,130
TOTAL	26,229	97,948	21,817	53,029	48,046	150,977	31,285	122,232	30,083	61,623	61,369	183,855

Table 1.7: cont.

	1881						1891					
	Males		Females		Total		Males		Females		Total	
	under 20	over 20	under 20	over 20	under 20	over 20	under 20	over 20	under 20	over 20	under 20	over 20
CLASS I:												
1.	266	2,058	20	103	286	2,161	485	3,074	84	182	569	3,256
2.	3	332			3	332	327	853			327	853
3.	1,679	3,897	1,737	1,848	3,416	5,745	1,995	6,067	2,249	3,082	4,244	9,149
Total	1,948	6,287	1,757	1,951	3,705	8,238	2,807	9,994	2,333	3,264	5,140	13,258
CLASS II:	186	1,620	4,445	12,162	4,631	13,782	673	3,315	6,044	19,290	6,717	22,605
CLASS III:												
1.	2,859	8,441	313	387	3,172	8,828	4,633	12,953	761	990	5,394	13,943
2.	5,437	15,119	1,098	73	6,535	15,192	7,579	22,040	2,010	506	9,589	22,546
Total	8,296	23,560	1,411	460	9,707	24,020	12,212	34,993	2,771	1,496	14,983	36,489
CLASS IV:												
1.	34	358	19	146	53	504	72	856	23	178	95	1,034
2.	90	595		4	90	599	11	231	1	3	12	234
3.	2	19			2	19	1	21		1	1	22
Total	126	972	19	150	145	1,122	84	1,108	24	182	108	1,290
CLASS V:												
1.	1,047	2,491	1,191	590	2,238	3,081	1,094	3,726	1,337	1,214	2,431	4,940
2.	1,986	8,879	105	158	2,091	9,037	3,943	13,431	110	155	4,053	13,586
3.	2,822	15,567	408	706	3,230	16,273	2,850	17,062	602	977	3,452	18,039
4.	175	1,096	3	5	178	1,101	270	1,476	20	30	290	1,506
5.	266	1,374	1		267	1,374	260	1,772	5	48	265	1,820
6.	231	1,204	95	117	326	1,321	253	1,475	90	140	343	1,615
7.	106	568	353	317	459	885	78	569	562	711	640	1,280
8.	2,436	10,082	899	3,565	3,335	13,647	3,000	11,895	2,003	4,654	5,003	16,549
9.	1,832	8,741	8,643	16,031	10,475	24,772	1,897	8,676	7,861	13,022	9,758	21,698
10.	1,394	8,354	4,199	11,660	5,593	20,014	1,231	8,453	6,154	13,595	7,385	22,048
11.	276	1,199	136	288	412	1,487	281	1,416	263	402	544	1,818
12.	712	3,204	1,064	882	1,776	4,086	879	4,256	1,352	1,439	2,231	5,695
13.	5,282	22,741	493	608	5,775	23,349	6,013	28,398	854	1,008	6,867	29,406
14.	2,079	13,483	1,991	3,778	4,070	17,261	3,037	17,653	2,045	3,882	5,082	21,535
15.	27	293	30	155	57	448	22	326	68	214	90	540
Total	20,671	99,281	19,611	38,860	40,282	138,141	25,108	120,584	23,326	41,491	48,434	162,075
CLASS VI:	608	2,376	3,882	94,356	4,490	96,732	444	4,558	6,433	125,113	6,877	129,671
TOTAL	31,835	134,096	31,125	147,939	62,960	282,035	41,328	174,552	40,931	190,836	82,259	365,388

Table 1.7: cont.

| | 1901 | | | | | |
| | Males | | Females | | Total | |
	Under 20	over 20	under 20	over 20	under 20	over 20
CLASS I:						
1.	708	3,033	23	135	731	3,168
2.	235	575			235	575
3.	775	6,100	726	5,019	1,501	11,119
Total	1,718	9,708	749	5,154	2,467	14,862
CLASS II:	231	1,622	5,118	18,976	5,349	20,598
CLASS III:						
1.	4,115	16,593	2,258	3,000	6,373	19,593
2.	9,411	29,577	2,585	690	11,996	30,267
Total	13,526	46,170	4,843	3,690	18,369	49,860
CLASS IV:						
1.	51	852	42	132	93	984
2.	8	214		5	8	219
3.		14				14
Total	59	1,080	42	137	101	1,217
CLASS V:						
1.	1,063	5,439	3,222	3,357	4,285	8,796
2.	7,176	31,339	272	359	7,448	31,698
3.	4,610	24,771	1,027	1,320	5,637	26,091
4.	376	2,410	21	40	397	2,450
5.	541	2,469	15	13	556	2,482
6.	359	2,838	397	538	756	3,376
7.	84	722	1,248	752	1,332	1,474
8.	3,626	17,469	3,837	7,560	7,463	25,029
9.	1,556	7,613	6,512	11,874	8,068	19,487
10.	1,236	9,504	7,108	16,684	8,344	26,188
11.	226	1,368	395	522	621	1,890
12.	816	3,642	158	130	974	3,772
13.	3,182	17,056	896	1,006	4,078	18,062
14.	2,453	18,199	859	2,404	3,312	20,603
15.	41	634			41	634
Total	27,345	145,473	25,967	46,559	53,312	192,032
CLASS VI:	4	4,458	20	6,638	24	11,096
TOTAL	42,883	208,511	36,739	81,154	79,622	289,665

Table 1.8: Percentage of Total Labour Force, by Sex and Category

	1841			1851			1861		
	Male	Female	Total	Male	Female	Total	Male	Female	Total
CLASS I: Professional									
1. Government	.59		.59	.76		.76	.76		.76
2. Army & Navy	1.00		1.00	.41		.41	.55		.55
3. Other	1.36	.71	2.08	1.75	.40	2.14	1.84	.46	2.30
Total	2.96	.72	3.68	2.92	.40	3.31	3.18	.47	3.65
CLASS II: Domestic	1.10	10.23	11.32	.50	9.94	10.44	.44	7.11	7.55
CLASS III: Commercial									
1. Commercial	3.37	.09	3.43	2.59	.21	2.80	2.98	.58	3.56
2. Conveyance	3.98	.12	4.10	6.00		6.00	6.49	.45	6.94
Total	7.32	.21	7.53	8.59	.21	8.81	9.47	1.02	10.49
CLASS IV: Agricultural									
1. Agriculture	2.91	.06	2.97	1.23	.14	1.38	.58	.21	.79
2. About Animals	.03		.04	.01		.01	.23		.23
3. Fishermen	.01		.01	.05		.04			
Total	2.95	.06	3.01	1.29	.14	1.43	.81	.21	1.02
CLASS V: Industrial									
1. Books, Maps	1.62	.12	1.74	1.26	.12	1.38	1.39	.29	1.68
2. Machines & Implements	1.42	.11	1.53	2.29	.01	2.36	2.65	.01	2.66
3. Houses, Furnishings	7.07	.08	7.15	6.88	.15	7.03	6.52	.32	6.84
4. Carriages & Harness	.39		.39	.38		.38	.38		.38
5. Ships & Boats	.30		.30	.27		.27	.79		.79
6. Chemicals & Compounds	.17	.15	.32	.65		.65	.92	.16	1.08
7. Tobacco & Pipes	.40		.40	.21		.21	.32		.32
8. Food & Lodgings	4.07	1.16	5.23	5.57	1.53	6.68	4.96	1.81	6.77
9. Textile Fabrics	14.55	16.03	30.61	11.83	16.61	28.44	8.69	13.41	22.10
10. Dress	5.63	4.68	10.30	5.30	6.45	11.75	5.10	9.01	14.11
11. Animal Substances	.54		.54	.46		.46	.44	.11	.55
12. Vegetable Substances	1.18	.09	1.27	1.76	.26	2.48	1.89	.58	2.47
13. Mineral Substances	6.23	.15	6.38	9.47	.35	9.82	10.52	.43	10.95
14. General or Unspecified	7.66	.46	8.12	3.78	.54	4.31	4.30	2.04	6.34
15. Refuse Matters	.10		.10	.08	.07	.14			
Total	51.33	23.13	74.46	49.73	26.27	76.00	48.95	28.32	77.27
Per cent of Total	65.66	34.34		63.03	36.97		62.87	37.13	
Ratio, under 20 to over 20	23.83	51.34	31.74	29.23	46.97	35.27	26.92	42.12	31.82

Table 1.8: cont.

	1871 Male	1871 Female	1871 Total	1881 Male	1881 Female	1881 Total	1891 Male	1891 Female	1891 Total	1901 Male	1901 Female	1901 Total
CLASS I:												
1.	.79		.79	.95	.05	1.00	1.14	.09	1.23	1.04	.04	1.08
2.	.36		.36	.14		.14	.38		.38	.23		.23
3.	1.63	.50	2.13	2.29	1.47	3.76	2.59	1.72	4.31	1.92	1.60	3.52
Total	2.79	.51	3.29	3.38	1.52	4.90	4.11	1.80	5.91	3.19	1.64	4.83
CLASS II:	.67	5.77	6.43	.74	6.81	7.75	1.28	8.14	9.43	.52	6.73	7.25
CLASS III:												
1.	3.36	.17	3.54	4.64	.29	4.93	5.65	.56	6.22	5.78	1.47	7.25
2.	7.54	.72	8.26	8.43	.48	8.91	9.52	.81	10.33	10.89	.91	11.80
Total	10.91	.89	11.80	13.07	.77	13.84	15.17	1.37	16.55	16.67	2.38	19.05
CLASS IV:												
1.	.26	.01	.27	.16	.07	.23	.30	.06	.36	.25	.05	.30
2.	.29		.29	.28		.28	.08		.08	.06		.06
3.												
Total	.56	.01	.57	.44	.07	.51	.38	.06	.44	.31	.05	.36
CLASS V:												
1.	1.32	.39	1.07	1.45	.73	2.18	1.55	.82	2.37	1.82	1.84	3.66
2.	3.46	.01	3.55	4.46	.11	4.57	5.58	.09	5.67	10.75	.18	10.93
3.	7.60	.13	7.79	7.54	.46	8.00	6.40	.51	6.91	8.20	.66	8.86
4.	.42		.42	.52		.52	.56		.56	.78		.78
5.	1.19		1.19	.67		.67	.65		.65	.84		.84
6.	.82	.21	1.03	.59	.09	.68	.56	.07	.63	.89	.26	1.15
7.				.28	.27	.55	.21	.41	.62	.23	.56	.79
8.	4.77	6.72	11.49	5.14	1.83	6.97	4.79	2.14	6.93	5.89	3.18	9.07
9.	5.33	12.27	17.60	4.34	10.12	14.46	3.40	6.71	10.11	2.56	5.13	7.69
10.	3.88	7.22	11.10	4.00	6.51	10.51	3.11	6.35	9.46	3.00	6.64	9.64
11.	.46	.11	.57	.61	.17	.78	.55	.21	.76	.45	.26	.71
12.	1.76	.64	2.41	1.61	.80	2.41	1.65	.90	2.55	1.24	.08	1.32
13.	12.09	.49	12.58	11.50	.64	12.14	11.06	.60	11.66	5.65	.53	6.18
14.	5.41	1.02	6.43	6.38	2.37	8.75	6.65	1.91	8.56	5.77	.91	6.68
15.				.13	.08	.21	.11	.09	.20	.19		.19
Total	48.56	29.30	77.87	49.21	23.99	73.20	46.83	20.83	67.67	48.25	20.25	68.50
Per Cent of Total	63.49	36.51		66.84	33.16		67.77	32.23		68.94	31.06	
Ratio, under 20 to over 20	25.82	52.00	34.26	233.71	50.84	31.55	24.05	52.49	31.98	21.01	49.28	28.57

decline occurred in the industrial sector, where the percentage of women decreased from a peak of 29.30 per cent in 1871 to an all-time low of 20.25 per cent in 1901. In particular there was a dramatic decline in the number of women engaged in textiles from 16.61 per cent in 1851 to 5.13 per cent in 1901. Domestic service, another traditional female employment area in general declined throughout the century, though there was considerable fluctuation from decade to decade, with an extremely low point in 1871, a depression year. Females gained in the professions, especially school teachers, and commercial occupations, though their gains in these areas were not as significant as the gains for males. The percentage of males in commercial activities more than doubled during the century from 7.32 per cent in 1841 to 16.67 per cent of the total labour force in 1901. As far as the industrial sector is concerned, males as a percentage of the total labour force decreased only slightly, with the average for the time period being approximately 49 per cent.

Some interesting patterns also emerge with respect to age distribution, which also cast a clearer light on the male-female ratio. The ratio of males under the age of twenty to those over the age of twenty peaked in 1851 at 29.23 per cent and decreased thereafter to 21.01 in 1901. The same ratio for females fluctuated throughout the period, but averaged 49.29 per cent. Clearly women were inclined to leave the labour force after the age of twenty, whereas men stayed in the labour force. This, of course, is not surprising. The proportion of females to males under the age of twenty in the labour force also fluctuated wildly, with an average rate of 87.45, while the same proportion for those over the age of twenty averaged 44.35, with a dramatic drop to 36.51 per cent in 1901. If this information is compared with the last two columns of Table 1.3, it is clear that the participation rate for males was higher than for females for both age groups, but significantly greater for males over the age of twenty. From this it is possible to conclude that, 1) women of marriage age were forced out of the labour force, 2) a major emphasis was placed on males over the age of twenty as the 'breadwinner', and this was a post-1851 phenomenon, and 3) after 1871, people entered the labour force at an older age, as a result of the introduction of general education.

C: Summary

The above statistics on population and employment indicate the changing nature of Glasgow. During the nineteenth century there were significant changes within the age structure, the age cohort and sex ratios. To some extent these changes were a reflection of the modifications within the infrastructure of Glasgow's economic activity. New industries replaced older ones; residential areas shifted, and so too did industrial location, both largely a result of developments within the transportation sector. Glasgow's well-being depended upon its ability to adopt to new situations.

Notes

1. Andrew Gibb, *Glasgow: The Making of a City* (Croom Helm, Beckenham, 1983).
2. W. Forsyth, 'Urban Economic Morphology in Nineteenth-Century Glasgow', in A. Slaven and D. Aldcroft, eds., *Business, Banking and Urban History* (John Donald, Edinburgh, 1982), pp. 166-92.
3. S.G. Checkland, *The Upas Tree: Glasgow, 1875-1975* (University of Glasgow Press, Glasgow, 1981).
4. A. Slaven, *The Development of the West of Scotland, 1750-1960* (Routledge & Kegan Paul, London, 1975), pp. 92-3.
5. Z. Grosicki, 'Cotton and Woollen Spinning and Weaving', in J. Cunnison and Gilfillan, eds., *Glasgow*, pp. 241, 243.
6. *Ibid.*, p. 243.
7. *Ibid.*, p. 241.
8. Sarah C. and James Orr, 'Other Engineering: Development in the Nineteenth Century', in J. Cunnison and Gilfillan, eds., *Glasgow*, pp. 211-2.
9. *Ibid.*, p. 215.
10. W. Forsyth, 'Urban Economic Morphology', pp. 168-70.
11. J. Cunnison and J.B.S. Gilfillan, eds., *The Third Statistical Account of Scotland, Glasgow* (Collins, Glasgow, 1958), p. 787.

Chapter Two

HOUSING

John Butt

Almost without exception visitors to Glasgow in the eighteenth century commented upon the elegance of the city; individuals as diverse as Daniel Defoe (1727)[1], Thomas Pennant (1772)[2] and Dr Samuel Johnson (1773)[3] thought it well-built and closely knit, and they were unaware of particular or unusual problems relating to the housing of the working classes. In 1750 the old regality consisted of ten major streets, and the western limit of building was Candleriggs (c.1724), which up to the third decade of the century had been a cornfield. Indeed, the rural aspect remained significant, but as construction proceeded in the last half of the century, it gradually covered more and more of the large common which extended westward from the present Queen Street to where the 'townherd led the cows of the citizens in the morning by the west port and brought them in the evening to be milked at the Cowcaddens'.[4] John Gibson (1777) was representative of the early tradition of pride associated with histories of, and guides to, Glasgow:

> Every stranger is charmed with the appearance of Glasgow; the streets are clean and well paved. . . the houses are all (excepting a very few) built of free stone, well hewed; few of them exceed four floors in height, and many of them are in exceeding good taste.[5]

Andrew Brown and James Denholm, respectively the authors of the most authoritative history and tourist guide circulating at the turn of the century[6], support Gibson's testimony, and had all three been asked, they would have undoubtedly commented upon the apparent lack of residential segregation in the city. Most Glaswegians, although aware of material differences, found themselves living in close proximity with those in different social orders. This pattern was being broken as the eighteenth century proceeded, but social homogeneity as well as rural surroundings was an important characteristic of urban life which the expansion of trade only slowly transgressed.

Daniel Campbell of Shawfield with his magnificent mansion (1711) and garden west of Candleriggs set a new fashion, and in the Malt Riots of 1725 such ostentation attracted a popular reaction; an attempt was made to fire it and the windows and furniture were damaged.[7] Amid the barns and malt kilns of Argyle Street, John Murdoch (1709-1776), one of the original partners in the Glasgow Arms Bank, built an elegant mansion c.1750, later to become the Buck's Head Inn.[8] Others also had their rural retreats; the connections between Glasgow's mercantile elite and landed society in the western lowlands were close.[9] But Campbell and Murdoch were representative of the developing trend of residential segregation, of the wealthy's flight from the confines of the old regality of Glasgow to western suburbs.

At first this movement was not merely slow; it was also relatively short distance. The New Town of Glasgow did not represent so obvious a geographical or class boundary as Edinburgh's New Town betokened. Builders such as Robert Smith, Dugald Bannatyne and Company and William Horn opened up Virginia Street (c.1756), Queen Street (1770s), Dunlop Street (1770), Miller Street and Buchanan Street (1780s) for the exceedingly affluent, but Smith also built houses on the west side of North Frederick Street for respectable tradesmen which were given the nickname of Botany Bay by their snobbish neighbours later. Campbell of Shawfield's house was purchased by the great tobacco lord, John Glassford, and later still, in 1791, sold with its garden (over 15,000 square yards in all) for £9,850 so that the development of Glassford Street could occur.[10]

A filtering-up process—and a making-down—happened in the older areas of the city being abandoned by the elite. Drygate, Saltmarket, High Street, Bridgegate, for example were increasingly the province of working-class families living mostly in one-room tenement dwellings which were either created anew in the erstwhile gardens of wealthy burghers or made-down from properties which had been previously occupied by single families. Wynds and vennels also in tenement form added to the density of the old city, and there was little regard for the provision of additional sanitary facilities or water supply.

An increasing population postulated a growing demand for accommodation, but there was no break in the mood of complacency for developing residential segregation was a piecemeal and novel process which stored problems for later generations. Gibson commented in 1777 that 'new streets have been laid out, and houses built with a taste and elegance unknown in former times'.[11] He detected no reason for alarm and expressed no concern for the new inhabitants of the old streets; this was not an expression of short-sighted prejudice but rather an indication that as yet no major problem had emerged.

Concomitant with the expansion of the built-up area of the city proper was the emergence of industrial villages beyond the periphery which by 1914 might reasonably be regarded—at least in some cases—as central areas: Calton, Bridgeton, Anderston, Finnieston, Brownfield, Pollokshaws, Hutchesontown and Tradeston.[12] Often their growth was associated with the textile industries: weaving, bleaching, dyeing and finishing. The long established independent burgh of Gorbals with its fine houses and wide streets ominously had begun to expand its coal production and output of metal goods. In the north the driving of the Monkland and Forth and Clyde canals provided the incentive for the building of Port Dundas, and the emergence of St Rollox chemical works at the end of the century was another signpost pointing to the overthrow of the 'merchant city' by the industrial city.[13]

The purpose of this chapter is to examine some of the principal changes arising from industrialisation: what problems arose from the operations of the free market in working-class housing; what attempts were made to solve them and for what reasons; what was the experience in housing for working-class groups and how did this change over the period down to the First World War. An essential background for these discussions remains to be considered: the supply of and demand for houses.

I: The Market for Working-Class Housing

In any discussion of this issue it is important to emphasise the deficiencies of data and to indicate that even census enumeration after 1801 left much to be desired from the point of view of the historian investigating this topic. Valuation rolls available from 1855 require more scientific examination before certainties about ownership can be established. How much darker is the gloom around the pre-1801 story!

In the industrial villages one can be reasonably certain that the landowners played the major part in providing houses and often these were also industrialists. When Archibald Ingram began the development of Pollokshaws in the 1740s, he was compelled to provide houses for his workers in the textile finishing trades.[14] Camlachie was populated mainly by coalminers who lived in tied housing.[15] Much the same might be said of parts of Calton as John Orr of Barrowfield developed it from the late 1730s.[16] Later in the century Tollcross was projected by the Dunlop family of Clyde Ironworks, and fire insurance records confirm that twenty-two small thatched houses 'in tenure of labourers' were valued at £200 in 1800.[17] Nearby at 'Little Tollcross' were five more substantial stone and slated dwellings valued at £50.[18]

The proto-industrialists in the textile industry of these suburbs were investing in house property for the working classes. Some were relatively humble. William Watson, for example, described as a Glasgow manufacturer in the insurance records, lived on the south side of Kirk Street, Calton in 1800 and insured two tenements and a weaving shop 'all communicating thatched in tenure of himself and others' for £300.[19] Alexander Norris insured a thatched tenement in Calton for £60 and a weaver's shop for £20 and clearly was an even smaller landlord.[20] David Addam, however, owned three tenements, one of which he occupied himself, and another small house, total insurance value for his house property being £810.[21] Bright Langley, also a Calton manufacturer, owned two tenements in Cross Loom Street 'in tenure of himself and others' and four tenements in Mile End occupied by weavers. The insurance valuation of his house property was £800.[22]

In Anderston three similar examples can be found as indicated in Table 2.1.

Table 2.1: Tenements owned by Manufacturers in Anderston, c.1800

Name	Number of Tenements	Insurance Valuation (£)
John Wright	2	450
John Neilson	2	200
John Glasgow	5	300

Source: Guildhall Library, Sun Fire Policy Registers

The case of John Glasgow illustrates a common feature of proto-industrialists' investment. Commonly, the work place was part of a tenement in which the manufacturer lived, and thus close regard could be paid to stock and utensils. The warehouse for the sale of cloth was often in central Glasgow, in John Glasgow's case on the west side of Old Wynd.[23]

More data are available for the city proper and these are given in Table 2.2. From these data and others given in Table 2.3 it is clear that industrialists' investment in house property for rent was less important than that of builders, merchants and retailers generally. The value of tenement property varied according to the number of dwellings contained therein and also the district. Better districts where artisans and craftsmen were likely to be tenants were valued more highly than property in less salubrious areas. Nature of construction—whether tiled or thatched, for instance—would also affect replacement cost and therefore insurance value; it might also reflect a demand from a different part of the market.

Table 2.2: Tenements owned by Industrialists in Glasgow, 1793-1801

Year	Occupation	Number of Tenements	Insurance Valuation ($£$)
1793	Coachmaker	1	300
1793	Manufacturer	2	150
1795	Manufacturer	3	450
1795	Calico Printer	1	100
1795	Oil & colourman	3	850
1795	Manufacturer	4	440
1796	Manufacturer	8	400
1800	Instrument-maker	1	150
1800	Manufacturer	3	350
1800	Manufacturer	2	640
1800	Rope maker	7	999
1800	Inkle-weaver	3	320
1800	Wire worker	4	650
1800	Saddler	4	560
1801	Rope spinner	3	880

Source: Guildhall Library, Sun Fire Policy Registers

The fifteen individuals whose property assets are given in Table 2.2 owned forty-nine tenements, an average of slightly more than three per individual. Twenty-six of these tenements were either adjoining to others owned by the same proprietors or 'backjams' built backwards from a front tenement. Only one was thatched, indicating that even in the older parts of the city some replacement of older materials and structures did take place. Most were in the area bounded by Trongate and Drygate and Saltmarket, Bridgegate, High Street and the wynds and vennels running from these main streets. Most of these landlords lived among their tenants, ten of the fifteen. Four also owned tenement properties elsewhere, three in Anderston and one in Calton.

Table 2.3 gives data over a longer period relating to the investment in tenement property by builders, merchants and a range of retailers. Obviously, the builders were a special interest group, often concerned with property development on 'green field' sites and holding their insured assets—by no means all of which were intended for working-class occupation—as speculative ventures. James Gemmill, for instance, insured a tenement at Brownfield for £750 in 1794,[24] and it must have been both large and intended for affluent owners/tenants. Similarly, the flight westward of the wealthy can be traced in the case of John Morrison who in 1796 insured (£500 with the Sun Office, and £1,000 with the Edinburgh

Friendly Office) two large tenements 'communicating on the north side of
Argyle Street not quite finished'.[25] But there were many instances in the
forty-six tenements listed of properties which by their value and location
were intended for working-class occupation, including the derided Botany
Bay tenements in Frederick Street, four of which George Bell insured for
£999 in 1800.[26]

Table 2.3a: The Building Trade and Tenement Property, 1793-1800

Year	Occupation	Number of Tenements	Insurance Valuation (£)
1793	Brickmaker	3	550
1794	Wright	3	1,050
1795	Bricklayer	6	540
1795	Wright	2	300
1796	Wright & Builder	2	1,500
1796	Wright	4	395
1796	Wright	1	450
1796	Plasterer	3	750
1796	Brickmaker	6	700
1799	Wright (partnership)	2	225
1800	Bricklayer & Thread Manufacturer	4	999
1800	Builder (partnership)	1	200
1800	Wright	2	1,400
1800	Wright (partnership)	2	310
1800	Plasterer	2	350
1800	Mason	2	200

Source: Guildhall Library, Sun Fire Policy Registers

   Sixteen individuals and partnerships owned these properties, an average of three tenements per insurer. The small-scale nature of most
building enterprises and their capital weaknesses are too well known to
be worthy of much comment; however, in the circumstances of the French
Wars—and higher public sector borrowing requirements—interest rates
may have operated against this group particularly severely, and thus this
snapshot of holdings may be uncharacteristic. Yet a number held property in closes and others in the form of 'backjams', indicating the trend to
greater building density per acre in some parts of the city and suburbs.

Table 2.3b: Merchants and Tenement Property, 1793-1823

Year	Number of Tenements	Insurance Valuation (£)
1793	2	100
1796	9	1,820
1796	3	1,100

1800	3	450
1800	8	1,900
1820	8	2,156
1820	2	800
1820	2	1,300
1820	5	1,500
1821	1	200
1821	11	7,600
1822	9	1,400
1822	6	1,800
1823	12	4,250

Source: Guildhall Library, Sun Fire Policy Registers

The range of mercantile investment in tenement property was more varied and, despite excluding their own premises (as was done in all other cases), it is likely that some of these assets were used wholly or partly for commercial purposes. Equally, even allowing for changes in the value of money over time, there is much to suggest that many merchants were investing in properties not likely to be occupied by working-class families. However, there were certainly others who did. For example, Alexander Cameron, 'Broker and Dealer in Cloths' in 1793 insured two tenements in Calton for £50 each, one stone and thatched and the other brick and tile in construction, and both occupied by weaving families.[27] In the Saltmarket John Burnside insured seven tenements whose average insured value was £90 in 1796; clearly here was an investor in old town properties while he lived in Charlotte Street in reasonable style.[28]

Although the designation 'merchant' often conceals more than it reveals, this group definitely owned much residential property in addition to those assets intended for their own private and business use. Where they owned houses occupied by working-class families—and they often did—the economic spectrum of their tenantry was often apparently wide as the location and valuation of their properties indicate. Not all were like John Burnside, and even he owned substantial tenements outside the Saltmarket area. The fourteen merchants whose properties are listed in Table 2.3b owned a total of eighty-one tenements, an average of nearly six each.

The retailers formed an even larger group, twenty-eight in all with ninety tenements, an average of just over three per insurer. William McEchnie, the barber listed in Table 2.3c, owned most of his property in Calton and it was occupied in 1796 mainly by weavers,[29] the small insurance valuation per tenement being a good guide to their modesty. On the other hand, Robert Jamieson, a baker who lived on the east side of King Street owned a large backjam insured in 1800 for £600.[30]

Table 2.3c: Retailers and Tenement Property, 1795-1823

Year	Occupation	Number of Tenements	Insurance Valuation ($£$)
1795	Grocer	1	300
1795	Merchant & Spirit Dealer	1	1,000
1796	Baker	4	500
1796	Tobacconist	2	580
1796	Barber	9	1,150
1800	Baker	1	600
1800	Grocer & Spirit Dealer	2	200
1800	Dealer in old clothes & furniture	1	300
1800	Gunsmith	1	600
1801	Grocer & Spirit Dealer	3	700
1801	Drysalter	5	700
1801	Watch & Clock Maker	1	300
1801	Tailor	7	1,550
1801	Baker	2	400
1820	Shopkeeper	2	200
1820	Spirit Dealer & Cowfeeder	1	400
1820	Tobacconist	3	1,000
1820	Cowfeeder	7	900
1820	Grocer	2	350
1820	Grocer & Spirit Dealer	1	350
1821	Tobacconist	4	1,100
.1821	Haberdasher	2	460
1821	Grocer	5	1,600
1821	Grocer	1	600
1822	Pastry Cooks (partnership)	3	800
1822	Baker	2	700
1823	Watchmaker	5	1,100
1823	Baker	11	1,670

Source: Guildhall Library, Sun Fire Policy Registers

Apart from Glasgow cottonmasters with mills located in the country or in the growing suburbs, there was little investment by the new industrialists in working-class housing in the city. David Dale in 1795 owned two tenements and a row of houses (total insurance valuation £400) and this compares with his Glasgow investment in commercial property and stock worth £9,600; his own house in Charlotte Street was insured for a further £2,000, and his household goods and wearing apparel for another £600.[31] The old established Glasgow soapwork company owned two tenement courts and a small house in 1796 valued at £1,050. But generally, the new cotton magnates, such as Henry Houldsworth at Anderston, William Gillespie at Woodside and John Dunlop at Bridgeton, only diverted their capital into housing on a modest scale because they established their businesses in villages on the edge of the city.

The merchants and retailers generally did not require to make substantial outlays on capital equipment and buildings. Their trading surpluses were easily and moderately tapped when demand for housing was buoyant, and thereby they diversified their sources of income. Rents provided a useful income in old age or for a widow with dependent minors. Assuming good tenants (and some would be employees), returns from rentals were more secure than investments in business ventures and greater than might be earned from gilts. Moreover, investments were near at hand, and their well-being could be constantly monitored.

How does this pattern relating to working-class housing survive the test of time? There were certainly cycles of investment and building, great additions being made to total stock between 1866 and 1877 and from 1893 to 1904; there was little activity in the 1880s and virtually none after 1904. Earlier, census and other data are so fraught with deficiencies that it is difficult to do more than guess: there was almost certainly a scarcity of accommodation in the second decade and the fourth. There was a constant problem of quality and standard which gradually provoked civic concern. From 1851 to 1914 the major speculators in working-class housing were the shopocracy, including spirit dealers and publicans, but the initial spark in areas outside the old city often came from the builders who financed their activities by borrowing on bond, a long-established technique derived from landed society. George Eadie, a builder who had lived in Glasgow since 1851, told the Municipal Commission in 1902 that he had built about two hundred tenements intended for working-class occupation, averaging twelve dwellings per tenement, mainly for shopkeeper-landlords.[32] Increasingly, builders imposed larger ground annual rents (in perpetuity) upon properties as they sold them to landlords as a means of raising a steady supply of cash to finance their operations, and when pressed, they would sell the right to such ground annuals to individuals or institutions.[33]

Because many builders were relatively small businessmen, their creation of ground annuals was often a deliberate tactic to raise working capital from their rapid sale. They seldom built houses to rent on their own behalf and rarely undertook the total financial outlay required for tenements which in the 1880s might average £72 per room.[34] Shopkeepers supported these building operations by taking interest-bearing bonds, often up to two-thirds of the value of each completed tenement; their bonds guaranteed them the right to final purchase or could be transferred profitably to others. Thus, eventually private individuals would generally become the landlords, not builders.

This process can be illustrated by reference to the working-class district of Polmadie which was investigated by John McKee.[35] Beginning in 1874 this district was built rapidly, forty-six tenements being completed by 1886, and the last at 12 Polmadie Street being erected much later in 1903. The group completed by 1886 consisted of 569 separate working-class dwellings in grey sandstone tenements, three storeys high with the number of houses per close varying from nine to sixteen, twelve (corroborating Eadie's experience) being the most common. The builders proceeded on one or two blocks without regard to completing one street at a time. Building followed a clear cycle as indicated in Table 2.4. Two years in the 1880s, 1882 and 1884, saw no houses completed, and this district stumbled to completion.

Table 2.4: Tenements and Houses in Polmadie, 1874-1886

Period	Number of Tenements	Number of Houses
1874-1879	33	398
1880-1886	13	171
Totals	46	569

Source: McKee, 'Working-class Housing', p. 47, and Scottish Record Office Valuation Rolls, VR114, 1874-1886.

The Valuation Rolls reveal that builders were often involved as first owners. John Paterson, a local landowner, brickmaker and builder, probably built at least ten of these tenements and was involved with a joiner, Breckenridge, in another four or five. Robert Bell, housefactor, and John Hornsby, mason, were first joint proprietors of another five tenements, and since they were partners in a building firm, it seems likely that they were the builders. Archibald Morrison, mason, was listed as first proprietor of eight tenements, John Morrison, mason, of one and Robert Wilson, mason, of one. In all, at least thirty-four tenements were built by the first proprietor. By 1910 only one builder remained as proprietor; there were four house factors, nine shopkeepers, one trust and three owners who could not be readily classified.[36]

In the independent burgh of Maryhill, Stewart Whitehouse found a more variegated ownership of house property, using valuation rolls for 1861 and 1891; his results are summarised in Table 2.5.[37] Here the 'shopocracy' was the largest group from 1861 together with trusts and lawyers (who commonly managed trusts). Firms in the area declined in significance as this suburb expanded, being owners of about a sixth of the property in 1861 and a twentieth by 1891. Housing as a safe home for small savings before the era of the great building societies is amply demonstrated by Table 2.5; the trusts often being a canny provision for dependents, including widows and children.

Table 2.5: Ownership (Percentage of Houses) of Working-Class Housing in Maryhill, 1861-1891

Owner	1861 (%)	1891 (%)
Companies in area	16	5.5
Trusts and lawyers	28	36.2
Widows	8	10.0
Builders	4	1.5
Farmers	4	0.0
Church	4	4.0
Merchants & Shopkeepers	36	42.8

Source: Whitehouse, 'Working Class Housing', p. 37, and Valuation Rolls.

Daunton and Morgan examined the structure of rented (not working-class) accommodation in Glasgow in 1900-1, also using valuation rolls.[38] They found that 56.1 per cent of the properties representing 58.9 per cent of annual rentals were owned by private individuals, trusts being a poor second with 25.5 per cent of properties and 25.7 per cent of rentals. Property companies, a recent development in the Glasgow context, were relatively unimportant as owners, accounting for only 3.8 per cent of properties and 4.2 per cent of rentals. The railway companies owned 674 properties including substantial groups in Springburn and Corkerhill. Industrial firms were unimportant also, although in the Clydeside burghs such as Govan, Clydebank, Dalmuir and Yoker they were significant.

Table 2.6 includes data relating to categories of housing and also details about the number of families in the city. It has many deficiencies, mostly arising from the nature of census enumeration before 1881, although I have attempted to offset these by reference to the social and economic statistics produced by the City Chamberlains in the Victorian period.[39] Briefly, the major problem arose because the census enumerators before 1881 were left to their own devices in determining what constituted a house, since the defining principle, the external walls of a property, was not very well suited to the tenement context. From 1881 the census procedure was amended to count every separate residential part of a building.

The 1712 data, given merely to establish the early eighteenth century context, arose from a decision to use rentals as a tax assessment mechanism. Householders included also tenants; there were 855 landholders among 3,669 householders—23.3 per cent—and only 2,455 houses were liable for house duty—67 per cent.[40] Taking account of the green belt and river, the city was a pleasant place to live with a low population density. Assuming about 4,000 families in 1712, by 1780 there had been a doubling, and Smellie's survey of 1785, thought to be very accurate by Denholm, revealed a 250 per cent increase in the number of houses. The growth of the city and suburbs up to the first census of 1801 was rapid and accompanied by a substantial expansion in the supply of houses.

Table 2.6: Population, Land Area and Housing in Glasgow, 1712-1911

Year or Census	Total Population	Acreage City & Suburbs	Population Density Per Acre	Inhabited Houses	Uninhabited Houses	Under Construction	Total Houses Available for Occupancy	Total Families	Percentage of Families above Inhabited Houses
1712	14,000	1,768	17.9						
1753	18,336	1,768	10.4	3,669				8,144	
1765	28,100	1,768	15.9						
1780	32,576	1,768	18.4	9,102					
1785	36,139	1,768	20.4						
1791	41,777	1,768	23.6	10,291					
1801	77,385	5,063	15.2	20,276	1,184		21,460	20,967	3.41
1811	100,749	5,063	19.9	17,543	706	72	18,249	23,567	34.34
1821	147,043	5,063	29.0	31,644	1,917	244	33,561	31,956	1.00
1831	202,426	5,063	40.0	41,598	1,759	156	43,357	41,965	0.88
1841	274,324	5,063	54.2	52,441	2,337	529	54,778	55,309	5.46
1851	329,096	5,063	63.0	63,153	1,547	1,032	64,700	64,854	2.62
1861	395,503	5,063	78.0	82,609	4,022	962	86,611	83,588	1.17
1871	477,732	5,063	94.0	100,876	2,134	1,025	103,010	106,861	5.60
1881	511,415	6,111	84.0	106,238	12,264	377	118,502	112,710	5.74
1891	565,714	11,861	93.0	134,339	6,491	768	140,830	144,828	7.24
1901	741,124	12,687	58.0	155,526	7,225	1,535	162,751	163,548	4.90
1911	784,496	12,975	62.0	163,057	20,903	487	183,960	167,896	2.90

In this period many handloom weavers were building their own houses and loomsheds; within a generation their decline became precipitous, and loomsheds in the housing shortage following 1811 were converted into dwellings for the working classes.[41] Evidence from the house market of the prosperity of the weavers in the late eighteenth century can be garnered from a number of sources. For instance, when the lands of Dowhill, including many small houses, were sold in 1780, it was revealed that most of the tenants were prosperous weavers.[42] The sale of building plots in Tradeston proceeding in 1792 similarly attracted the better paid among this occupational group.[43]

The housing stock came under severe pressure in the French Wars, although the census data relating to houses for 1811 may be wildly inaccurate for reasons already given. However, James Cleland (1820) corroborates these, and the low rate of 'empties' and the slackness in the building cycle confirm the suggestion of a house famine. Moreover, there was a survey, for the city only, undertaken in 1819 under Cleland's supervision: this revealed the data given in Table 2.7. The 16,478 householders were divided roughly three to one, with the males, as might be expected, predominating; however, the size of the female contingent is worthy of comment, not only as reflecting female survival rates under the pace of industrialisation—what the Victorians called the excess of females—but also the demographic characteristics of a city heavily committed to the production of textiles where men found jobs harder to acquire. There were 8,065 lodgers, with males outnumbering females by a proportion of roughly three to two. For every two householders there was one lodger. Since the distribution of lodgers was not even throughout the social structure, an overcrowding problem and a houseless group almost certainly strained the seams of the city's social fabric.

Table 2.7: Householders and Lodgers in the City of Glasgow, 1819

Male Householders		Female Householders		Male Lodgers		Female Lodgers	
Number	(%)	Number	(%)	Number	(%)	Number	(%)
11,950	72.5	4,528	27.5	4,671	57.9	3,394	42.1

Source: Cleland, *Rise and Progress*, p. 288.

Cleland was deeply conscious of the problem, the first city servant to leave record of his concern:

It has long been matter [sic] of regret to the Philanthropist, and to every man of feeling, that the houses of the lower classes should be huddled together, in the narrow and ill ventilated closses[sic] of the more ancient part of the town, amid nuisance and filth, by which diseases are caught, and contagion generated.[44]

Migration and immigration added to demand pressures on an even greater

scale after 1820, and by 1841 lodgings were in short supply, and overcrowding of families had become a major concern for those interested in the
health of towns and people. As Dr Robert Graham, Professor of Botany
in the University of Glasgow and Cleland's contemporary, noted in 1818
cellars and lodging houses were crammed; 'the hovels they inhabit are
collected into dense masses of very great size between some of the larger
streets'.[45]

J.C. Symons, 'Assistant Commissioner on the Condition of Handloom
Weavers', in a celebrated passage from his report to Parliament graphically
described conditions twenty years later:

> These districts (the low districts of Glasgow) contain a motley popula-
> tion, consisting in almost all the lower branches of occupation, but chiefly
> of a community whose sole means of subsistence consists in plunder and
> prostitution. Under the escort of that vigilant Officer, Captain Miller, the
> superintendent of the Glasgow Police, I have four times visited these dis-
> tricts, once in the morning and three times at night; I have seen human
> degradation in some of its worst phases, both in England and abroad,
> but I can advisedly say, that I did not believe, until I visited the wynds
> of Glasgow, that so large an amount of filth, crime, misery, and disease
> existed on one spot in any civilised country. The wynds consist of long
> lanes, so narrow that a cart could with difficulty pass along them; out
> of these open the 'closes', which are courts about fifteen or twenty feet
> square, round which the houses, mostly of three storeys high are built;
> the centre of the court is the dunghill. . . In the lower lodging houses,
> ten, twelve, and sometimes twenty persons, of both sexes and all ages,
> sleep promiscuously on the floor in different degrees of nakedness. These
> places are generally as regards dirt, damp, and decay, such as no per-
> son of common humanity would stable his horse in. Many of the worst
> houses are dilapidated and in a dangerous state, and are condemned by
> the Dean of Guild Court, a sentence of which the execution appears to
> be generally postponed, and which renders these abodes doubly desirable
> to the occupants, as the passing of sentence prevents the levy of rent.[46]

Much the same kind of comment was made by Captain Miller himself
in a paper delivered to the British Association for the Advancement of
Science, at its Glasgow meeting in 1840. The centre of the old city contained 'an accumulated mass of squalid wretchedness'; 'places filled by a
population of many thousands of miserable creatures'; 'houses unfit even
for styes, and every apartment is filled with a promiscuous crowd of men,
women and children, all in the most revolting state of filth and squalor'.[47]
For a substantial group of Glasgow's working-class population, penury,
low incomes, irregular and casual work rendered demand for reasonable
accommodation ineffective.

The major provision within the tenement was the one apartment
dwelling, commonly known as the 'single-end'. Until late in the century

it was as much as most respectable working men were able to afford, and at times of economic crisis, as Table 2.6 indicates for 1881, even this went by the board for many families. The fluctuations in the number of uninhabited houses reflect the changing levels of ineffective demand, for at no time did the number of inhabited houses match the number of families. The total available for occupancy very occasionally did equal the number of families, as for instance in 1841, 1851 and 1911, but 'empties' and the number being built, especially in 1911, indicate the slackness of the market.

II: Problems and Solutions

For civic officials and professional men involved with the general care of the community, their general commitment to a free market for housing was gradually modified as the city's population density increased. Habits common in rural societies—either in Ireland or the Highlands—were transferred to urban housing and concentrated so as to affront men like Graham, Symon and Miller. The district surgeons in their reports to the city authorities linked epidemics of typhus and later cholera with the housing and general environment of the central city slums.

Dr Robert Cowan (d.1841), like Graham, related housing and epidemic disease closely together;[48] Symon and Miller were more committed to an analysis based upon human failings—immorality, vice, drunkenness, mendicity, and criminality. These central slums were dangerous not only as centres of contagion, but also as the repositories of depravity and delinquency. Increases in the incidence of typhus and more particularly cholera alarmed the bourgeoisie most, but they recognised also that there was a law and order problem.[49]

Mostly, they favoured selective demolition of the worst dens of iniquity. Graham advocated opening up the homes of the poor to better ventilation and also the charitable involvement of the middle classes in 'the building of houses for the poor on an approved plan, and in a good situation'.[50] Cleland also favoured a charitable—but profitable—building society: he thought this should be established 'among the sons of humanity, who know that house rents to this description of people, are frequently higher than they can afford'. A sum of £21,000 (equivalent to the relief distributed in the city in 1818 and 1819) should be applied to building '600 houses, consisting of a kitchen and a small room, and 600 houses of one apartment'. The room and kitchen dwellings could be let from 1s. per week and the 'single-ends' at 6d. per week. These dwellings should be scattered over three parishes so that any prospective burden on parish poor rates would not be concentrated. Thereby about 5,000 people would be rehoused and 5 per cent retained after all expenses as 'interest on their capital'.[51] This idea became relatively commonplace in the late nineteenth century, but it provided no permanent solution to the housing of the poor.

Its principal expression in the city was the Glasgow Workmen's Dwellings Company which was established in 1890 with capital of £40,000. The Glasgow Social Union had revived Cleland's idea, and from this group came the directors and secretary, John Mann. By 1902 this company owned 669 houses and had spent £54,000 in providing accommodation for over 2,000 people. The average return on capital was 4 per cent. Its annual rent roll, according to Mann, was £4,600, collected weekly every Monday rather than nightly or monthly. Rents were very cheap for the kind of accommodation required: 1s. $9\frac{1}{2}$d. to 2s. $9\frac{1}{2}$d. per week for one-apartment houses and 3s. $2\frac{1}{2}$d.. to 4s. $2\frac{1}{2}$d. for two apartments in new tenements, less for rooms in converted or repaired property. This company had rehabilitated four properties in need of repair from the stock acquired by the Corporation's Improvement Trust and made them profitable.

'Four per cent philanthropy' also aimed to demonstrate that housing built to reasonable standards could be made to pay: that there was a class of 'industrious poor' prepared to meet the obligations of rent and reasonable tenant behaviour. The operations of this company were designed to encourage the private market to operate more perfectly—to supply more houses at reasonable rents for working people to occupy.[52]

By the 1830s and 1840s the lodging houses were regarded as a major menace to law and order, civic health and hygiene and morality by an increasingly influential group of citizens: 'a large part of the dwellings of the poor in the Wynds and Streets upon the south side of the Trongate, Gallowgate, Calton. . . consist of lodging houses, and constitute the very worst part of these localities'.[53] Increasingly, the City's Police Acts and later its Improvement Acts conferred legal powers to control these premises. However, provision was necessary for transient labourers on their way to jobs; the labour market could not operate effectively without lodgings, but action was necessary on two counts. First, private lodgings were often of a very low standard, and secondly poor rates, it was thought, could be kept to a minimum by establishing accommodation for a poor, but temporary lodging house population.

The Night Asylum was opened in 1838 as an act of charity and was the real beginning of the model lodging house movement in the city.[54] In 1847 the Glasgow Association for Establishing Lodging Houses for the Working Classes was formed with the aim of providing 5,000 beds per night, 'comfortable and cheap accommodation for the Working Classes including strangers to the city in search of employment or in course of transit to other places'. Single beds cost 3d. per night and double beds 4 $\frac{1}{2}$d. Soap and towels were free, and basic food provided at cheap prices. Powers against unfit lodging houses based on the Calton Burgh Act of 1840 had been taken under the Glasgow Police Act (1843), but enforcing these would have put more people onto the streets and stairways of the city. This number was estimated at 5,000; hence the objective of the Glasgow Association to provide accommodation on that basis.[55]

The first house in Mitchell Street was rented and provided accommodation for sixty individuals, but in 1849 a house was bought in Greendyke Street. In 1856 purpose-built properties in McAlpine Street and Carrick Street were added, and extensions undertaken at Greendyke Street. By that date these properties could provide accommodation for about 650 people nightly,[56] but they were rarely full over long periods: in 1874, for instance, the average occupancy was about 500 per night and in 1875, 515.[57] The regime, perhaps rightly, was authoritarian coupled with an emphasis on sobriety, cleanliness and religion which might not have appealed to transients accustomed to other ways and standards.[58]

The Corporation opened its first lodging house in 1871 under the terms of Clause 23 of the City Improvement Act of 1866, and under the Police Acts of the 1860s acquired more controls over the private sector. There was some reluctance by its sanitary inspectorate to use these powers to the full for fear that the number of homeless would increase as a result. In 1878 despair about the state of the common lodging houses and their inhabitants was voiced in their professional journal:[59]

> the state of the lodging houses, and the cellars especially, beggars description, the floors thereof being packed at night with human beings—men, women and children like so many bundles of rags, and the walls and roof black with vermin.

All the economic advantages were placed with lodging house keepers, and this occupation was regarded as the possible route to higher things. In 1860 it was estimated that 6,000 people lived in lodging houses registered with the Corporation and about as many again in unregistered premises.[60] Billy Toye, a celebrated Irish lodging-house keeper of the 1840s and 1850s, earned 10s. per night for beds and retired to farm after nine years in Glasgow.[61]

Corporation lodging houses also showed substantial profits, running at over £4,000 per annum in the late 1880s and early 1890s,[62] and this provided the financial basis for further developments. Additions and extensions were made to several of the lodging houses, and the decision was taken in 1894 to build a 'Family Home' in St Andrews Street. This cost £12,000 and opened in 1896 to cater for widowers with young children.

A Sinking Fund was established in 1890 to plan the repayment of capital expenditure, which by 1914 had reached nearly £113,000, of which £78,443 was then outstanding. Full capacity working (97 per cent of total beds) brought constant profitability throughout the 1890s and only in the depression after 1908 did the current account move temporarily into deficit.[63]

Undoubtedly, the major achievement of the city's own lodging houses was not financial but social: they acted as an agency for the improvement of the private sector. So did a system of regular inspection and tighter local control.

Another major problem was overcrowding in ordinary houses to which the city authorities responded by a system of ticketing, the powers for this being acquired under the Glasgow Police Act of 1862.[64] Any dwelling house in the city with three rooms or less and not exceeding 2,000 cubic feet was measured, and the capacity inscribed on a metal ticket, fixed to the outside door or lintel, together with the number of occupants allowed by law at the rate of 300 cubic feet for every person over the age of eight. This minimum occupancy level was regarded by the authorities as being too low for healthy existence, but it was felt that any higher requisition would either be disregarded or add to the problem of the homeless.

There were 23,228 ticketed houses in Glasgow by the 1880s, 16,413 of which were 'single-ends' and the remaining 6,815 two-apartment. Less than half of Glasgow's one-roomed houses were ticketed, but about 75,000 people, one-seventh of the total population of the city in 1881, occupied ticketed accommodation.[65]

Almost without exception ticketed houses were 'made-down', i.e. they were subdivisions of existing property which until the Building Regulations Act of 1892 required no approval from the Dean of Guild Court. Many 'made-down' houses escaped ticketing, for often the ceiling heights in dwellings once owned by the wealthy were such that their capacity was above the prescribed limit. Ticketed houses were regularly inspected, generally at night, and the sanitary inspectors occasionally waived ticketing to avoid the humiliation of respectable working people living in sub-standard but well-kept accommodation.[66]

Closing houses and demolition were extreme measures taken by the Dean of Guild Court with greater regularity from the late 1840s, but the two City Improvement Acts of 1866 and 1897, the Glasgow Police (Amendment) Act and the Housing of the Working Classes Act of 1890 gave specific and additional powers. About 16,000 houses were demolished between 1866 and 1914 and a further 5,000 closed.[67]

The City Improvement Trust was at first reluctant to build houses, intending as a general policy to provide land for property developers to exploit. However, paralysis in the land market in the 1880s caused the Trust to rethink its policy. By 1914 the Improvement Trust had added 2,199 houses to the stock of the city: 592 one-apartment houses, 1,344 two-apartment, 257 three-apartment and 16 larger than three-apartment houses. Probably about 10,000 people were housed in consequence, fewer than were housed in any one year by private builders in the periods 1867-78 or 1893-1902.[68]

For most working-class families the private market for housing was their only recourse. As Table 2.6 indicates, the total housing stock greatly increased in the nineteenth century as did the city acreage after 1871, which substantially altered average population density per acre, but there was a growing accommodation crisis measured by the percentage of families above the number of inhabited houses until 1891. In the following decade about 30,000 houses were added to the city's net housing stock, and by 1911 there were more homes available for occupancy than families.

Over 80,000 houses of three-apartments or less—85 per cent of all authorisations granted by the Dean of Guild Court—were built between 1862 and 1901. Of these 18 per cent were one-apartment houses, 48 per cent two-apartments and 19 per cent three-apartments.[69] An increasing scale of municipal intervention after 1871 reflected more closely defined Public Health requirements and tighter building regulations. Increased costs of building houses resulted, and since the supply of houses tended to outstrip effective demand, profitability began to decline, especially from the late 1890s. This was most marked in the cheaper end of the market, and there was, therefore, a decline in the building of 'single-ends'.[70] The free market ran out of steam.

III: Working-Class Experience, Some Conclusions

From discussions so far it is more than apparent that working-class experience in the housing market varied from the extremes of accommodation in lodging houses and the night asylum to a fairly comfortable, in relative terms, existence in three or more apartments. Job opportunities, habits, health and income determined how effectively the working-class family coped with the whole urban experience which Glasgow represented; nowhere is this more true than in housing.

Homelessness was a problem for a minority whose plight attracted at-

tention occasionally from religious groups such as those concerned with the
City Mission movement of the 1850s and 1860s. These individuals often
took a radical stance on the importance of the working classes. William
Logan, writing in 1863, remarked that the working classes were the 'foundation of society', upon which 'all the higher orders rest'. He reminded the
wealthy that they could not cope with the living and housing conditions
which the working classes were expected to endure: 'The wonder is not
that there are recklessness and immorality among the labouring classes,
but that there is a spark of virtue left at all'.[71] The houses of the poor
were 'slaughter pens'.[72] Familiar with the activities of the Night Asylum,
the Glasgow Benevolent Society and Police, Logan knew that sleeping on
tenement stairs or in more exposed places was commonplace.[73]

In addition, there were many who, because of their poverty, could
not afford more than the barest accommodation. Logan advanced the
notion that work should be provided for all 'and wages sufficient for all
the necessities of life'.[74] The reality was very different: much work was
casual and temporary; more was subject to downturns in the trade cycle
and seasonal variations; income was occasionally insecure for even the best
paid working man. The pattern of residence and room occupancy reflected
these underlying circumstances.

Transients and casual workers dominated the lodging house population. Not all lodging house keepers were like Billy Toye, who, according
to Hawkie, a celebrated Glasgow character, would evict any lodger who
did not pay his or her nightly rent promptly.[75] Mary Giliespie, who kept
a lodging house in the Gorbals, earned plaudits in a Glasgow broadsheet
for her honest and caring approach to her professional duties, but she was
obviously exceptional.[76] Most lodging houses—at least until the advent
of Corporation inspection—were very crowded and dirty. The price per
night varied from 2d. to 4d., and in many houses the floor served as the
bed. Shelter was thus of a minimal character; but it is important to remember that general housing conditions in the poor areas of the city were
no better.[77]

The model lodging house movement of the 1840s undoubtedly pointed
the way to improvement, but the pressure on accommodation was such
that progress was slow and erratic. Moreover, the disciplined life-style
imposed on those who entered these houses often acted as a deterrent to
those who found it unacceptable or uncompromisingly severe. The Carrick
Street female lodging house matron, Miss Wilson, during the 1870s, pursued a deliberate policy of excluding known and potential trouble-makers
with the approval of the Directors.[78] There were regular religious services
and tight discipline in the City Improvement Trust's lodging houses, and

a deliberate attempt to provide superior accommodation: individual cubicles and iron bedsteads with spring wire mattresses; washing facilities with the charge for a bath of $1\frac{1}{2}$d. also included the necessaries for laundering clothes.[79]

In the 1870s the average nightly attendance at the Corporation's lodging houses was over 500 and after the expansion of the 1890s over 1,900. Many were regulars, and this had been the pattern for many years set by the Model Lodging House Association. At the Carrick Street house, the 1875 Report reveals there were six women who had spent more than three continuous years in residence, and one woman who had lodged there for fifteen years. This degree of continuity was more common in the male establishments: at Greendyke Street and McAlpine Street lodging houses there were twenty-eight and fourteen residents of more than three years stay respectively.[80]

Evidence given to the Municipal Commission on Housing in 1903 by John Stirling Duncan, the superintendent of Portugal Street Model, is instructive about conditions in a newer establishment. There were 468 beds let at $3\frac{1}{2}$d., 4d. and $4\frac{1}{2}$d. The men cooked for themselves, and the majority bought their food from the store in the lodging house. A sample survey taken when the house was full on the night of 22 January 1903 revealed that 113 inmates (24 per cent) were skilled men and 355 (76 per cent) unskilled. The latter could earn in good times between 22s. to 25s. per week, but they rarely worked a full week, and therefore average earnings were 18s. per week. Duncan estimated that the inmates could live on 7s. per week and their rent. He thought they preferred the lodging house to private lodgings because of the relative freedom and modern surroundings. Most of his customers were single men, he was sure, and they were much addicted to drink, their frailty acting against marrying and setting up in homes of their own.[81]

There is much more substantial and less partial evidence about those who lived in ticketed houses. In 1881 Glasgow had 16,413 'single-ends' in this category and 6,815 two-apartment houses, a total of 23,228 properties. About 75,000 people or one-seventh of the city's population in 1881 occupied this type of accommodation, but it should be noted that only 35 per cent of those living in 'single-ends' were ticketed and about 14 per cent of those occupying two-apartment dwellings.[82] Regular inspection at night was a feature of working-class experience in ticketed properties, and 40,000 visits per annum were made in the 1880s.[83] Overcrowding, however, remained a persistent problem right up to 1914, and ticketed houses, therefore, were a matter of civic concern throughout this period. There were fluctuations in the degree of the problem—8 per cent in 1866 down to 5 per cent in 1885 to 12.74 per cent in 1901 and 6 to 8 per cent in the decade before 1914.[84] By then there were six inspectors instead of the original two, and they operated from 11.30 pm to 5 am in their unavailing attempts to eliminate overcrowding.

The occupational pattern of the heads of households in ticketed houses is also clear. About 70 per cent were unskilled labourers, 22 per cent were skilled workers or artisans, while the remainder had no definite occupation.[85] Dr J.B. Russell argued in 1888 that they all paid more than those living in City Improvement Trust model property *pro rata*, and the quality of their accommodation was much inferior.

Nonetheless, Russell believed that the principal problem was human weakness:[86]

> He (the inhabitant of the ticketed house) not only pays interest on his poverty, but on his character. Those 75,000 people comprise not only the criminal class, but the whole social *debris* of this large city; some who are bravely struggling with poverty, and far more who are alike bankrupt in character and in fortune. They are the nomads of our population. If we could see them in their constant movements from place to place the sight would resemble nothing so much as that which meets our eye when we lift a stone from an ant's nest. The City Assessor will tell you that they change their location in hundreds every month.

Misallocation of income may have occurred, especially in the case of skilled men, but they were a clear minority, and irregularity of earnings and income commonly resulted in grinding poverty which sapped health, stamina and ambition. This affected most of this group.

'House-farmers' provided furnished accommodation for those who could not get access to unfurnished rented properties. Usually, this accommodation was of a primitive kind in poor property in the older parts of the city, for which the owners received a fixed rent and yet managed to avoid responsibility. House-farming increased in the 1890s and in the period up to 1914 as the standard of living for many Glasgwegians deteriorated. House-farmers by 1902 controlled 617 'single-ends' and 322 two-apartment dwellings, accommodating 2,695 adults and their children. These sub-tenants lived, on average for six months in 'farmed' accommodation, and it seems that transients and other poor people found it useful or necessary.[87]

'House-farmers' found it very profitable to provide this service. £3 per room might be spent on furniture; rent paid to the owner might reach £6 per annum; sub-tenants paid at least £20 per house per annum.[88] These houses were occupied by people 'with no furniture and . . . practically bankrupt in estate'.[89] They usually paid their rent nightly as couples—in 1902, 8d. for old customers and 10d. for new; cots were provided for children at a nightly rate of 4d. and 6d. respectively for old and new sub-tenants.[90] When in employment many of these people earned relatively good wages, but according to the 'house-farmers' drink was the main reason for their downfall. A few could certainly earn as much as £2 per week in 1902, but many inhabitants of farmed properties were seasonal or casual workers and most were unskilled. A sample of 909 sub-tenants taken in 1902 revealed that 186 males were dockers, 279 other types of unskilled labourers, 79 in unskilled trades, 66 carters and vanmen, 35 street musicians and vendors, 48 without precise occupations and 156 artisans. Of the 60 women heads of households in the sample 22 worked as charwomen, and the rest were divided in small numbers: 7 unskilled, 2 machinists, 2 seamstresses, 2 laundry workers, 5 hawkers, and 5 caretakers.[91] Perhaps more unexpectedly, occupants of farmed houses were asked to give their own reasons for living in these places. Nearly 60 per cent gave drink as the reason, 18 per cent 'want of a factor's line or reference', nearly 12 per cent unemployment, nearly 6 per cent illness and about the same proportion gave no clear reply.[92]

The vast majority of those seeking accommodation in the private market rented property unfurnished, but there were many constraints. It was vital to be able to secure an acceptable reference or a factor's line before a house could be obtained. Some factors charged key money and then demanded a month's rent in advance. Factors operating on behalf of property owners could pick and choose tenants for good properties at most periods of the nineteenth century, and the City Improvement Trust and the Glasgow Workmen's Dwelling Company in the later period could select those in steady employment and of good character. Rising rents placed tenants under pressure in the period 1866 to 1901—55 per cent increase for single-ends and 38 per cent for two-apartment dwellings.[93] It should, therefore, occasion little surprise that Glasgow had a persistent problem of overcrowding and slum landlords.

By 1914 there had been some improvement in working-class experience of the housing market, and general measures taken to improve environmental and living conditions were beginning to take effect. By the Census of 1911, 20 per cent of families were living in 'single-ends' compared with 34.1 per cent in 1861; 46.3 per cent lived in two-apartment houses compared with 39.3 per cent at the earlier date; 18.9 per cent in three-apartment dwellings compared with 12.6 per cent. The city authorities were well versed in the problems posed by the private housing market, but they had no magical cure.[94]

Notes

1. Daniel Defoe, *A Tour thro' the Whole Island of Great Britain*, G.D.H. Cole, ed. (1927), II, pp. 746ff.
2. Thomas Pennant, *A Tour in Scotland and Voyage to the Hebrides*, 5th edition (1790), II, pp. 145ff.
3. J. Boswell, *Journal of a Tour to the Hebrides with Samuel Johnson, 1773*, F.A. Ottle and C.H. Bennett, eds. (1963), p. 364.
4. A. Brown, *The History of Glasgow*, (Glasgow, 1795), II, p. 86.
5. J. Gibson, *The History of Glasgow*, (Glasgow, 1777), p. 132.
6. J. Denholm, *The History of the City of Glasgow and Suburbs to Which is Added a Sketch of a Tour to the Principal Scotch and English Lakes*, 3rd edition (Glasgow, 1804).
7. Senex (Robert Reid), *Glasgow Past and Present*, (Glasgow, 1884), I, pp. 114, 274, 455.
8. James Gourlay, *The Provosts of Glasgow, 1609-1832*, (Glasgow, 1942), pp. 69-70.
9. T.M. Devine, 'Glasgow Colonial Merchants and Land, 1770-1815', in J.T. Ward and R.G. Wilson, eds., *Land and Industry*, (Newton Abbot, 1971), pp. 205-35.
10. Senex, *Glasgow*, II, pp. 101ff, 243, 316; *Glasgow Mercury*, 9 July 1778; *Glasgow Journal*, 3 April 1777 and 14 August 1777.
11. Gibson, *History of Glasgow*, p. 115.
12. Brown, *History of Glasgow*, pp. 100-16, 212; *Glasgow Mercury*, 11 September 1792; Senex, *Glasgow*, II, p. 514, III, p. 10, I, pp. 61-2; Denholm, *City of Glasgow*, pp. 141-9.
13. Denholm, *City of Glasgow*, p. 149; G. Stewart, *Curiosities of Glasgow Citizenship* (Glasgow, 1881), pp. 40-1; J.D. Porteous, *Canal Ports*, (1977), p. 42; A. & N. Clow, *The Chemical Revolution* (1952), p. 193.
14. Brown, *History of Glasgow*, p. 212.
15. Denholm, *City of Glasgow*, p. 149.
16. *Ibid.*, p. 148.
17. London Guildhall Library, Sun Fire Assurance Policy Registers (hereafter GH), vol. 11937/31, Policy No. 701669, 21 April 1800.
18. GH 11937/31, Policy No. 703487, 7 June 1800.
19. GH 11937/34, Policy No. 705757, 29 July 1800.
20. GH 11927/34, Policy No. 701042, 27 March 1800.
21. GH 11927/34, Policy No. 701038, 27 March 1800.
22. GH 11937/32, Policy No. 701319, 7 April 1800.
23. GH 11937/10, Policy No. 640581, 20 April 1795.
24. GH 11937/4, Policy No. 623974, 8 February 1794.
25. GH 11937/14, Policy No. 653101, 10 February 1796.
26. GH 11937/35, Policy No. 708486, 11 October 1800.
27. GH 11937/2, Policy No. 620190, 8 October 1795.
28. GH 11937/14, Policy No. 656965, 18 July 1796.
29. GH 11937/11, Policy No. 651033, 13 January 1796.
30. GH 11937/34, Policy No. 705741, 29 July 1800.

31. GH 11937/11, Policy No. 649605, 29 December 1795.
32. Glasgow City Archives (GCA) C3/2/18, Minutes of Evidence taken before Glasgow Municipal Commission on Housing (1902-3), p. 339.
33. *Scottish Land. The Report of the Scottish Land Enquiry Committee* (1914), liii, pp. 289, 307,ff.
34. A. Slaven, *The Development of the West of Scotland* (1975), p. 179.
35. J. McKee, 'Glasgow Working-class Housing with Special Reference to the Polmadie District, 1870-1910', (BA Honours Dissertation, University of Strathclyde, 1976).
36. Scottish Record Office (SRO), Valuation Rolls, 1880-1910, VR 114 and VR 102; Trade Directories, 1870-1910.
37. S. Whitehouse, 'Working Class Housing in the Burgh of Maryhill, 1856-1891', (BA Honours Dissertation, University of Strathclyde, 1976).
38. M.J. Daunton, *House and Home in the Victorian City: Working-Class Housing, 1850-1914* (1983), pp. 119-20.
39. Sources for Table 2.7: Population figures from Brown, *History of Glasgow*, II, p. 88; Denholm, *City of Glasgow*, pp. 226-7; J. Cleland, *The Rise and Progress of Glasgow* (Glasgow, 1820), pp. 288-9; *The Census of Scotland*, 1801-1911; acreage, families, and housing from W.W. Watson, *Vital, Social and Economic Statistics of Glasgow* (Glasgow, 1880); J.A. Nicol, *Vital, Social and Economic Statistics of Glasgow* (Glasgow, 1891); GCA, Municipal Minutes, *passim*, and *Municipal Glasgow*, 1914.
40. Brown, *History of Glasgow*, II, p. 88.
41. N. Murray, *The Scottish Hand Loom Weavers* (Edinburgh, 1978), p. 153.
42. *Glasgow Mercury*, 19 October 1780.
43. *Ibid.*, 11 September 1792.
44. J. Cleland, *The Rise and Progress of Glasgow* (Glasgow, 1820), pp. 158-9.
45. R. Graham, *Practical Observations on Continued Fever* (Glasgow, 1818).
46. British Parliamentary Papers, 1839 (195) LXII; J.C. Symons, *Reports from Assistant Handloom Weavers' Commissioners*, 1839.
47. *Proceedings of British Association* (Glasgow, 1840), p. 170.
48. Edwin Chadwick, *Report on the Sanitary Condition of the Labouring Population of Great Britain, 1842*, M.W. Flinn, ed. (Edinburgh, 1965), pp. 5, 98n, 214; R. Cowan, *Vital Statistics of Glasgow* (1838).
49. A.A. McLaren, 'Bourgeois Ideology and Victorian Philanthropy: the contradictions of Cholera', *idem, Social Class in Scotland* (Edinburgh, 1976), pp. 43ff.
50. R. Graham, *Practical Observations*.
51. Cleland, *Rise and Progress*, pp. 159-60.
52. O. Checkland, *Philanthropy in Victorian Scotland* (Edinburgh, 1980), pp. 293-4; J. Butt, 'Working-class Housing in Glasgow, 1851-1914', S.D. Chapman, ed., *The History of Working-class Housing* (Newton Abbot, 1971), p. 79.
53. S. Laidlaw, *Glasgow Common Lodging Houses and the People Living in Them* (Glasgow, 1956); *Report of the Glasgow Association for Establishing Lodging Houses for the Working Classes*, 1847, p. 5; O. Checkland, *Philanthropy*, pp. 285ff.

54. J. Goodwin, *A History of the Glasgow Night Asylum for the House-less, 1838-1887* (Glasgow, 1887).
55. Report of the Glasgow Association, 1847.
56. *Glasgow Herald*, 2 October 1860.
57. Report of the Glasgow Association, 1875.
58. O. Checkland, *Philanthropy*, p. 286.
59. *Sanitary Journal*, 1878.
60. *Glasgow Herald*, 2 October 1860.
61. Laidlaw, *Common Lodging Houses*, p. 17.
62. J. Nicol, *Vital, Social and Economic Statistics of the City of Glasgow* (Glasgow, 1891), pp. 134-5.
63. *Municipal Glasgow, 1914*, pp. 53-4; Municipal Commission Minutes, p. 104.
64. Glasgow Police Act 1862, clauses 385-388.
65. Glasgow City Archives Miscellaneous prints, vol. 36, p. 368; J.B. Russell, 'On the Ticketed Houses of Glasgow', A.K. Chalmers, ed., *Public Health Administration in Glasgow* (Glasgow, 1905), pp. 206-28.
66. Municipal Commission Report, p. 2; Russell, 'Ticketed Houses', p. 216.
67. Municipal Commission Minutes, pp. 100ff; *Municipal Glasgow, 1914*, pp. 259-260; Chalmers, *Public Health*, pp. 95ff.
68. Butt, 'Working-class Housing', pp. 62-3.
69. Municipal Commission, p. 81.
70. Butt, 'Working-class Housing', pp. 73-5.
71. A Sabbath School Teacher (William Logan), *The Moral Statistics of Glasgow in 1863* (Glasgow, 1864), p. 21.
72. *Ibid.*, p. 25.
73. *Ibid.*, pp. 59-60.
74. *Ibid.*, p. 61.
75. J. Strathesk, *Hawkie, the Autobiography of a Gangrel* (Glasgow, 1888), p. 58.
76. Mitchell Library, Glasgow. Broadsheet: 'Molly's History'.
77. Laidlaw, *Common Lodging Houses*, pp. 17-8.
78. *Report of the Annual General Meeting of Glasgow Model Lodging House Association* (Glasgow, 1875), pp. 5-6. The need for this approach was demonstrated by *The North British Daily Mail*, 29-30 August 1871, whose correspondent stayed in this lodging house.
79. GCA, City Improvement Trust Minutes, 1877-9, *passim.*
80. *Report of AGM of Glasgow Model Lodging House Association*, 1875, p. 7.
81. GCA, Minutes of Municipal Commission, pp. 126-8.
82. Russell, 'Ticketed Houses', pp. 206-208.
83. Dilke Commission, 1885, p. 49.
84. Municipal Commission Minutes, p. 42; *Municipal Glasgow, 1914*, p. 240.
85. Municipal Commission Minutes, p. 122.
86. Russell, 'Ticketed Houses', pp. 220-1.
87. Municipal Commission Minutes, pp. 17-8, 32-3, 44.
88. *Ibid.*, pp. 85-9, 544.
89. *Ibid.*, p. 44.
90. *Ibid.*
91. Butt, 'Working-class Housing', pp. 76-7.

92. *Ibid.*, p. 77.
93. *Ibid.*, pp. 74-85.
94. *Ibid.*, p. 81 and *idem*, 'Working-class Housing in Glasgow, 1900-1939',
    I. MacDougall, *Essays in Scottish Labour History* (Edinburgh, 1978), pp.
    143ff.

Chapter Three

HEALTH IN GLASGOW

R.A. Cage

At the beginning of the nineteenth century mortality rates for Glasgow were similar to the surrounding areas. Indeed, the mortality rate for children under the age of five was showing a downward trend. Glasgow, like the remainder of Scotland, was not experiencing the mortality crises which had been a major feature of the seventeenth and early eighteenth centuries. However, during the 1820s the situation reversed, as there was a significant increase in the death rate for all age groups. It was not until the beginning of the twentieth century that mortality rates for Glasgow returned to their pre-industrial levels. The purpose of this chapter is to examine the trends in mortality and morbidity to try to discover the major underlying causal factors.

I: Mortality Rates

Numerous studies undertaken in Glasgow during the first half of the nineteenth century provide some of the best statistical information on mortality and morbidity rates for any city in Britain. These studies have recently been analysed and updated by the Edinburgh-based study of Scottish population history.[1] One feature emerges from this study—nineteenth century mortality crises were not unique to Glasgow, most of Scotland also experienced them, though urban areas, and especially Glasgow, were the hardest hit. The principal villain was the return of the fever epidemics, mainly typhus and cholera. The annual mortality in Glasgow in 1820 was about 25 per thousand and rose to 30 per thousand by 1840. The mortality crises could take the annual mortality to very high levels, reaching 49 per thousand in 1832 and 56 per thousand in the years of cholera and typhus, such as in 1847.

> With the retreat of cholera at the end of 1832, mortality returned for the time being to pre-epidemic levels. For the next quarter-century, however, there were to be no more long stretches—whole decades, as in the first third of the century—free from crises. The period from 1832 to 1855 was to be one of the worst in modern Scottish history, with frequent, severe crises rising to a peak in 1847, and only falling away in the late 1850s. The crises were largely, though not exclusively, confined to urban areas, and were the product of the failure of municipal governments to cope with the public health problems arising from urban populations of unprecedented size and density. Urban populations grew at a pace that outran the ability of city governments to provide the essential services of housing, drainage, cleansing and water supplies. These fundamentally 'public health' failures created an environment in which repeated epidemics of cholera, typhus and other infectious diseases were inevitable. The frequent sharp peaks drove mortality for the decades of the 1830s, 1840s and 1850s to levels reminiscent of the seventeenth century.[2]

As can be seen from Table 3.1, sudden increases in mortality rates were not confined to these decades. In 1808 there was a 33 per cent increase in the number of deaths over the previous five-year period; the prime factor was a sharp rise in the number of children under the age of ten dying from measles.[3] A typhus epidemic in 1818-19 resulted in a 42 per cent increase in deaths over the previous five-year average.[4] An outbreak of measles and smallpox in 1871 was the last major epidemic to hit Glasgow; it caused mortality to increase only 15 per cent above the average of the preceeding five years.[5] These crisis periods, however, were minor compared to those of the 1830s and 1840s. For example in 1836 there was a dramatic increase in the number of deaths recorded in Glasgow. There had been an average of 7,069 deaths between 1833 and 1835, which jumped to 9,141 in 1836 and 'to 10,886 in 1837—a greater total than in the cholera epidemic of only five years earlier. Typhus was largely responsible for the increased mortality in Glasgow. 412 had died of typhus in the city in 1835: the toll rose to 841 in 1836, and to 2,180 in 1837'.[6] During 1843 for the period 'from August to November deaths ran at almost 50% above their usual monthly levels. Most of the additional deaths were due to relapsing fever and over the whole year burials were 30% higher than in the previous year'.[7] 'Burials in Glasgow, which had averaged 8,452 during the non-crisis years 1838-42 and 1844-45, more than doubled to 18,071 in 1847.'[8] The last serious cholera epidemic to hit Scotland was in 1853-54, with Glasgow suffering the major impact, as an estimated 4,000 Glaswegians died out of a possible 6,000 for the whole of Scotland.[9]

Table 3.1: Causes of Death, Children under 10, Total Burials, 1783-1812

Year	Smallpox	Measles	Fevers	Other	Under 2	2-5	5-10	Total under 10	Total burials
1783	155	66	118	366	479	174	66	719	
1784	425	1	146	309	671	161	45	877	
1785	218	0	292	380	576	126	42	744	
1786	348	2	177	386	706	179	56	941	
1787	410	23	240	421	746	205	65	1,016	
1788	399	1	302	388	770	221	68	1,057	
1789	366	23	135	471	794	188	76	1,058	
1790	336	33	155	593	903	247	86	1,236	2,079
1791	607	4	132	560	984	320	63	1,367	1,912
1792	202	58	205	461	664	184	45	893	2,190
1793	389	5	183	441	807	239	80	1,126	2,445
1794	235	7	126	340	553	144	62	759	1,700
1795	402	46	92	462	761	225	62	1,048	2,297
1796	177	92	137	392	562	181	54	797	1,813
1797	354	5	183	373	586	241	57	884	2,064
1798	309	3	107	425	642	181	41	864	2,181
1799	370	43	180	564	783	244	78	1,105	2,499
1800	257	21	125	304	545	148	53	746	2,096
1801	245	8	89	388	494	211	61	766	1,928
1802	156	168	247	477	544	326	155	985	2,325
1803	194	45	242	468	610	243	87	940	2,438
1804	213	27	146	468	583	192	88	863	2,224
1805	56	99	116	550	616	188	80	884	2,389
1806	28	56	151	564	517	188	81	786	2,280
1807	97	16	163	574	595	211	93	899	2,463
1808	51	787	180	697	1,079	521	175	1,775	3,265
1809	159	44	147	784	782	287	118	1,187	2,368
1810	28	19	97	801	765	169	93	1,027	2,367
1811	109	267	175	657	769	341	164	1,274	2,622
1812	78	304	105	584	804	371	103	1,278	2,716

Source: J. Cleland, *Statistical Tables Relative to Glasgow*, 1828, pp. 16, 23.

Table 3.2 presents estimated crude death rates for Glasgow for the nineteenth century. It can clearly be seen from this table that the crude death rate for Glasgow in the nineteenth century peaked during the 1845-9 time period. Moreover, it was not until 1891 that the average crude death rate for Glasgow was below the rate for the period 1821-4. Thus, it can only be concluded that the maintenance of health was a major problem for Glasgow, and that dramatic improvements did not occur until after 1871. The worse decades occurred between 1821 and 1861. Table 3.3 provides more detail for these crucial decades.

Table 3.2: Crude Death Rates, per thousand, Glasgow, 1821-1911

Period	Rate
1821-4	24.8
1825-9	26.8
1830-4	31.5
1835-9	33.0
1840-4	31.0
1845-9	39.9
1850-4	38.2
1855-9	29.6
1860-4	30.5
1871	30.6
1881	25.6
1891	22.7
1901	21.1
1911	17.3

Source: Flinn, *Scottish Population History*, pp. 377, 383.

Table 3.3: Age-Specific Death Rates, per thousand, Glasgow, 1821-1861

Age-Group	1821	1831	1841	1851	1861
0-4	70.4	66.1	112.8	110.1	96.4
5-9	11.9	9.8	16.1	16.3	11.5
10-19	6.6	6.6	9.3	7.2	7.7
20-29	10.2	8.7	11.1	9.5	10.2
30-39	13.9	11.8	17.3	13.0	13.4
40-49	16.7	19.3	26.0	18.1	17.5
50-59	26.2	30.2	38.2	28.2	27.7
60-69	42.8	49.0	65.8	48.3	51.7
over 70	117.1	151.2	160.6	126.0	129.8

Source: Flinn, *Scottish Population History*, p. 378.

The figures in Table 3.3 illustrate that no age group escaped the mortality crises. The 0-4 age group was the hardest hit, however, those in the 40-49 age bracket also experienced a disproportionately large increase. The fact that all age groups fell victim to increasing mortality rates suggests that the causes of the mortality crises were not age-specific related, but rather were the result of a general, overall worsening of conditions, be they economic or social. Indeed, one possible explanation is readily apparent from an examination of Table 3.4. This table illustrates a very close relationship between mortality rates and population density, even in a period of time when the overall mortality rates were improving.

Health in Glasgow

Table 3.4: City Sanitary Districts: Comparative Density & Mortality, 1871 & 1881

Name	Density per Acre		Death Rate per 1000	
	1871	1881	1871	1881
Springburn & Maryhill	17	26	28.4	22.4
Greenhead & London Rd.	36	52	31.1	26.7
Kelvinhaugh & Sandyford	37	43	20.4	17.2
Bellgrove & Dennistoun	37	47	29.4	23.1
Monteith Row	39	42	23.5	21.0
Port Dundas	73	64	33.9	27.3
Woodside	81	134	25.5	20.9
St Enoch Square	93	44	31.3	26.7
Hutcheson Square	99	121	26.4	24.9
Kingston	100	97	25.6	21.8
Exchange	123	96	22.0	21.7
Blythswood	126	101	20.6	16.1
Barrowfield	245	233	31.2	30.3
Anderston	249	229	32.5	28.4
Laurieston	251	186	29.8	27.2
St Rollox	289	316	30.8	21.8
High St & Closes West	301	239	45.7	29.9
Cowcaddens	316	249	33.9	32.0
Brownfield	337	348	38.3	30.7
Gorbals	350	274	38.5	29.0
High St & Closes East	351	155	40.7	37.8
St Andrews Square	365	189	38.3	28.7
Calton	388	335	36.7	30.9
Bridgegate & Wynds	408	223	42.3	38.3

Source: A. Gibb, Glasgow: The Making of a City (Beckenham, 1983), p. 131.

II: Morbidity Rates

As with mortality rates, numerous statistics were kept for Glasgow on the causes of death before civil registration was required after 1855. The information is contained in Table 3.5, allowing some observations to be made about morbidity rates during the first half of the nineteenth century.

Table 3.5: Crude Death Rates from Selected Diseases, Glasgow, 1800-1865

Cause of Death	1800-10 (%)	1836-42 (%)	1855-65 (%)
Fever	9.8	16.1	9.5
Whooping-cough	6.8	5.3	5.6
Tuberculosis and Bronchitis	22.8	16.8	29.6
Smallpox	6.6	5.0	1.9
Measles	7.5	6.6	3.1
Bowel diseases	8.9	12.1	11.4
Total of above	62.4	61.9	61.1

Source: Flinn, *Scottish Population History*, p. 389

As useful as they are, it is necessary to treat these statistics with some care.

These figures are subject to a number of severe limitations and may be taken as only a very rough guide to the actual causes of death at the period. First, they are drawn from three quite separate sources—the parish registers, the bills of mortality, and the civil registration returns, respectively—each employing different sources of information. Second, classification is subject to the acute deficiencies of diagnosis of causes of death: bronchitis, for example, was often confused with, and classified as consumption (tuberculosis); typhus and typhoid were not differentiated and separately entered in the official returns until 1869. Third, these deficiencies were not constant over the period, being presumably somewhat reduced as medical knowledge improved. Fourth, there were severe problems of terminology: tuberculosis, often called consumption or phthisis, was nearly always what was meant when death was attributed simply to 'decline'; dysentery was commonly called 'flux'; but not all such popular usages may so readily be identified with their modern equivalents. Fifth, the populations in each of the three periods have not been age-standardised: because of the high degree of age-specificity in the incidence of certain diseases, changes in age-structure alone must affect the proportion of fatalities from various diseases.

A few conclusions emerge fairly clearly. First, throughout the first half of the nineteenth century, the common infectious diseases regularly accounted for over 60% of all deaths. Second, tuberculosis, under-registered as it almost certainly was in these sources, was overwhelmingly the largest single killing disease. Third, the lethal impact of smallpox and, to a lesser extent, of measles, declined significantly during this period. Fourth, fever and whooping cough, important killers at all times in the nineteenth century, did not noticeably diminish during this period.[10]

During the second half of the nineteenth century tuberculosis remained the major killer. It accounted for 39 per cent of all deaths in Glasgow in the 1860s, 43 per cent in the 1870s, and even though it began to decline after that, it still remained at nearly 39 per cent in the 1890s.[11] The explanation for the increase and then decline of tuberculosis remains a mystery, especially when it is realised that,

> during the last four decades of the nineteenth century at least, the reduction of mortality from tuberculosis was slower in Scotland than in England and Wales. This serious failure is not easily explained, though it is clear that, for once, Glasgow—for all its high rate—cannot take all the blame. Mortality from tuberculosis declined faster in Glasgow than almost anywhere else: it had, of course, further to fall.[12]

III: Causes

It is very easy to state with a high degree of certainty that the epidemics and resulting increases in the mortality rates for Glasgow were simply the result of overcrowded, filthy conditions. To a large extent this is true, however, some qualifications must be made. Even in those years which did not experience epidemics, the death rate on average was considerably higher than at the beginning of the century, thus other reasons must exist.

The state of nineteenth century Glasgow is well known. It was a city which suffered all the traumas experienced by a rapidly growing industrial area.

> Although population increased 5-fold between 1801 and 1861, the whole of the Glasgow of 1775 remained geographically intact. There was in the centre of this rapidly expanding conurbation a medieval city covering about 100 acres with narrow winding ill-paved streets which were quite unsuited to the requirements of an industrial city. The central business district, including the new City Chambers, had moved west, and much of the new industry had fanned out along both sides of the Clyde and to the north. The middle classes had moved west, leaving the declining areas to the poorest classes. Virtually no demolition took place, and indeed the demand for cheap dwellings was so great that former middle-class gardens were filled with jerry-built back-tenements.[13]

The rapid growth brought about sections of Glasgow which had a population density of 500 to 1,000 per acre in 1860. Census returns for 1861 show that 'In Glasgow 100,000 people lived in one-room houses; of these one-room houses, 1,253 housed 7 persons each, 596 had 8 persons, 229 had 9 persons, 84 had 10 persons, 30 had 11 persons, 11 had 12 persons, 5 had 13 persons, 3 had 14 persons, and 2 housed 15 persons'.[14] These figures are probably underestimated, as many families took in lodgers on a daily basis. The situation which existed can best be illustrated with an 1870s quotation from J.B. Russell, Glasgow's first full-time Medical Officer.

It is in those frightful abodes of human wretchedness which lay along the High Street, Saltmarket, and Briggate, and constitute the bulk of that district known as the 'Wynds and Closes of Glasgow', that all sanitary evils exist in perfection. They consist of ranges of narrow closes, only some four or five feet in width, and of great length. The houses are so lofty that the direct light of the sky never reaches a large proportion of the dwellings. The ordinary atmospheric ventilation is impossible. The cleansing, until lately, was most inefficient, and, from structural causes, will always, under existing arrangements, be difficult and expensive. There are large square midden-steads, some of them actually under the houses, and all of them in the immediate vicinity of the windows and doors of human dwellings. These receptacles hold the entire filth and offal of large masses of people and households, until country farmers can be bargained with for their removal. There is no drainage in these neighbourhoods, except in a few cases; and from the want of any means of flushing, the sewers, where they do exist, are extended cesspools polluting the air. So little is house drainage in use, that on one occasion I saw the entire surface of a back yard covered for several inches with green putrid water, although there was a sewer in the close within a few feet into which it might have been drained away. The water supply is also very defective; such a thing as a household supply is unknown, and I have been informed that, from the state of the law, the water companies find it impossible to recover rates, and that, had the cholera not appeared, it was in contemplation to have cut off the entire supply from this class of property.

The interior of the houses is in perfect keeping with their exterior. The approaches are generally in a state of filthiness beyond belief. The common stairs and passages are often the receptacles of the most disgusting nuisances. The houses themselves are dark, and without the means of ventilation. The walls dilapidated and filthy, are in many cases ruinous. There are no domestic conveniences even in the loftiest tenements, where they are most needed, except a kind of wooden sink placed outside some stair windows, and communicating by a square wooden pipe with the surface of the close or court beneath. Down this contrivance, where it does exist, is poured the entire filth of the household or flat to which it belongs, and the solid refuse not unfrequently takes the same direction till the tube becomes obstructed.

Another matter connected with these districts, and their peculiar liability to epidemic disease, is the great and continually increasing overcrowding that prevails. I have been credibly informed, that for years a population of many thousands has been annually added to Glasgow by immigration without a single house being built to receive them. The great proportion come from Ireland. Every cabin in that wretched country that is razed to the ground sends one or more families to find house-room in the cities of England and Scotland, and of this element of disease Glasgow obtains its full share.

The overcrowding and wretchedness of late years has brought typhus with it, a disease that not long ago was almost as rare in the large Cities of Scotland as ague now is; and wherever typhus has prevailed, there cholera now prevails, or has done so recently.[15]

It is obvious from the above that Glasgow sufferred the ill-effects of overcrowding and the lack of proper sanitary conditions, especially in the densely populated working-class sections of the city. But, can these factors be the only ones to blame for the sharp secular increase in mortality which Glasgow experienced? Indeed, can they even be considered as the most important? David Hamilton has analysed the statistics of the Glasgow Royal Infirmary with respect to compound fractures, primary amputations of the upper limb, and common leg ulcers. He argues that a study of the incidence of these three types of cases exhibits a pattern similar to that for the fever epidemics, and thus it may be possible to determine the reasons for the improvement in health which seems to occur in Glasgow after the 1870s.[16]

Hamilton states that 'The death rate from these [compound] fractures in the 1840s was low, rising to higher rates in the 1860s, but showing a steady fall in the later part of the century. Superimposed on this trend are a number of peaks and troughs of mortality. High death rates occurred in 1847-49 and 1861-62'. 'The annual death rate from primary amputation of the upper limb was low in the 1840s and rose to a peak in the 1860s, falling steadily thereafter until the end of the century. Significant elevations of mortality above the trend occurred in 1849-50 and 1867-68.' Admission figures for leg ulcers show a secular increase until the mid-1860s and a decline thereafter, with peaks in 1845, 1855, 1865 and 1872. What accounted for the nearly identical patterns and subsequent improvements? Hamilton argues thus:

> . . . two factors may have brought about the improved results. The first, which is the traditional explanation, is that they resulted from the appearance of antiseptic methods around 1867, which were pioneered by Lister, and which were then slowly adopted by other surgeons. . . This explanation fails to account for a number of the main findings above, most notably that the early nineteenth-century results were so good before antiseptics. It also fails to explain the slow fluctuations in surgical results—the good and bad spells. As an additional explanation, therefore, the idea that the host defenses of the patient played an important part in the surgical mortality is worth exploring. A rising standard of living from mid-century onwards is suggested by the rapid disappearance of typhus and 'common' leg ulcers. Real wages rose, and there was new security

of employment. Moreover, typhus was not common in the early part of the nineteenth century, and its return in Glasgow is usually explained by the appearance of starvation or malnutrition; resistance to infection may have been high in early nineteenth-century Glasgow.

This 'nutritional' argument fits the observed facts in several ways. Firstly, it can be argued that nutrition was good in the early part of the century, surgery was quite successful, and typhus deaths were low. The fluctuations in death rates in the earlier part of the century can be explained by the effects of fluctuations of the trade cycle in an increasingly urban society, and also by the influx of starving Irish and Highlanders into Glasgow. The steady rise in surgical mortality in the middle part of the century can be seen as the result of the steadily worsening conditions of the working class, conditions which allowed the return of repeated epidemics of typhus. This can explain the observed association between typhus and surgical deaths, not on the basis of hospital overcrowding, but as a result of under-nourishment, of both the typhus victims and the surgical patients. Lastly, the nutritional argument explains the fall in mortality in the latter part of the century as the result of better host defenses, not only because of better living conditions, but also by the appearance of social buffers against starvation, such as unemployment benefits and pensions. This explanation also rehabilitates the reputation of opponents of Lister who were puzzled at the lack of success with his methods. It may also suggest that the reason for the better surgical results in private practice and cottage hospitals compared to those in city hospitals was because the private or rural patients were better fed. In addition, it explains why earlier use of antiseptics, including carbolic acid, failed. Lastly, it should be said that, although Lister's support of the germ theory was correct, it does not follow that his treatment was effective.[17]

Even though Hamilton's arguments have elements of historical inaccuracy, such as the timing of unemployment benefits and pensions, his case cannot readily be discounted. The clustering of epidemics and other indicators, each displaying similar cyclical patterns, must surely negate the idea that a virulent micro-organism was fortuitously present, or that environmental conditions such as sanitation, poor housing and exposure to infection had temporarily turned for the worse. The clustering of epidemics instead suggests that other factors known to influence disease were perhaps more important in the nineteenth century than has been thought, notably that nutrition played a major role in the pattern of disease. The nutrition of the working class was dependent on the business cycle. This nutritional factor was a prominent explanation at the time. The local opinion on the causation of typhus outbreaks was often that it was a product of hard times. The managers of the Royal Infirmary often remarked in the Annual Reports on the link between bad trade and typhus epidemics, a link which they regarded as obvious and self-evident. This empirical grasp of the link between malnutrition, diminished host resistance and disease was seen within the hospital when nutritious diets were part of therapy. Outside the hospital many doctors urged that the poor law should provide food along with medicine, and the poor law reformers in Scotland urged that the priority in public policy should be to maintain the income of the poor, rather than simply the grand schemes for sanitation proposed by Chadwick.

Other quantitative hospital data from the mid-nineteenth century also suggest a deterioration in health. The Glasgow Maternity Hospital experienced an increase in maternal mortality, and the hospital work shows that the deformity of rickets was increasingly a problem in obstetrics. Rickets, a deformity resulting from childhood deficiency of vitiman D, caused a deformed pelvis and obstructed labour. Rickets had been unremarkable in Glasgow and elsewhere, but in the later nineteenth century obstetricians in Glasgow quickly acquired a reputation for the Caesarian section operations which had to be used to meet the need. The increase in rickets in Glasgow is usually blamed on the lack of sunlight, resulting from the industrial haze, rather than to a dietary deficiency; but rickets declined in Glasgow towards the end of the century, yet the smoke problem increased. A dietary deficiency seems, therefore, to be a likely major factor in rickets.

The deterioration in health in mid-century, as judged by the town statistics and the hospital records, has usually been related to overcrowding, lack of sanitation, and less often to malnutrition. There is no lack of literary descriptions of poor nutrition in nineteenth century Glasgow. Chronic malnutrition is suggested by descriptions of the appearances of the people and periods of famine elsewhere, such as the Highlands and Ireland, might drive starving people to seek the towns of Lowland Scotland. Estimates are that 50 per cent of the Scottish weavers were beneath the poverty line in 1834, and hence underfed. In these times even the idea of a steady income or average income is misleading. Employment opportunities varied with trade, and there were no financial buffers during times of unemployment. Old age, illness or debility also meant loss of income. For women, widowhood or desertion meant poverty. Poor relief was minimal, offering relief at below subsistence levels.

IV: Factors Responsible for Improvements

Three general areas were crucial for reversing the increasingly adverse movement in mortality rates. They were water supply and sewers, the Improvement Trust, and the establishment of the Health Department. Each will be examined in turn.

A. Water Supply and Sewers

At the beginning of the nineteenth century Glasgow was entirely dependent on thirty public wells and numerous private wells for its source of water. This had severe limitations, as the increased population and resulting
demand for new buildings put to task the ability to site wells. Moreover,
the waste from the teeming masses and industry was dumped into streams
and drainage ditches. This sewage eventually found its way into the water
courses. Thus, not only were Glasgow's inhabitants forced to queue for
and carry water for their household use, they were also subjected to the
adverse effects of consuming polluted water. The problem intensified with
the previously unknown rapid increases in population which happened in
the first half of the nineteenth century.

It was in this environment that private water merchants emerged,
selling spring water. Then, in 1806 Parliament passed a law creating the
Glasgow Water Company, a limited liability company. The Company established filtration ponds first on the north side, and then larger ponds on
the south side of the Clyde. As a result of ingenious engineering by Telford
and Watt, the Company was able to provide a steady, though variable,
supply of water during the day. However, the system was not entirely satisfactory, as even this amount was insufficient to meet Glasgow's growing
needs, and large quantities of the water were never filtered.

In 1808 an Act of Parliament created the Company of Proprietors of
the Cranstonhill Water Works. They established operations on the Clyde
at the western edge of the city. The authorised capital was about half
that of the Glasgow Water Company, located on the eastern side of the
city. Both companies competed with each other for the same customers,
rather than apportion the city into districts. The Cranstonhill's decision
to locate their works downstream of the city was a major mistake, for by
1820 the water was so polluted it could not be used for drinking purposes.
They were forced to move their works to a site near the Glasgow Water
Company's.

In 1838 Parliament allowed the two companies to amalgamate. Even
with united efforts, sufficient quantities of good quality water were not
forthcoming. In 1845 the Loch Katrine scheme was floated, but was abandoned when the Glasgow Water Company received the approval of Parliament to bring water from Loch Lubnaig. This scheme, however, eventually
proved to be too ambitious. A series of bitter disputes followed, but finally
in 1855 Parliament approved the Loch Katrine scheme. In 1860, for the
first time since rapid urbanisation began, the citizens of Glasgow received
pure water.

There were no sewers in Glasgow before 1798. In that year the first was constructed, though its benefits are doubtful, for it also emptied its contents into existing streams and drainage systems, in this case the Molendinar Burn. The Police Act of 1800 gave the town council the power to construct common sewers. By 1816 nearly 5 miles of sewers had been built. The Police Act of 1843 made provision for the ordering of properties to be connected to common sewers, and that no property could be connected without approval.

The building of sewers was a slow process, especially for the established, densely populated areas of the city. The new, middle-class suburbs were the first to receive the extensive benefits. The older sections of the city still relied heavily upon the earthern closet and the accompanying income-producing midden. Water closets did not come into common usage until after the bountiful supplies of water from Loch Katrine. In 1850 there was 40 miles of sewers, and 100 miles by 1890. The miles of sewers, however, was in actuality a mute issue, dwarfed by the fact that all effluent from Glasgow's residents and industries found its way into the River Clyde. Effective sewage treatment and disposal did not come to Glasgow until May, 1894, when the Dalmarnock works were opened. Thus, the introduction of pure water into Glasgow in 1860 was much more important to general health than was the introduction and expansion of the sewer system.

B. The Improvement Trust

As the population increased at remarkable rates, the housing stock did not keep pace. Limited accommodation led to high rents and the establishment of the infamous lodging houses and the building of the even more infamous backlands. The filth and overcrowding of the area in proximity to Glasgow Cross is well-documented and mentioned elsewhere in this volume. Not much was done to alleviate these deplorable conditions, in spite of the fact that these were the areas of highest mortality. Ironically, slum clearance did begin with the arrival of the railways in the 1830s, for these neighbourhoods were desireable sites for stations, yards, and tracks. Though, those dispossessed were probably forced into even more overcrowded conditions.

The preamble of the City Improvement Act of 1866 states, 'Various portions of the City of Glasgow are so built, and the buildings so densely inhabited, as to be highly injurious to the moral and physical welfare of the inhabitants'. The importance of this statement cannot be over-emphasised, for it was a recognition that the sacred rights of private property must be broken. Given the power of landlords, there was little people could do other than suffer in hopeless misery. The City Improvement Act gave the Lord Provost, magistrates and town council, as trustees, a set of compulsory powers to enable them to begin the task of eliminating the worse slum areas of the central district of the city, an area of approximately 88 acres containing a population of 51,000 people. The Act provided the power of compulsory purchase of properties within a five year time period; this was extended for a further five years in 1871. In brief the Act empowered the trustees

> to acquire houses and land within certain defined compulsory areas, to purchase other lands by agreement, to alter, widen, and divert existing streets, and to form new streets as shown on the plans submitted to Parliament, to take down existing buildings and to sell the materials thereof, to lay out lands so opened up of new, and to sell or dispose of the grounds and buildings they may acquire on lease or on feu as they may deem proper. Power was also given to the trustees to erect buildings on their lands, and to sell or lease the same. Under certain restrictions power was given to the trustees to eject tenants from the properties they acquired, and generally, it may be said, they were endowed with all the powers and rights of any ordinary Glasgow land and house owner.[18]

Such a grand scheme as the Improvement Trust was not without its opposition. Even though the proposal moved through the town council and Parliament without any trouble, opposition arose when rates were levied to provide revenue. The assessment fell not upon the landlords, but rather upon the occupiers of the areas concerned. This created a great deal of resentment.

During its first four years the Trust concentrated on acquiring properties. Large-scale demolition did not begin until 1870. Work then proceeded quickly, for by May, 1874 the Trust had demolished houses that had been occupied by 15,425 people.

> The policy of the Trust was to scatter as far as possible the dislodged population, to encourage the erection of houses where they might find employment. The trustees did not then contemplate the erection of dwellings for the working population, being of opinion that such was the function of private enterprise, and they deemed it impolitic to compete with or in any way discourage the building trade. To become philanthropic landlords they reasoned would be unjust competition with and discouraging to private builders who necessarily sought a return for their investments, and an unfair burden on the citizens generally. The trustees, however, purchased the estates of Overnewton and Oatlands, situated respectively in the western and south-western districts of the City, laying them out for building on a liberal plan; and the sites were speedily bought up and occupied with a good class of dwelling-house.[19]

Thus, the Trust eliminated some of the worse housing areas within Glasgow. However, a problem emerged. They did not, at least immediately, replace many of these houses. Indeed, they held as vacant lots expensively acquired land in the central city. Nor did the Trust concern itself with providing decent housing on a large scale to the low-income groups. In 1870 the Trust constructed two model lodging houses, which it was hoped would be copied by other builders. Then in the 1880s, it was realised that private builders were not supplying sufficient new houses. The Trust then began a building scheme, providing 2,199 houses.[20]

The impact of the Glasgow Improvement Trust can only be viewed with mixed feelings. Undoubtedly, the worst section of Glasgow was cleared by their operations. Thus, there were certainly benefits to the general state of health in Glasgow. Yet, the housing stock did not increase adequately, creating overcrowded conditions elsewhere. Nonetheless, it must be remembered that

> Glasgow was the pioneer city in its improvement policy, and its example has been followed by many others. Possibly our need was the sorest; for that a deadly gangrene was eating into the very heart of the City was obvious, clear also it was that the evil could be alleviated only by the strenuous surgery that had been exercised. The experiences of the Improvement Trustees have taught the Town Council valuable lessons. They led directly to the enactment of the Buildings Regulation Act of 1892, and armed with its powers the Corporation can effectually prevent the recurrence of conditions in any part of the City such as the Improvement Trustees had to face. But there is no finality in the City Improvement work. The standard of decency and comfort in house accommodation has been enormously elevated since 1866; every victory won by the sanitarian and by the social reformer only increases their demands and their beneficent pretensions; the poor themselves are awakening to a healthy instinct for improvements, and what is deemed good enough for the close of the nineteenth century will certainly be rejected early in the twentieth. The City Improvement Trustees have still ample work in store for them.[21]

C. The Health Department

When epidemics arrived, concerted effort was exerted to meet the problem. Yet, the daily nuisances and threats to life were largely neglected, other than the provision of sewers and drains and the paving of streets. Police Acts were passed in 1800, 1807, 1821, 1830 and 1837 which introduced measures for the cleaning of streets and public places by the town council and private closes by the occupiers. In 1843 an inspector of cleaning was appointed to oversee the provisions of the various acts and to ensure the cleaning of closes and the removal of middens, and to license lodging houses to prevent overcrowding. However, the inspector lacked effective administrative machinery and powers. Thus, the inspector was not entirely successful, especially in dealing with the removal of middens, which were considered as private property and jealously guarded as an important source of income.

It was only in 1857 that recognition was given to the fact that the introduction of constant environmental controls should be utilised to help stop the cycle of epidemics. A committee was appointed to investigate the sanitary conditions and local powers of the major towns in Britain. The result was the Police Act of 1862.

> Judged by present-day standards the powers sought under that enactment were modest and meagre. These embraced the obligatory appointment of a medical officer or officers, and permission to appoint one or more inspectors of nuisances, and one or more inspectors of common lodging-houses. The specified duties of the medical officer embraced the reporting on districts, streets, or courts in which it appeared to him advisable to adopt special sanitary measures, with the view of preventing the occurrence of epidemics and contagious disease. He was also called on to report the prevalence or threatened prevalence of such disease in any district, and the existence of any nuisance which tended to cause or to aggravate disease, or otherwise was hurtful to the health of the community, and he had to specify the measures he would recommend for the prevention or abatement of any outbreaks. To the magistrates committee was given the power to proclaim, after due public notice, any district reported on by the medical officer; proprietors or occupiers were to be called on to cleanse, whitewash, ventilate, and disinfect according to the instructions of the inspector of nuisances, and such then exceptional powers were to continue for a period fixed, and specified in the magisterial edict. Further, during that period, but with the concurrence of the Privy Council only, the magistrates were entitled within the proclaimed district to institute house-to-house visitation, for preventing overcrowding, for prevention and removal of nuisances, for preventing the spread of disease, and for giving medical treatment, and, when needed, accommodation to the sufferers from infectious disease. Regulations were also enacted for lodging-houses, under which their keepers became bound to report every case of fever or serious disease among the inmates of their houses, they were obliged to deliver daily a list of the names and addresses of the lodgers of the previous night, and they were at all times bound to receive the visits of the medical officer or inspector of lodging-houses.[22]

In 1868 the Cleansing Department was established. Since 1800 it had been recognised that the cleaning of streets was a public responsibility, and this activity was administered by the Commissioners of Police. With the formation of a separate department came the recognition of the extreme importance of cleaning and rubbish disposal. In 1870 a permanent statutory Sanitary Inspector was appointed and a permanent fever hospital was opened. In 1878 Glasgow's first public baths and wash house was opened at the Green; several more were put in operation during the 1880s. In 1881 it was decided that all cases in city hospitals be treated free of charge, regardless of class or condition. The Police Amendment Act of 1890 further enhanced the statutory powers of the sanitary officials and legislated for the provision of sufficient water closets for all occupants.

And what is the outcome of the stupendous work of the Municipality of Glasgow towards improving the health and bettering the conditions of life of the vast lower stratum of the community? Between the Improvement Trust and the Police Commissioners millions of money have been expended, and for thirty years an increasing warfare has been kept up against dirt, darkness, and disease. Has the result been commensurate with the effort and the expenditure? Before answering the question, it is well to bear in mind that frightful as were the conditions thirty years ago, there is no reason to believe that the City had sounded the lowest depths of possible human existence. Indeed it is perfectly certain that with a policy of *laissez-faire*, the evils amid which the poor lived and died would have increased in accelerating ratio. There is nothing in the form of a shelter into which human beings will not creep and seek to establish themselves, no structure is too mean, dirty, disreputable, and broken down to be an object of the avarice of rapacious and unprincipled owners. What might have been, to what depths of deadly misery the meaner parts of the City might have sunk, it is almost impossible to imagine. The conditions were already on the score of public safety unbearable in 1866, and the drastic remedies of the municipality were not applied a day too soon.

A brief study of the record of mortality from zymotic diseases for forty years, from the period when the Scottish Registration Act came into operation in 1855 to the end of 1894, affords a most striking and satisfactory justification of all that has been done and expended in Glasgow by the sanitary authorities. Dividing the period into decades we get ten years of presanitary experience, ten in which the sanitary authorities were groping their way towards system and order, and two lapses of ten in which results began to manifest themselves. For the purposes of comparison Dr. Russell has reduced the total mortality to a standard of death-rates per million, bringing out the following remarkable figures:

	Zymotics	Phthisis	Other Diseases of Lungs	Other Causes	All Causes
1855-64	7,841	3,918	5,170	13,121	30,050
1865-74	7,377	3,940	6,522	12,692	30,530
1875-84	5,056	3,396	6,322	12,113	26,886
1885-94	3,822	2,458	5,329	11,566	23,175

Contrasting the experience of the first and last ten years of the period we have a decrease of 23 per cent. on the total death-rate, almost entirely due to zymotics and phthisis, the decrease in the former alone being no less than 51 per cent., and on the latter it amounts to 37 per cent. on the mortality. In 1864—the year previous to the beginning of hospital work—in a population of 420,738 persons, there were 13,674 deaths; thirty years later, in a population increased to 686,820, almost 60 per cent., the number of deaths reached precisely the same figure, 13,674.

There is not in the list a single infectious disease which has entirely resisted the ameliorative efforts of the sanitary authorities. Some have proved themselves much more amenable to control than others, a circumstance which is sufficiently accounted for by the peculiarities of the diseases themselves. Typhus may be said to be practically extirpated. In the ten years, 1855-64, the deaths from that disease numbered 5558; in the decade ending 1894 they were only 167. From small-pox the deaths in the first period were 2197, in the last they were reduced to 45. Enteric fever was not separately registered till 1865. In the ten years, 1865-74, the deaths it caused numbered 2251; for 1885-94 the deaths registered were 1138. With children's diseases the success is not so striking. Scarlet fever is the most formidable of all the enemies with which the sanitary powers have to cope. It is never absent, and in spite of all precautions it becomes epidemic in unexpected quarters. Yet it also has been sensibly curbed. In the first decennium, 1855-64, it contributed a total of 4770 deaths; in the next period, 1865-74, epidemics raised the deaths to 6607; but thenceforth a notable decrease set in, and for 1885-94 the total deaths amounted only to 2269. Of all zymotic diseases measles appears to be the least amenable to public control. In the ten years ended 1865 measles caused 3474 deaths; in the ten years ended 1894 the deaths 4642. It would thus appear that measles is the one zymotic disease which has baffled the efforts of the sanitary officials, and the reason is not far to seek. 'The acute stage of infectivity,' says Dr. Russell, 'is over before the acute stage of the disease is fully established.' Before the case is removed the most of the damage is done. The record of whooping-cough is also one of obstinate tenacity, and it is not a little remarkable that this disease, popularly regarded as more troublesome than dangerous, is the most persistent, formidable, and fatal of all our zymotics. In the ten years, 1855-64, it claimed 6377 victims; in the decennium ended in 1894 it was the cause of 6223 deaths, and taking the increase of population into account—in the end nearly double—the decreased mortality cannot be regarded as other than highly satisfactory. The course of diarrhoeal disease has in Glasgow been more influenced by water supply than by any other cause. From 1860 Loch Katrine water, probably the purest supply in the world, has been turned on in Glasgow. The cholera epidemic of 1854, when part of the water of the City was drawn from the Clyde, carried off 3886 victims, 12 per thousand of the population; cholera again broke out in 1866, but then it caused only 68 deaths in all, and obtained no real hold on the people. The deaths from diarrhoea, dysentery, and cholera in the ten years ended 1864 came in all to 4049, 2719 in the first five years when water supply was impure; in the ten years, 1885-94, there occurred 3034 deaths from this class of disease. It is in the case of children under one year of age that these diseases maintain a high and persistent average death-rate, and with these the sanitary authorities are comparatively powerless—'the mother,' as Dr. Russell remarks, 'is after all the domestic sanitary inspector'.

In 1874 a simple tract on the necessity of domestic cleanliness in air, clothes, and food was drawn up by Dr. Russell, and with the permission of the Registrar General, a copy is given to every person who in Glasgow registers a birth. In dealing with such intimate domestic matters as the care of children, it is found that the services of the female Sanitary Inspectors are of great value. Diphtheria was not recognized and separately classified till 1857, and it has been steadily increasing since, but apparently at the expense of its ally croup. Summing the deaths under these two diseases together, a distinct but not notable decrease in the proportion of fatal cases is brought out. For the ten years, 1855-64, they together were responsible for 2327 deaths; in the ten years ended 1894 they caused 2581 deaths. Of the minor zymotics, erysipelas, puerperal fever, influenza, etc., it is sufficient to say that the ten years, 1855-64, record of deaths amounted to 4330; while for the later ten years 1885-94, in the greatly increased population, they occasioned 4044 deaths.

The aggregate of disease, suffering, and deadly misery which has been warded off has surely been a sufficient sanction for the expenditure by the Health Committee and an ample reward for their labours. And be it remembered it is not in zymotic diseases alone that the beneficial influence of the public sanitary work has been experienced. It is with such diseases that the department is primarily concerned, but whatever tends to diminish and check infection, in like manner reduces the potency and fatality of every other class of disease. The stamina of the entire population has been improved, their vitality has been quickened, and the average longevity has been distinctly increased. Glasgow, from being an unhealthy City with an annual death-rate per thousand of from 30 to 33, has become a really healthy community with a death-rate ranging from 20 to 23, a fairly satisfactory condition as great urban populations go. The Police Commissioners, aided by the Improvement Trustees and the Water Trustees, the Municipality of Glasgow in fact, for under different names they are the same body, have taken away the reproach from the City; they undoubtedly faced a Herculean task— they have cleaned an Augean stable. Their labours are by no means at an end, nor has the goal been reached. What they have accomplished only points hopefully to what is possible yet to do. Every coign of vantage secured, every repulse of the dread foe effected, gives new opportunities of successful attack, and increases the hope of ultimate victory all along the line. It has been demonstrated that zymotic diseases can be curbed and controlled—already their fatality in Glasgow has been decreased by 50 per cent. The contest in which these results have been attained has developed the aggressive skill of the assailants, and with their increased knowledge and improved methods it should be possible in the future to work even greater havoc in the weakened strongholds of the foe. That a community living under the highly artificial conditions of modern city life should attain entire immunity from disease is too much to expect. We shall have the sick and the feeble as well as the poor always with us. But that fact notwithstanding every citizen should have at least the possibility of living a healthy, comfortable, and useful life, and towards that ideal condition, yet in the dim and distant future, the efforts of the Sanitary Department are entirely directed.[23]

There is no simple explanation as to the worsening of mortality rates in Glasgow beginning about 1820 and then the subsequent improvement after 1870. Overcrowding and lack of adequate sanitation certainly contributed to the cause. So too a decrease in nutrition; it has been stated in the Introduction that real wages in Glasgow fell after 1815, leading to a logical conclusion that nutrition must have suffered. Sanitary improvements and a decrease in overcrowding occurred after 1870. Thus, just as the causes of increased mortality were the function of several inter-related factors, improvements resulted from the interaction of a number of factors. Certainly, after 1870 the working classes enjoyed conditions less detrimental than those that existed during the height of working-class exploitation in the first half of the nineteenth century.

Notes

1. M. Flinn, ed., *Scottish Population History* (Cambridge University Press, 1977).
2. *Ibid.*, pp. 370-1.
3. *Ibid.*, pp. 368-9.
4. *Ibid.*, p. 369.
5. *Ibid.*, p. 376.
6. *Ibid.*, pp. 371-2.
7. *Ibid.*, p. 372.
8. *Ibid.*, p. 373.
9. *Ibid.*, p. 375.
10. *Ibid.*, pp. 388-9.
11. *Ibid.*, pp. 411-2.
12. *Ibid.*, p. 413.
13. C.M. Allan, 'The Genesis of British Urban Redevelopment with Special Reference to Glasgow', *Economic History Review* 18 (1965), p. 603.
14. Thomas Johnston, *The History of the Working Classes in Scotland* (Glasgow, Forward Publishing, n.d.), p. 294.
15. As quoted in Olive Checkland and Margaret Lamb, eds., *Health Care as Social History: The Glasgow Case* (Aberdeen University Press, 1982), pp. 1-2.
16. David Hamilton, 'The Nineteenth-Century Surgical Revolution—Antisepsis or Better Nutrition?', *Bulletin of the History of Medicine* 56 (1982), pp. 30-

40. I am grateful to David for supplying me with additional information, especially about rickets.
17. *Ibid.*, pp. 39-40.
18. James Bell and James Paton, *Glasgow: Its Municipal Organization and Administration* (Glasgow, 1896), p. 221.
19. *Ibid.*, p. 224.
20. See Chapter 2.
21. Bell, *Glasgow*, p. 232.
22. *Ibid.*, pp. 185-6.
23. *Ibid.*, pp. 214-7.

Chapter Four

THE NATURE AND EXTENT OF POOR RELIEF

R. A. Cage

By 1878 the industrial might of Glasgow was an accomplished fact. The city was a major international industrial centre. Fortunes had been made, and more would be made. Yet, the years 1877-79 found Glasgow in the grips of a severe depression; the immediate cause was the failure of the City of Glasgow Bank. At the height of the depression in the winter of 1878-79, 37,904 individuals, including dependents, received assistance from the Glasgow Unemployed Relief Fund. In all there were 13,960 applications for relief; of these 710 were under 20 years of age, 7,389 from 20 to 40 years, 4,991 were from 40 to 60 years, and 870 were over 60 years; 4,099 claimed to be natives of Glasgow, 3,425 were natives of different parishes in Scotland, 306 were natives of England and Wales, and 6,074 were natives of Ireland, with 62 foreigners; 3,837 were skilled male workers, and 6,654 were unskilled; 1,206 were skilled female workers, and 2,263 were unskilled; 8,080 were married men, 2,411 were single men, 877 were single women, and 2,592 were widows and deserted wives. There were 22,109 dependents of married men, 464 of single men, 253 of single women, and 3,667 dependents of widows and deserted wives. The number of cases refused was 1,294, leaving the number relieved as 12,666. The occupations of the recipients were extremely varied, with 2,010 being out-door labourers, and the remainder representing nearly every other trade and occupation in the city. Of the trades, the weavers were the most numerous. There were 461,787 two pound loaves of bread with a total value of £4,861 19s. distributed, along with 596,960 pounds of oatmeal with a value of £2,593 19s. 7d., 144,165 rations of soup valued at £798 11s. 10d., 1,524 tons of coal valued at £618 17s. 10d., 4,804 tickets for provisions valued at £142 17s. 1d., and 7,568 articles of clothing and boots. Total expenditure was £27,208 10s. 4d., and total revenue was £29,225 16s. 1d.[1]

Was this an unusually high period of unemployment, or was it a common occurrence? How did Glasgow cope with such situations? Even during times of normal business activity, there was the need for poor relief. What was the mechanism for catering for Glasgow's poor? These questions form the central issues for discussion.

For the purpose of this chapter, Glasgow will consist only of the traditional City or Royalty; the Barony, Gorbals, and Govan will be excluded. The reason for this restriction is mainly for simplicity, as the Scottish poor law was complex in nature, establishing different administrative procedures for rural and urban parishes.[2] Within the Glasgow metropolitan area there were two systems in operation, as Glasgow City was an urban parish, and the suburban areas were rural parishes. The issue was complicated even further with a change in the law in 1845, which established the Parochial Board, whose members were elected, as administrators.

An indication of the pattern of poor relief in Glasgow is obtained from an examination of the relevant statistics (number of inmates, number of out-pensioners, receipts and expenditure). The information is presented in Table 4.1. The data reflect only the activities of the official guardians of the poor; excluded are the immeasurable and all-important activities of the private charities.

Examining first the data with respect to the number of inmates of the Town's Hospital (a workhouse), there was a very slight upward trend from 1790 to 1845, and then a sudden increase, followed by a more pronounced upward trend, though one with considerable cyclical variation. The sharp jump after 1845 can be explained in several ways. Firstly, the number of inmates at any given time was limited by the availability of accommodation. Thus many deserving cases were not granted indoor relief simply because of the lack of facilities. In 1841 the Hospital directors purchased the Royal Lunatic Asylum, eventually moving the Hospital to that site, and substantially increasing the amount of accommodation available. Secondly, the change in the Scottish poor law in 1845 placed a greater reliance upon legal assessments, thus increasing the amounts available for expenditure. The Parochial Board, therefore, took advantage of both increased accommodation and funds by helping to meet the needs of the deserving poor. The ability to accommodate more inmates also can account for the striking cyclical patterns emerging after 1845. The Hospital was continually used as the basis for applying the 'means test'. Hence, during downturns in business activity, or unusual conditions such as epidemics or severe winters, marginal cases would apply for assistance, staying in the Hospital until conditions outwith improved.

The pattern with respect to out-pensioners is even more striking. There is a slight upward trend from 1790 to 1841, and then an amazing increase until 1850, followed by a downward trend for the remainder of

Table 4.1: Poor Relief Statistics—Town's Hospital and Parochial Board, 1791-1898

Year	Recipients		Revenue				Expenditure			
	Inmates	Out-pensioners	Assessment (£)	Government Grants (£)	Other (£)	Total (£)	Relief (£)	Management (£)	Other (£)	Total (£)
1791	335	337	1,480	740	477	2,697				2,699
1792	363	341	1,673	738	612	3,023				2,737
1793	375	352	1,610	735	551	2,896				2,923
1794	384	563	1,993	740	452	3,185				3,939
1795	384	926	3,387	740	348	4,475				4,795
1796	377	903	3,861	740	467	5,068				5,187
1797	387	710	3,958	740	479	5,177				4,774
1798	396	699	4,195	740	634	5,569				4,460
1799	397	674	3,920	740	671	5,331				4,139
1800	395	728	4,534	740	578	5,852				6,409
1801	426	1,050	7,180	728	646	8,554				9,188
1802	380	1,128	7,955	674	854	9,483				7,020
1803	336	711	3,940	674	847	5,461				4,664
1804	381	784	4,350	704	1,060	6,114				5,329
1805	395	800	5,265	704	1,038	7,007				6,061
1806	390	859	4,865	704	1,263	6,832				5,982
1807	394	651	4,815	704	1,502	7,021				6,519
1808	427	882	5,220	704	1,491	7,415				7,057
1809	412	818	6,000	704	1,606	8,310				7,426
1810	420	932	5,770	704	1,524	7,998				7,425
1811	441	969	5,740	704	1,628	8,072				8,036
1812	470	1,333	7,480	704	1,372	9,556				10,332
1813	482	1,329	10,273	641	1,836	12,750				12,521
1814	430	1,409	10,709	704	1,935	13,348				11,566
1815	436	1,208	9,940	704	2,025	12,669				10,883
1816	426	1,201	9,063	649	1,610	11,322				9,684
1817	497	1,079	10,535	693	1,342	12,570				14,753
1818	499	1,088	11,864							
1819	441	1,088	10,303							

Table 4.1: cont.

Year	Recipients Inmates	Recipients Out-pensioners	Revenue Assessment (£)	Revenue Government Grants (£)	Revenue Other (£)	Revenue Total (£)	Expenditure Relief (£)	Expenditure Management (£)	Expenditure Other (£)	Expenditure Total (£)
1820	368	1,072	13,136							
1821	347	1,008	12,560							
1822	340	1,016	9,213							
1841	419	1,276								
1842	414	1,334								
1843	416	1,584								
1844	411	1,561								
1845	447	1,793								
1846	517	2,376								
1847	673	4,724	41,091			41,091				
1848	700	5,687				67,771				
1849	1,138	6,424								
1850	815	6,313								
1851	973	5,286								
1852	1,052	5,417								
1853	1,084	4,960								
1854	951	4,682								
1855	1,046	4,831								
1856	892	4,663								
1857	888	4,998	47,240	958	71	48,269	33,268	5,862	1,322	40,452
1858	947	5,137	38,752	942	18	39,712	33,276	6,349	1,609	41,234
1859	771	4,030	39,605	723	14	40,342	30,965	5,603	1,251	37,719
1860	770	3,574	37,300	697	23	38,020	31,434	5,497	1,345	38,276
1861	855	4,427	38,478	678	76	39,232	32,137	5,048	1,623	38,808
1862	931	5,226	38,989	675	68	39,732	32,623	6,219	1,643	40,485
1863	1,009	4,938	38,602	682	116	39,400	32,337	5,762	1,214	39,313
1864	914	5,146	38,902	669	32	39,603	33,750	5,792	1,247	40,790
1865	991	5,043	40,051	689	114	40,854	32,453	7,996	1,531	41,980
1866	957	4,069	42,694	666	26	43,386	33,868	5,765	1,462	41,095
1867	1,111	4,191	43,179	612	0	43,791	35,724	7,502	1,902	45,128
1868	1,136	4,118	44,839	606	89	45,534	39,186	6,503	1,613	47,302
1869	1,012	3,923	47,564	645	4	48,213	37,386	6,092	1,665	45,143

Table 4.1: cont.

Year	Recipients		Revenue				Expenditure			
	Inmates	Out-pensioners	Assessment (£)	Government Grants (£)	Other (£)	Total (£)	Relief (£)	Management (£)	Other (£)	Total (£)
1870	1,401	4,099	50,248	643	2,270	53,161	36,477	8,323	1,490	46,290
1871	1,428	4,041	47,019	645	5,280	52,944	36,070	7,652	1,511	45,233
1872	1,254	3,486	44,189	647	4,254	49,090	35,851	7,414	1,487	44,752
1873	1,342	3,471	43,086	575	4,542	48,203	34,507	6,567	1,328	42,402
1874	1,361	3,366	42,418	567	3,956	46,941	35,587	6,613	1,799	43,999
1875	1,316	2,338	42,653	563	4,381	47,597	35,475	6,755	1,743	43,973
1876	1,329	2,314	41,012	562	3,771	45,345	34,996	7,700	1,727	44,423
1877	1,266	3,075								
1878	1,539	3,118								
1879	1,361	3,494	41,666	4,042	2,856	48,564	43,303	9,915	597	53,815
1880	1,322	3,469	43,579	6,104	3,824	53,507	41,276	8,183	1,301	50,760
1881	1,345	3,330	47,263	5,102	2,820	55,185	43,302	8,439	762	52,503
1882	1,359	3,344	45,988	5,050	2,566	53,604	43,176	8,241	619	52,036
1883	1,387	3,372	46,129	6,314	2,821	55,264	45,703	9,656	754	56,113
1884	1,505	3,189	45,593	6,289	3,322	55,204	46,133	9,418	626	56,177
1885	1,375	3,247	45,448	6,416	3,984	55,848	45,856	9,642	666	56,164
1886	1,222	3,106	46,551	6,575	3,900	57,026	46,377	9,050	846	56,273
1887	1,335	3,088	45,865	6,707	3,485	56,057	45,235	8,474	661	54,370
1888	1,325	3,039	45,140	6,496	3,714	55,350	46,338	8,690	740	55,768
1889	1,171	2,901	44,014	10,951	3,024	57,989	44,348	8,246	640	53,234
1890	1,146	2,847	37,565	6,400	2,796	46,761	41,546	7,663	635	49,844
1891	1,226	2,847	38,125	6,350	2,433	46,908	40,658	8,030	695	49,383
1892	1,265	2,936	42,400	10,117	2,749	55,266	43,191	8,167	896	52,254
1893	1,327	3,019	42,866	9,996	2,882	55,744	44,052	7,692	897	52,641
1894	1,416	3,071	43,454	9,720	2,444	55,618	44,479	8,073	889	53,441
1895	1,305	3,083	43,904	9,733	2,587	56,224	45,360	8,168	913	54,441
1896	1,329	3,117	42,715	9,625	4,808	57,148	49,363	10,128	0	56,117
1897	1,457	3,245	43,623	9,695	4,788	58,106	49,766	9,418	0	59,184
1898	1,500	3,327	46,412	9,786	3,947	60,145	54,396	9,765	0	64,161

Source: Computed from the records of the Glasgow Town's Hospital and the Glasgow Parochial Board.

the period. At all times considerable cyclical variation is observed. Peaks coincide closely with downturns in business activity, bad harvests, fever epidemics, and severe winters. The radical increase in 1845 was a direct result of the change in legislation in that year, with peaks after that date representing economic recessions, until 1870. In that year a Select Committee strongly recommended against the practice of providing the unemployed with assistance from the public funds. Moreover, in the same year the Board of Supervision ordered a more strict adherence to the 'means test'. As a result, the Glasgow Parochial Board generally offered every applicant relief in the Hospital. Thereafter, there is a noticeable drop in the number of out-pensioners, with cyclical patterns being considerably less obvious.

An examination of expenditure and receipts shows that the two move in a similar fashion, with total receipts generally exceeding total expenditure. Relief accounted for approximately eighty per cent of total expenditure, with the cost of management and buildings consuming the remainder. As out-pensioners received very small sums, the bulk of relief expenditure was on the inmates of the Hospital. Thus, it is not surprising that the expenditure pattern generally closely correlates with the pattern for the number of inmates. There was a dramatic increase in relief expenditure per recipient, from £5 10s. in the 1850s and early 1860s to an average of £10 10s. in the 1890s, in money terms. One should be cautious about making hasty conclusions that the recipients were materially better off, for the increased expenditure could simply have been the result of price inflation. The little evidence that is available suggests that price inflation does account for the rise, at least until 1870. Indeed, it has been argued elsewhere that the real income of the unskilled workers in Glasgow did not increase in the period up to 1870.[3] For the remainder of the nineteenth century the information is too sketchy to arrive at any conclusions. Finally, another item worthy of note is that government grants as a percentage of total revenue increased dramatically (from about 1.5 per cent to over twenty per cent) after 1879, allowing the amount raised by assessment to stabilise. Increased government allowances were a reflection of national British trends to reduce the burden of local rates by shifting finance to the central government, with its larger and more varied tax base.

A final point must be made. The data represent only the activities of the Glasgow Town's Hospital. Besides this organisation, there were two other workhouses in the Glasgow area, the official activities of the Established Church before 1845, and the numerous private charities. Thus, the data can only provide a hint of the extent of pauperism in the Glasgow area; the nature of the problem would be grossly underestimated by sole reliance on this data. In fact, during years of high unemployment, at least twenty per cent of the population received some form of assistance. One can only conclude that the survival of the working classes frequently depended upon private charity, for the legal structure prevented public support.

I: Provision for the Legal Recipients

The Scottish poor law before 1845 established as the administrators of poor relief in burghs the magistrates and town councils. Many burghs, including Glasgow, delegated responsibility to other organisations. Prior to 1731, poor relief in Glasgow was administered by the following four groups: the Town Council, the General Session of the Established Church for Glasgow, the Incorporated Trades, and the Merchant's House. Each of these worked independently of the others, administering relief mainly to those for whom it was directly responsible. Under this framework an effective unified system of relief was impossible. In 1731, because of increasing problems of destitution and begging in Glasgow, the magistrates and town council initiated discussions with the other groups providing relief. The purpose of these talks was to develop a new system of administering poor relief in Glasgow. The result was the creation of the Town's Hospital,[4] bringing about two institutions for the supplying of relief in Glasgow, the new Hospital and the General Session. Although these two organisations administered their respective funds independently of each other, persons could not be placed on the roll of the Town's Hospital without being referred by their individual parish kirk session.

The General Session was a policy formulating organisation composed of the minister and elders from each of the *quoad sacra* parishes within Glasgow.[5] As was the general rule in Scotland, each parish was divided into 'portions', with an elder responsible for its poor assigned to each. Persons first applied for assistance to their elder, who gave the applicant temporary aid while investigating the claim. The elder did this by determining the applicant's need, and whether the applicant had been an industrious resident of the burgh of Glasgow for at least three years. If these conditions were met, the applicant was placed upon the session rolls and received a monthly allowance, of which there were thirteen payments during the year. Recipients remained on the session rolls until the maximum amount which the session could give was insufficient to maintain them; they were then transferred to the rolls of the Town's Hospital, their names being removed from the session's rolls.

. The Hospital was managed by a group of forty-eight directors and the Lord Provost. Twelve directors were elected by the Town Council, twelve by the Merchants' House, twelve by the General Session, and twelve by the Incorporated Trades. Hence, all the groups providing relief prior to 1731 were equally represented in the new system, and any change in the Hospital rules and regulations had to be ratified by three of the four electing societies. From the forty-eight directors a weekly committee of eight was elected; it was responsible for handling the admission of the poor and the daily business.

On 15 November 1733 the Hospital was opened. It was capable of maintaining 300 persons. Benefit of the Hospital was extended to all sorts of poor belonging to the city. Each inmate was instructed in the principles of the Christian religion and taught to read and write, and such as were capable did some work suitable to their age and ability to help defray their expenses. Upon entry each was examined by the surgeon for contagious diseases, washed, and given new clothes. They arose at six in the morning during the summer months and at eight during winter. Bedtime was at nine in the evening during winter and at ten during the summer.

Prior to 1774 only the indigent, orphans, or other children (if a payment of £25 was received) were accepted into the Hospital; no outdoor relief was given. On 19 August 1756 the directors decided that the Hospital was too crowded, therefore, they were forced to refuse relief to a great number of poor even though they had a very good claim and 'their poverty and distress pleads strongly for them'. The directors claimed that they were able to maintain the poor at a lower expense than if they were maintained in their own homes. As the number of poor increased sharply and the Hospital was filled beyond capacity, on 11 June 1773 it was agreed to provide the city's begging poor with badges entitling them to three meals a day for three months at the Hospital. It was thought that this would be a method of restraining all begging, except from the city's poor. Finally, in 1774, relief was extended to out-pensioners by allotting them an allowance in meal. Ironically, this was also the first year of a regular assessment, applied according to the principles of the Act of 1574. The assessment was levied on the inhabitants by valuation of heritable and of personal property, according to the individual's wealth, circumstances, and ability.

These were the major items of administration during the period up to 1818. As can be seen, they represent primarily decisions on how better to administer relief to the poor of the city. During this period there was a close and harmonious relationship between all four societies that had entered into the agreements in 1731. There was a gradual movement from a position of not granting out-pensions to one of granting them. Thus, the sphere of individuals eligible for relief was expanding, leading to a need to introduce assessments in order to finance the additional expenditure.

The system did not produce serious complaints until about 1818. It is ironic that this first period of dissent against the system was instigated by increasing costs due to rising prices and increasing numbers of paupers as a result of war, industrial depression, and epidemics—factors beyond the control of the directors.

A change in the system as above described can be dated from 23 April 1818. It was agreed that by 1819 all out-pensions would be paid in money instead of meal. The committee argued that meal was easily exchanged for whiskey and that the practice of giving meal was too inconvenient. For example on one Saturday a total of 3,802 pounds of meal was distributed among 512 paupers—201 received six pounds each, 276 received eight pounds each, ten pounds each was given to 16 persons, and 19 received twelve pounds each. The meal was distributed by the Hospital inmates, who were not supervised, and there was no check on the quantity distributed. The committee estimated that the expense of giving meal was 50 per cent more than if money was given. Secondly, it was decided to end the practice of having boarders, individuals who paid from £18 to £20 per year to live in the Hospital, but who did not have to follow the rules. Thirdly, the Hospital had the following three classes of children: 1) orphans—children who either had no parents or who had been deserted and were at the age of education; 2) exposed children—foundlings given out to nurse until six or seven years of age and kept on the funds until the age of ten for boys and eleven for girls and then apprenticed; and 3) adopted children—those admitted as infants with a payment of £30, no questions asked. The practice of keeping the last category was begun in 1802, and as over half of the children had died, was considered as a source of revenue. Indeed, a profit of £1200 was derived from this category between 1802 and 1818. Nonetheless, it was decided to discontinue the acceptance of adopted children. The practice, however, was reinstated in 1823, since its discontinuance had caused the Hospital to sustain financial losses.

These changes were but a prelude to what was to follow. With the inception of St John's Church on 29 September 1819 and the beginning of the Rev. Dr Thomas Chalmers' famous scheme, the break-down of the old system was accelerated, finally coming to an end on 15 February 1821, when the General Session submitted their resignation as administrators. The resulting major change in management was that the individual sessions no longer gave their collections to the General Session to be distributed to the parishes according to their proportion of paupers. Each parish session administered its own funds, any surplus of revenue over expenditure being retained. If a session's funds, consisting of the church door collections, were not adequate, it drew from the Hospital's funds, which were composed primarily of the revenue from the assessment. Of the ten parishes forming the Parish of Glasgow, only four drew from the funds of the Town's Hospital immediately after the General Session resigned, being the following: College, St Andrew's, St Mungo's, and Tron. The other six eventually sought aid from the Hospital; a list with their date of assumption follows: Outer High–1826, St George's–1827, St James'–1831, St Enoch's and St David's–1832, and St John's–1836.

Important changes in the director's attitudes become apparent in the early 1840s. In 1841 they agreed that the city's able-bodied unemployed had a right to relief, and they proposed a House of Industry for this class. In 1842 they agreed to allow £200 to be used in co-operation with the magistrates and heritors in the suburbs to provide a temporary House of Industry for the vagrant poor. The following year £500 was given for the relief of able-bodied unemployed, who suffered from the 'great stress on business'. But the final impetus to provide more liberal relief payments was provided by a Court of Session decision. On 15 February 1843 the Court of Session in Widow Duncan *against* the Parish of Ceres decided that 3s. 6d. per week for six children was not needful sustentation according to the statutes *anent* the poor. Accordingly, on 5 June 1843 the directors adopted a new and higher scale of relief payments. Moreover, children were continued on the roll until the age of ten and were provided with school fees from the age of six until the age of ten.

The minutes of the directors of the Hospital end soon after the passage of the Poor Law Amendment Act (Scotland) in 1845. On 23 June 1845 the directors sent a memorial to the Lord Advocate of Scotland expressing their general approval of the proposed bill. In particular they stated their satisfaction in allowing parishes to combine, stated they felt that each session should be allowed to keep their own collections to be applied to the relief of their indigent members and the education of the parish poor and such other parochial purposes as the sessions may direct, and they stated a belief that a clause should be added forcing Irish authorities to accept poor Irish deported from Glasgow. On 17 November 1845 the directors attended their first meeting as members of the new Parochial Board. They held office until 11 December 1846, when the first election of the Parochial Board members occurred.

At its meeting of 29 December 1846 the Board received a report on the course of pauperism in Glasgow, which stated that 'Pauperism is increasing with fearful rapidity in this City'.[6] The Board was urged, in spite of the seemingly more generous provisions for poor relief intended by the framers of the new poor law, to reinforce a major underlying principle of the old poor law that the amount of relief given should be below the subsistence level. It was argued that such a policy was essential in order to curb the flood of applications from the undeserving and to raise the level of moral standards among the lower classes. Members of the Board soon learned that the mechanism of pauperism was not that simple. On 5 March 1847 the members of the Board were forced to make an additional assessment on account of the high price of provisions and the increasing number of paupers, causing the assessment to jump from £24,750 in 1846 to £48,000 in 1847. The assessment in Glasgow was now based on the value of rental; under the old mode of means and substance the number of individuals assessed was 4,000, while using the new mode of rental value the number was 14,000.

The year 1847 was a particularly bad one for the Board because of a fever epidemic and a business recession. At a meeting on 11 November of that year it was stated that because of '. . . the want of employment among the working classes, and the pressure of disease, the Board's weekly payments to out-door and incidental poor has risen from an average of £25 per week, to an average for the last six months of £230'. As the Board was also responsible for the health standards of the city, it was forced to cope with the fever epidemic. Its first action was to vote an additional £300 to the Royal Infirmary in order to supply more beds for fever patients. That action was taken toward the end of May, along with a decision to re-open the old Hospital buildings for use as a fever hospital. On 4 June the Board sent a petition to Parliament stating that because of a great influx of Irish into the city, which was causing overcrowding and the rapid spread of fever, the Board requested that all west of Scotland ports be given the right to search vessels from Ireland and refuse to admit the ill. This request seems reasonable when it is realised that from 1 January 1847 to 13 November, the number of destitute Irish who landed in Glasgow was 49,993, resulting in an additional expenditure of £21,243.

The Board continued to feel that the new poor law was threatening the moral standards of the lower classes. On 13 April 1850 they petitioned the Commons, arguing that the present laws cause 'the feelings of self reliance which formerly existed amongst the labouring classes in Scotland have since the passing of that Act [The Poor Law Amendment Act (Scotland), 1845], given place to feelings of dependence which have become as injurious to their own well-being as to that of the general community'. It is significant that the government did not act on this petition; the mood of the country was changing toward a more generous attitude with respect to poor relief provision; the administrators of relief within Glasgow had changed from progressive supporters to conservatives; Glasgow's position as a leader in poor relief reform had been lost. One reason for the change in viewpoint was the changing nature of the structure of the metropolitan area. The boundaries of the city expanded at a much slower rate than population increased. This caused extreme pressures, especially as the middle and upper classes were moving out of the city, resulting in an erosion of the assessment base. Thus, with an increasing number of applications for relief, the quality of assistance could not be maintained. To try to ease the pressure, the Board on 28 January 1851 sent a petition to Parliament requesting a bill which would allow the city and Barony to amalgamate for the purposes of poor law administration. The amalgamation, however, did not take place until 1898, when for purposes of poor relief administration the City Parish of Glasgow and the Parish of Barony became known as the Parish of Glasgow.

The Board constantly tried to find ways to reduce the burden of poor relief. For example the Board late in 1850 considered the feasibility of constructing a system of 'test houses' as a method of applying a means test; all applicants for relief would be offered indoor relief; if they refused, they would be denied assistance. This action was reinforced in December of 1850, when it was reported that monthly meal tickets had been found in the shop of James Steele, grocer and spirit dealer. It should be noted, however, that the 'test houses' were not constructed at this time. Another example occurred on 6 January 1852, when the Board ordered that a list of deserted wives and children be published as a means of reducing their numbers. At the same time they also decided 'to offer a reward of Ten shillings and sixpence, for such information as shall lead to the conviction of any person who shall have absconded, leaving a wife or family chargeable to the Parish'. Ironically, sometimes the Board's attempts to reduce expenditure actually increased them, as happened with the removal of non-resident paupers. On 25 March 1851, 'The Inspector stated that in granting warrants for the removal of Irish paupers, the Magistrates lay an obligation on the Board, to provide clothing for every pauper removed, and he requested the Board to make arrangements for procuring clothing for that purpose'. The Board was sometimes justified in being critical of applicants' need for relief, for on 1 November 1853 it was reported that one family who applied for relief had a weekly income of £1-1-6, of which 2s. was from lodgers; they had 13 people living in their one-room house of 13 feet by 9 feet, with a low ceiling. However, not all members of the Board followed a hard line, as for example Mr Kennedy charged on 5 October 1853 that the inmates did not receive sufficient sustenance, resulting in the appointment of a committee to investigate the charges; the committee never reported. On 4 May 1875 the Board decided that 'the food of the inmates should be as nearly similar as is compatible with health to that of the labouring classes whose position is next to that of paupers'. This represents a major shift away from the previous policy that the poor should receive below subsistence allowances in order to encourage help from their families and to ensure that only the deserving poor would apply.

Besides providing for paupers as inmates of the Town's Hospital and as out-pensioners, the Board also had paupers in the Insane Asylum, reformatory schools, the Deaf and Dumb Institution, the Blind Asylum, the Eye Infirmary, Lock Hospital, and various parish schools. The poor in Glasgow had always been catered for in these institutions at the expense of the poor's fund. By far the majority of applications for relief were from women with children and aged women, as had always been the case. Paupers could leave the Hospital at any time, and this is reflected in the fact that eighty per cent of all dismissals were at the inmate's request. Not all inmates wished to leave; though few would envy the record established by Janet Allan or M'Queen. When she died in the Town's Hospital on 6 January 1897, she had been a resident for a period of forty-two years.

A major characteristic of poor relief administration in Glasgow in the post-1845 period was the ever-increasing lack of local uniqueness. The Scotland-wide policies of the Board of Supervision created a greater degree of uniformity within the operation of the Scottish poor law. The autonomy of the administrators within Glasgow was lost. Even provision for the alteration of existing buildings had to be approved by the Edinburgh-based Board of Supervisors. For example, a letter from John Skelton, secretary to the Board of Supervisors, dated 1 June 1882, gave the Glasgow Parochial Board permission to modify a wing of the main building of the Town's Hospital into accommodation for male 'test cases', as long as a paid official was hired to be in charge of that department and to oversee the proposed adjoining stone-breaking yard.

By the last quarter of the nineteenth century, the Glasgow Town's Hospital was no longer regarded as a model institution. Even though the Hospital had moved to a new site in the early 1840s, by the 1880s that site was considered to be an unsuitable location, as it was in the midst of a densely populated area and surrounded on all sides by important manufactories. As a result the atmosphere was continually filled with smoke. Moreover, the Hospital buildings themselves were completely lacking in adequate sanitation facilities. Overcrowding was a perpetual problem, partly as a result of the Parochial Board's policy to use indoor relief as a means test. As a majority of applicants for relief were persons resident in lodging houses, about 97 per cent of them accepted the Board's offer for accommodation. This resulted in another major change in emphasis for the Hospital. In its operation until at least the 1860s, it was viewed primarily as a residence for the infirm aged. However, during the last quarter of the nineteenth century, emphasis was shifted to its use as a workhouse. A majority of the inmates performed some type of work, receiving in exchange an additional four ounces of meat at dinner. Inmates undertaking light voluntary work were not eligible for this additional food allowance. Effective discipline also became a major issue, and it was argued that poorhouses should be institutions of terror to the ill-doing and a home for the well-doing,[7] thus preserving the concept of the deserving poor.

II: Provision for the Able-Bodied Unemployed

In a growing industrial city such as Glasgow periodic problems arose as a result of downturns in business activity. Prior to 1845 the directors of the Town's Hospital frequently gave occasional relief to the able-bodied unemployed and their families in order to prevent them from becoming permanent burdens on the poor's roll. Generally, however, this practice was discouraged. A more acceptable practice was for the town council to try to find employment for the unemployed. Failing this, private charities were established for the sole purpose of providing assistance to these individuals and their families.

After 1845 the Glasgow Parochial Board took a firmer stance. The first indication of the introduction of a new, tougher policy occurred on 25 January 1848, when it was reported that the Sheriff of Lanark had ordered the parish of Gorbals to provide relief to the children of an able-bodied unemployed man; the Board agreed that they should fight the principle thus established. This action was followed on 11 August with a letter from the Board of Supervision, advising that the Glasgow Parochial Board should make interim provision for the able-bodied unemployed and their children until the Court of Session decision on the Sheriff's ruling. On 18 August it was noted there had been a dramatic increase in the number of orphans and children deserted by their parents. The Board therefore decided to ignore the order from the Board of Supervision to provide relief to the able-bodied unemployed, as these individuals had always been supported by means of voluntary charity. Nonetheless, on 9 February 1849 it was reported that since the decision of Sheriff Alison the previous October, 1,347 able-bodied unemployed men, who with their wives and children totalled 3,205, had been placed on the rolls of the parish. The issue finally was resolved on 6 April 1852, when the House of Lords concurred with the Court of Session ruling that able-bodied persons out of employment were not entitled to parochial relief for themselves or their children.

A severe downturn in business activity occurred in 1857, as a result of the collapse of the Western Bank of Scotland. In March of that year the

Board agreed to form a 'Relief Committee for the Unemployed'. As there was already in existence the Central Relief Committee, it was suggested that applicants first go to this voluntary group for temporary assistance, and that the parish of settlement later reimburse the Central Relief Committee. Furthermore, it was agreed that relief could only be supplied in the form of food, and that each recipient and dependent would have to do some work. The Board unanimously agreed that they could not '. . . recognise the right of able-bodied persons or their children, in any circumstances to parochial relief'. However, they could provide occasional relief to prevent them from becoming disabled and hence a burden on the parish, yet relief could only be given in kind and in exchange for work. Relief works were opened, funds collected, and 10,051 heads of families were assisted. It was estimated that not less than forty or fifty thousand persons received benefits from the funds collected.[8] This represented about fifteen per cent of the population

The nature of the workings of these special committees becomes clear with an entry in the minutes of the Glasgow Parochial Board dated 4 March 1862.

> The Unemployed—Able-Bodied—In consequence of the present distress, the great number of persons out of work and the Poor Laws of this country having made no provision for the relief of able-bodied persons, an arrangement was entered into with the Lord Provost, Magistrates and Parochial Boards, whereby all the above class requiring relief, should have their cases reported to, and their circumstances inquired into by the Officials of the Parochial Boards, and if found proper objects of charity, suitable relief should be granted for themselves and families, in return for which the men should be employed in such labour as could conveniently be obtained for them. Under this arrangement 1670 applications have been made at the offices of the City Parochial Board, 1028 of these were married men—112 were widowers; in the families of the above there were 1322 children under 12 years of age. The remaining number of applicants, 530 were single men. In investigating these cases it was painful to find nearly one-third of them single men. Most of them had left the parental roof as soon as their earnings were sufficient to maintain themselves—too selfish to allow any part of their income to contribute to the maintenance of other parts of the family—and too self-willed to submit to parental control—they left home—contacted unsettled habits—when in work, squandered their means—and when distress came, they were among the first to apply for charity.
>
> Of the above 855 were Scotch, 755 Irish, and 25 English; 280 were weavers, 766 labourers, 60 cloth lappers, 56 moulders; 508 were hammermen, printers, porters, clerks, hawkers, and various other trades; 622 were sent to work in the Public Park, or to sweep the streets; 145 were sent to the oakum rooms; 268 gave wrong addresses or could not be found; 40 never made their appearance after being visited; 28 were refused relief, having sufficient from the earnings of the rest of the family to support the whole; 3 were pensioners without families—one the family consisted

> of himself, wife and two sons whose united earnings were 30/- per week;
> 557 were offered the house; of this number only 163 accepted the offer,
> and the greater number of these left in a few days—to the families of
> men employed in the oakum room, and those whose circumstances were
> under investigation, 14,000 tickets for bread and soup have been given
> (value £116-13-1) besides £49-8-1 in money.

It is clear from this quote that the Town's Hospital was still being used as
a means test; individuals were offered accommodation in the Hospital, and
if they rejected this offer, relief was denied. During a period of two years,
£36,320 was collected and distributed, in addition to clothing, blankets,
coals, and food. Assistance was given to 18,797 persons. Nearly £2,000
was expended on emigration.[9]

In the above described periods of distress, relief operations were carried out by a combined committee of citizens and members of the town
council. The necessity of such groups was a result of restrictive interpretations of the poor laws. The Glasgow Parochial Board held the view
that, 'No doubt the Poor Law Act makes it lawful for Parochial Boards to
subscribe to certain public charitable institutions, such as infirmaries and
the like; but there is no authority for giving its funds to such an organisation as the Unemployed Relief Fund'.[10] However, these interpretations
were criticised.

> Having no statutory powers to raise the funds requisite for relief either
> by assessment or otherwise, without suitable work ready to offer at the
> moment, and the Poor Law having been rendered utterly inoperative
> by an adverse interpretation, in the House of Lords, of its originally
> intended provision to aid these 'occasional poor', the only resource left
> to the Magistrates' Committee was an appeal for help to the generosity
> of the citizens by voluntary subscriptions—a mode admittedly unequal
> to its burden for this purpose, but nevertheless, on each occasion, most
> liberally responded to.[11]

Beginning in 1878, the town council took charge of disbursing the funds
collected and in overseeing the establishment and operation of relief works.

The recession of 1877-79 was of particular note, as the Board stated
that the main category of unemployed was women, who were unable to
get work. The cause of this commercial depression was the failure of the
City of Glasgow Bank. Detailed operation of the relief programme can
be gained from an examination of the *Report of the Administration of the
Glasgow Unemployed Relief Fund, During the Winter of 1878-9*.

> The Sanitary Department, since its extension in 1870, has been the
> medium through which the required relief was granted, applications re-
> ceived, investigation as to the circumstances of each case made, and or-
> ders for work granted, while the Public Works, Public Parks, and Cleans-
> ing Departments arranged the work, and the Chamberlain's Department
> carried out the collection and disbursement of the funds.
>
> The work consisted of stone-breaking for the roads, earthworks at

the Public Parks, and scavenging in the streets, and never, in any case, yielded a return sufficient to recoup the outlay in wages; but continuance at it was generally found an effective test of the applicant's destitution and willingness to work.

Part of the wages was given in Benevolent Society's tickets, which procured food at certain selected provision shops throughout the city, and part in cash. The relief given to applicants' dependants, and those unable to work, was invariably by these tickets.

The subscriptions raised in these years fortunately more than met the required outlay, leaving balances in the Committee's hands sufficient, at least, to begin a distribution of relief at each returning demand, until new collecting arrangements were made.[12]

The following rules were adopted for the guidance of inspectors in receiving applications from the unemployed:

1. No applications will be received except from able-bodied men out of employment;
2. Unemployed women, and men disabled for work and in destitution, may apply at the Parochial Board offices of the parish in which they reside;
3. No application will be received from single able-bodied men, nor from men who have members of their families working and earning fair wages;
4. No application will be received from any person who resides outwith the City boundaries, nor from any one who has been less than three months resident in the City of Glasgow;
5. All applicants must provide themselves with a certificate of residence from their landlord or factor, and of character and length of service from their last Employer.[13]

It must be stressed that all means were avoided for the supplying of relief in the form of money; assistance was granted in the form of food, clothing, fuel, and employment on public works, such as earth digging, stone breaking, oakum picking and occasionally scavenging. No person who was on strike, or who declined employment at wages sufficient for maintenance, or a person in receipt of parochial or charitable relief was to receive assistance from the Relief Committee. Even though the Relief Committee was a voluntary charity, it was able to utilise existing departments within the city's governmental structure. This practice enabled the Committee to be more efficient.

The rules were strictly enforced, though there appears to have been few cases of an undeserving nature applying. One inspector stated, 'As yet comparatively few tradesmen have applied, the majority of the recipients of relief being labourers and millworkers. Occasionally an undeserving case is discovered; but the number of really bad characters who have turned up is very small . . . men six, eight, and ten weeks out of work, furniture sold or pawned, and wives and children on the brink of starvation'.[14] Most of the applicants, especially the women, stated they had been forced to dispose of most of their possessions.

Depressions occurred in 1884-87 and 1892-93, which were of sufficient severity to cause the town council to establish relief operations. The administrative structure and regulations were similar to those of 1878-9; the major exception was that the Charity Organisation Society, established in Glasgow in 1874, accepted responsibility for investigating all applicants for relief as to their character and needs. Selected information for these periods are contained in Table 4.2, along with the years 1878-80 and 1895. In all cases where a man was able to work, the labour test was enforced. Besides the official committee established by the town council, other voluntary organisations were providing assistance. For example, during the 1886-87 depression the Charity Organisation Society provided 627 pairs of boots and stockings and 100 pairs of trousers and shirts; the directors of the Night Asylum gave 5,420 rations of food; the United Evangelistic Association gave 22,636 rations of food.[15]

During the recession of 1895 new arrangements were made, as the Board in conjunction with the Lord Provost and magistrates decided on 19 February 1895

> that the arrangements be placed under the charge of the police, that soup kitchens be established in various districts of the city, that the police offices should be at the disposal of the poor as shelters in case of need, and that lines be distributed on shopkeepers to deserving families, and that the public should be invited to subscribe the funds required.

The major reason for the change was that there was such an influx of applications that the Charity Organisation Society was unable to investigate them. The cause of the sudden increase in unemployment was the prolonged severe cold weather. These unusual conditions meant that prime emphasis had to be placed on other forms of relief, other than providing for temporary employment in public work projects. Accordingly, soup kitchens were established, public buildings were used to house the homeless, food, coals and rent was provided, and medical relief was extended. The Lord Provost placed a letter in the local papers, asking for donations from the general public. Within a week, £9,586 had been collected, of which £4,532 was spent. It was estimated that over 330,000 meals were given, 4,839 persons used the night shelters, over 1,000 tons of coals were delivered to 13,151 households, and 22,666 food tickets were issued during February and March. Again, it must be remembered that besides these public bodies, there were numerous private organisations giving relief.

Table 4.2: Glasgow Relief Funds, 1878-1895

	1878-80	1884-85	1885-86	1886-87	1892-93	1895
Cause of distress	Depression after City of Glasgow Bank failure	Commercial depression	Commercial depression	Commercial depression	Depression in Iron and shipbuilding	Weather
Relief Works Opened	25 Nov. 1878	—	1 Dec. 1885	16 Dec. 1886	8 Dec. 1892	4 Feb. 1895
Relief Works Closed	31 Jan. 1880	—	1 May 1886	16 April 1887	4 Mar. 1893	16 Mar. 1895
Kind of work provided	Digger work, Stonebreaking, Scavenging Oakum picking	Stonebreaking	—	Digger work and Stonebreaking	Digger Work	Stonebreaking
Public subscriptions received	£17,752	£7,205	£675	£25	None	£9,586
Total amount spent on Relief and Wages	£33,333	£9,171	£12,860	£6,202	£3,103	£9,387
Value of work done	£13,590	£1,480	£11,283	£5,408	£996	£1,895
Applications for work	2,213	—	4,576	2,202	2,801	3,643
Orders for work given to	1,900	—	4,000	1,580	2,328	3,643
Orders for work refused to	313	—	576	622	473	None
Highest number working on one day	4,508	1,229	1,494	918	870	2,543
Average number working during whole period	303	—	—	—	466	1,036
Different occupations of men employed	110	231	—	117	110	231

Source: Glasgow Parochial Board Minutes, 2 May 1895

III: Conclusions

The administrators of poor relief in Glasgow during the nineteenth century cannot be given full marks. Prior to 1845, there is evidence which indicates that they were becoming more lenient toward the poor, making greater provision for the recipients and expanding the categories eligible for relief. However, after 1845 the attitudes of the administrators hardened and were reinforced by the decisions and actions of the central Board of Supervision. To some extent, therefore, the changing nature of the policies within Glasgow were a reflection of the change from local autonomy to one of central control. Nonetheless, it cannot be denied that the progressive leadership of Glasgow in poor relief reform was transformed into one of reluctant followers.

The percentage of population receiving public assistance in 1891 was slightly lower than the percentage in 1801 (2.25 per cent versus 2.35 per cent). This represents a considerable drop from the 1850-70 average of 3.2 per cent, reflecting the hardening of attitudes in the 1870s. The condition of the poor also deteriorated, as the accommodation in the Town's Hospital became so overcrowded and unsanitary that the Board of Supervision was forced in the 1890s to order improvements.

While the lot of the legal poor did not improve, the situation of the able-bodied unemployed was made unbearable. This category was allowed some assistance from the public funds before the 1860s; thereafter, they were denied public relief. Without the existence of private charities, the temporarily unemployed and their dependents would have perished. Machines received better care from factory owners than did their displaced workers.

Notes

1. *Report of the Administration of the Glasgow Unemployed Relief Fund, During the Winter 1878-9* (Aird & Coghill, Glasgow, 1879).
2. For a detailed description of the operation of the Scottish poor laws prior to 1845, see R. A. Cage, *The Scottish Poor Law, 1745-1845* (Scottish Academic Press, Edinburgh, 1981).
3. See Anthony Slaven, *The Development of the West of Scotland: 1750-1960* (Routledge & Kegan Paul, London, 1975), pp. 157-9.
4. Unless otherwise specified, information on the Glasgow Town's Hospital was obtained from the manuscript records housed in the Mitchell Library, Glasgow.
5. Unless otherwise specified, information on the General Session was obtained from the records of meetings housed in the Mitchell Library, Glasgow. In-

formation for each parish was obtained from the respective kirk session minutes, housed either in Register House, Edinburgh, or Glasgow University Library.

6. Unless otherwise stated, information concerning the activities of the Glasgow Parochial Board was obtained from the Parochial Board Minutes, housed in the Strathclyde Regional Archives, Glasgow.

7. *Ibid.*, 21 March 1895.

8. *Report of the Administration of the Funds for the Relief of the Unemployed and of the Distress Prevailing in Glasgow from January to March, 1895, Presented by the Committee Appointed by the Lord Provost and Magistrates,* 1895.

9. *Ibid.*

10. Glasgow Parochial Board Minutes, December, 1879.

11. *Report of the Administration of the Glasgow Unemployed Relief Fund, During the Winter of 1878-9* (Aird & Coghill, Glasgow, 1879), p. 1.

12. *Ibid.*, pp. 7-8:

13. Glasgow Parochial Board Minutes, 29 September 1879.

14. *1879 Report*, p. 22.

15. *1895 Report.*

Chapter Five

GLASGOW WORKING-CLASS POLITICS

I.G.C. Hutchison

I: Pre-1820 Radical Movements

Before the French Revolution, the Glasgow working classes manifested little interest in political questions, such incidents as the Calton weavers'
strike in 1787 probably best being interpreted as strictly an industrial
matter.[1] Cockburn in a well-known passage described the impact of the
French Revolution on Scottish politics: 'Everything rung, and was connected, with the Revolution in France; which, for above 20 years was, or
was made, the all in all. Everything, not this thing or that thing, but
literally everything, was soaked in this one event'.[2] The working classes
of Glasgow were rather slower than elsewhere to pitch themselves into
the tide of political activity unleashed in 1789. Moreover when they did
become active, it was generally in very close liaison with a broad swathe
of middle-class reformers, and the political ideas they expressed rarely
deviated from solidly constitutional doctrines.

The earliest responses in Glasgow to developments in France seem
to have come predominantly from middle-class reformers: a celebratory
dinner to salute the fall of the Bastille was organised by Professor Millar
and Lt-Col Dalrymple of Fordell.[3] 1792 was the year in which the first
impact of the Scottish working classes on the radical movement was felt. A
major political riot occurred in Edinburgh, but no such incident took place
in Glasgow.[4] Similarly, the symbolic gesture of planting Trees of Liberty
was made in a number of towns, including Perth and Dundee, but Glasgow
did not participate.[5] Again, the launching in Scotland of the major radical
organisation of the mid-1790s—The Friends of the People—was initiated
in the summer of 1792 in Edinburgh, while Glasgow did not move until

early in October.[6] After three months' existence the Glasgow branch had 1,200 members, when Edinburgh had around 1,000. Even so, the centre of the association in Scotland remained firmly in Edinburgh. At the first Convention of the Scottish Friends of the People held in December 1792, only 12 Glasgow delegates attended, the bulk of the total of 170 coming from Edinburgh and environs. At the second Convention, which met on 30 April 1793, Glasgow provided only 3 out of 93 delegates.[7] By the summer of 1793 the Glasgow society was finding it hard to keep going, but still managed to organise a petition protesting at Britain going to war against France. The arrest, trial and heavy sentence passed on Thomas Muir of Huntershill, the revered leader of the Glasgow movement, was initially a severe blow, but the sense of the injustice of the treatment meted out to Muir actually seems to have stimulated a revival of support.[8] Thus in October 1793, ten Glasgow branches were stated to be functioning, but the collapse in disunity shortly afterwards of the third Convention, and the arrest of the movement leaders throughout Scotland, virtually extinguished all life in Glasgow reform circles.[9]

In Glasgow the Friends of the People was a broad-based organisation. Among its supporters were some of the neighbouring gentry class: North Dalrymple, the future Earl of Stair, Col Dalrymple of Fordell and Muir of Huntershill. There was also a sizeable number of the solid urban bourgeoisie, including David Dale, the great cotton master, William Boal, the father of the founder of the Clydesdale Bank, and George Crawford, a prominent city lawyer.[10] Shopkeepers and lesser tradesmen played a major part in the Glasgow branches, but in addition many working-class men were active reformers. This was particularly true of the growing body of weavers, who were experiencing a sharp set-back in trade in 1792-93, and flourishing branches were situated in the weaving centres of Anderston and Calton.[11] The extent of support for the Friends of the People was in part due to a conscious decision by the middle-class founders, who put the quarterly subscription at the low level of 3d.[12] Nevertheless, as events in France moved in a more violent and radical direction, participation in the Glasgow society by the middle class became less pronounced, and an alliance of the lower middle class and handloom weavers predominated. But there was no overt ousting of the middle-class reformers as part of a growing sense of the separate identity among the working class.

The general harmony between the classes among the reformers was cemented by the political programme subscribed to by all sections. The historian of the Scottish handloom weavers stressed that at this time these key components of the working class did not express socialistic demands. Indeed, the target of their criticisms was not so much their employers as the landlord class.[13] In this they shared common ground with middle-class merchants and Dissenters, who objected to trading monopolies, the imposition of the corn duties, the retention of the Test Acts and the resistance to burgh reform. The refusal of the Government to act on these topics was blamed on aristocratic control and manipulation of the political system. Working and middle-class reformers therefore united in arguing that a fairer system of parliamentary representation and shorter parliaments would improve the economic condition of the people by ensuring that the level of taxation bearing down on both classes would be reduced.[14] Even when overtly Paineite ideas spread with the shift in the social composition of the reform movement in 1793, it was Paine's advocacy of tax cuts as the prelude to an age of plenty which was warmly endorsed. This theme of Paine's appealed to the ethos of self-help, to which handloom weavers were fully committed, whereas there was little interest in his more socialistic vision of a welfare state.[15]

The restoration of lost political rights was the abiding theme of the reform movement, and no serious hint of republican sentiment ran through its rhetoric; instead deep loyalty to the King was repeatedly stressed. Only at the weakest point of its existence, late in 1793, did the Friends of the People call for universal suffrage, a position far beyond anything acceptable to the Foxite middle-class Whigs.[16] Moreover, the reformers remained staunchly constitutional in their approach to the mode of attaining their objectives. Peaceful propaganda, not violence, was seen as the means whereby popular support would be won. The bulk of political activity accordingly took the form of petitioning, as it was believed that Parliament was bound to listen to and respond to the voice of the people. Therefore extra-legal acts were unnecessary and counter-productive, and members of the Glasgow branches had to swear to abjure violence and intimidation.

After 1793 there was a quiet period, until a brief resurgence of political activity flared up between 1797 and 1802. This was initiated by the United Scotsmen, a secret society functioning among weavers and other working-class occupations. The United Scotsmen had links with the United Irishmen and planned to liaise with a projected French invasion of Britain. The authorities in France had been assured by a spy as far back as 1792 that the working classes in the Glasgow area were ready to join a rising if the occasion arose.[17] The French accordingly included a landing near Glasgow in their invasion plans of 1796-97. In the event, however, the United Scotsmen were at first more of a presence in the eastern and central Scotland areas—especially Perth—than in Glasgow.[18] A very sharp deterioration in weavers' living standards in 1800-01 did help to increase the size of the Glasgow branch, but by the end of 1802 all signs of the United

Scotsmen had apparently vanished.[19] The secret cell structure and the administration of an oath endowed the United Scotsmen with revolutionary overtones, and the movement was avowedly republican. Moreover it called for annual parliaments, universal suffrage and the abolition of church patronage. But there was no interest in Paineite state welfare ideas, and equality of property was firmly repudiated. It would appear, then, that the weavers were still firmly wedded to their self-help values.[20]

With the eclipse of the United Scotsmen, little open working-class political activity occurred in Glasgow for over a decade. The worsening economic conditions endured by handloom workers in the second decade of the nineteenth century contributed to a re-awakening of political involvement, particularly as efforts to build a strong trade union organisation foundered, so stimulating a desire to seek redress by political means.[21]

Although Major John Cartwright had been in contact with Glasgow reformers in 1813 and visited the city at the end of the Napoleonic Wars, his reform schemes evoked no immediate response. Thus, there was little evidence of the spread in Scotland of the Hampden Clubs, which were so prevalent among the English working classes at the time.[22] The re-emergence of radical political awareness in Glasgow was marked by a mass meeting held on 29 October 1816. An estimated 40,000 attended this demonstration, held at Thrushgrove, a property owned by James Turner, a Glasgow shopkeeper and radical of long standing.[23] Those present were predominantly, but not exclusively working class, and a substantial number of shopkeepers and merchants took part, with several delivering speeches to the crowd. The demands made at Thrushgrove were firmly in line with the radical rostrums shared by middle- and working-class reformers. The corrupt political system placed crushing burdens on the population, who sought to have their lost political rights restored. Parliamentary reform was therefore necessary, and the extent of enfranchisement envisaged was restricted to the middle class. The vehicle by which reform was to be won was by sending mass petitions to Parliament.[24]

The indifference of Parliament and the hostility of the Tory party doomed the petitioning campaign to failure. It is illuminating that the sense of economic desperation and political frustration in the five or six years after the Napoleonic Wars was so strong that this was the only period in the time covered by this study that violent political action was plotted by a goodly portion of the Glasgow working class. In 1816-17 government spies disclosed the existence of a 500-strong underground organisation with a structure of constantly dividing cells, which administered oaths and devised secret signs. The society had up to a hundred pieces of arms, and planned to storm barracks to augment its holding, as part of its revolutionary scheme. Although a manufacturer, Robert Kerr, provided financial aid, the secret associations were otherwise strictly working-class in their composition, and were strongest in the city's weaving communities of Anderston, Calton, Tradeston and Camlachie. This Spencean revolutionary organisation was thwarted by the arrest in February 1817 of the ring leaders, including the key personnel of Andrew MacKinley, John Campbell and John Leith. The prosecution of the plotters was mishandled, and all were released on a verdict of not proven.[25]

There was then a lull of nearly three years before organised working-class demands for political reform were again raised in the city, perhaps because a mild economic upturn took place in 1817-19. There was less Scottish interest in the initial reform agitation of 1819 than was found in England. The most significant display in Glasgow came only after the Peterloo incident had shocked opinion into a public show of protest. A vast meeting on 21 August 1819 called for annual parliaments, universal suffrage and the ballot. The marchers were well disciplined, and many of the protestors were wearing revolutionary caps. However, it seems that this demonstration was primarily composed of handloom weavers, now a declining sector of the workforce, while the new factory workers, such as the spinners, were less involved.[26]

The climax of the post-war radical wave in Glasgow came in April 1820, when an abortive rising was staged. On 2 April 1820 a summons to launch a general strike was issued in posters which appeared throughout the city published by 'The Committee of Organisation for forming a Provisional Government'. The strike was well-supported, the call to stay away from work being observed by some 60,000 workers drawn from a wide range of occupations, including weavers, printers, colliers, spinners and machine makers. There was little violence, and only a few isolated instances of drilling were reported, while the local authorities imposed a curfew and rounded up the suspected instigators. When no news of the linked uprising which had been planned to take place simultaneously in various north of England cities came, most of the Glasgow insurgents decided to abandon their projected military action. A small group of intransigents, numbering perhaps 60, marched out of the city, and linking up with others from Strathaven, headed north. They were intercepted by troops at Bonnymuir and put to flight. The leaders, Baird, Hardie and Wilson were arrested, tried and executed.[27]

Several points may be made about the radical rising of 1820. It has been hailed as a pioneering effort by the working class both to found a socialist republic and to assert Scotland's right to independence from England.[28] It does indeed seem clear that the movement was essentially a working-class one: those taking part in the Bonnymuir fiasco were typically weavers, and very few middle-class reformers—apart from James Turner—were implicated. Moreover, the success in persuading so many workers to join in the general strike is most impressive. However, the degree to which the rising marked a breach in the middle- and working-class unity which had hitherto characterised Glasgow radicalism is less apparent.

The trial defence of Baird and Hardie was arranged by Robert Grahame, one of the city's eminent Whig reformers. Grahame had almost been arrested in 1793, when he had also been active for the defence of Muir of Huntershill's trial, and subsequently he helped form the middle-class Fox Club. Grahame was the first Lord Provost appointed by the Town Council elected under the 1833 Municipal Reform Act.[29]

The socialist content of the rising may be doubted. The demands made in the strike proclamation were not couched in very extreme terms. Ancient rights were said to have been lost and required to be regained, but this was a staple claim of moderate reformers. Moreover, the proclamation was careful to insist that 'Equality of Rights (not of property) is the object for which we contend', clearly ruling out any socialistic tendencies.[30] The idea that Scottish Nationalism lay behind the rising also faces difficulties. It is clear that the Glasgow uprising was to be part of a co-ordinated series of insurrections which would also take place in several English towns. To this end, careful pre-planning had been made on both sides of the border, with a lengthy correspondence being entered into to settle questions of finance.[31] Moreover, the demands made in the proclamation refer specifically and unequivocally to British rights and injustices. The committee called on all sympathisers to '. . . support the laudable efforts, which we are about to make to replace to BRITONS, those rights consecrated to them by MAGNA CHARTA and the Bill of Rights. . . .'[32]

It is also not likely that an incipient revolution enjoying mass support was stamped out in 1820 by the ruthless deployment of force by a repressive state. While it can be alleged the government spy system had been invaluable in uncovering the earlier plan of 1816-17, the authorities were far less well informed of developments in 1819-20. The police had no prior knowledge of which individuals were behind the latter rising, and they signally failed to avert the strike by a pre-emptive strike.[33] The extent of support received for the physical force element—as distinct from the mass commitment to the strike—suggests that there was little taste for violent revolution among the Glasgow working class. Certainly the mood in the period after 1820 was not one of simmering discontent. Reformers seem to have been pretty quiescent for the rest of the decade, only returning to public effort as the Reform Bill crisis deepened in 1820.[34]

II: Reformers & Chartists, 1830s & 1840s

Throughout the period between the campaigns to secure the first and second Reform Acts, the tenor of working-class radical politics in Glasgow was as a rule less hostile to middle-class liberalism, than was the case in many other parts of Britain. Co-operation was frequently sought, rather than confrontation, and when that proved unattainable, as in the Chartist phase, the working-class wing remained moderate, constitutional and gradualist in tactics and rhetoric.

There were three distinct organisations set up in Glasgow to agitate for the passage of parliamentary reform in 1830-32. The solid middle class supported the Reform Association: the lower middle class and artisan classes controlled the Political Union; while the factory operatives established their own committee composed of delegates representing trade unions and workshops. While these societies obviously had different social bases, this did not in itself indicate any class tension. Firstly, there was an overlap of personnel between the three bodies, as instanced by the shoemaker John MacAdam, who belonged to all three.[35] This helped to ensure that common approaches to the campaign and joint participation in meetings and demonstrations were standard features of the struggle waged in Glasgow. Thus a dinner in support of reform principles held on 3 January 1831 was initially arranged by the working-class radicals. They then extended an invitation to the middle-class Whigs who, led by Robert Wallace of Kelly (later M.P. for Greenock), turned up in considerable force.[36]

The reform ideology was also shared: working-class radical agreed with middle-class radical that the decay and malfunctioning of the constitution should be reversed at once, and that economic and social improvements would flow from parliamentary reform. The values of self-help and moral elevation were widely held by working men as well as by employers, and so there was no schism over the case for reform.[37] The moderation in conduct and politics of the Glasgow working-class reformers was favourably commented on by Cockburn, who witnessed a huge demonstration in the city on 2 October 1831. He noted the placards carried by the marchers, who were drawn from all the trades, called for peace, economy, reform, no borough-mongering and pledged loyalty to the King. The heroes of the reformers, as indicated by their banners, were not ultra-radicals like Hunt, but Whig leaders such as Grey, Russell and Brougham.[38] Cockburn was especially struck by the peaceableness of the whole demonstration, with no soldiers and very few police present. Whereas in most major English cities rioting broke out during the Reform crisis, there were no such incidents in Glasgow.[39]

Although disillusionment was felt by working-class reformers after the triumphal passage of the first Reform Act and the return of two Whigs for Glasgow, their alienation from the middle-class Liberals was a protracted process. Misgivings were expressed about the failure of middle-class voters and politicians to use their newly-won influence to champion working-class grievances. Thus factory reform, a pressing issue in Glasgow, with so many mills in the city, attracted little support from the local M.P.s. However, the spirit of amity remained in force until 1837. At a festival held on 29 October 1834 in honour of Lord Durham's visit to the city, reformers of both classes were present. John Tait, the working-class radical leader of the 1830s urged Durham to support the demands for shorter parliaments, household suffrage and the ballot. Although these were sweeping calls, the ends for which they were sought were not extreme. Tait explained that they were necessary to secure the abolition of placemen, and an end to both the Corn Laws and the taxes on knowledge. Durham affirmed his approval of these objectives, and they were evidently not unacceptable to Colin Dunlop, the city's next M.P., and the Whig city councillors, who also attended the proceedings.[40] Unity was preserved by anger at the circumstances in which Wellington and Peel were installed in office soon afterwards, and indignation meetings in Glasgow revealed a solid phalanx of reformers opposed to the Tory administration. The immediately succeeding general election of 1835 revealed no overt gulf between reformers, and instead the rather conservative-leaning M.P. James Ewing was replaced by the more radical Colin Dunlop.[41]

In the next two years, however, relations did deteriorate, as working-class impatience grew at the Whig government's inabililty to sustain the momentum of reform. Middle-class reformers became cooler towards calls for the ballot and an extension of the franchise. The existence of trade union violence which was brought out during the cotton spinners case in 1837-38 added to this unease, for it appeared that sections of the working class were turning to non-constitutional modes of action.[42] Moreover, the attention of middle-class radicals was increasingly consumed by the mounting crisis in the Church of Scotland, which absorbed the energies of most of them until the mid-1840s. Thus on the resignation of Dunlop as M.P. in 1836, the highly Whiggish Lord William Bentinck was chosed by the leading local Whigs as a replacement. He was opposed by a Radical, George Mills, who received the backing of Dissenters, as well as political radicals. Bentinck got 1,955 votes, Mills, 903. Yet when Mills ran again in 1841, this time as a Chartist, he was roundly denounced for allegedly colluding with Churchmen and Tories and collected only 355 votes.[43]

The rupture came at the very end of 1837 on the question of the extent of further political reforms to be sought. The disillusion of the working class with their erstwhile allies may explain the speed with which Chartism gained hold in Glasgow. The launching of the national Chartist agitation took place in Glasgow on 21 May 1838. The Birmingham-based initiators of Chartism chose Glasgow because of its record during the Reform crisis and because of the apparent unrest evinced by the cotton spinners trial. The Glasgow working-class reform bodies—the Political Union and the committee of trades delegates—were involved in staging the demonstration, at which perhaps 100,000 people were present. The venereable James Turner of Thrushgrove chaired the proceedings, so establishing the continuity of the Chartists with the reform movements of the preceeding 40 years. The main speech was delivered by Thomas Attwood, in response to an invitation issued after a meeting of 200 trades delegates.[44] The cause was warmly taken up by the city's Complete Suffrage Association, which claimed some 2,000 members within 5 months. 1839-42 proved to be the peak years for Chartism in Glasgow. Indeed, after a brief period in 1838-39, when Edinburgh provided the leadership, Glasgow was the mainstay of Scottish Chartist endeavour. The Scottish Central Committee in August 1839 consisted of 15 members, 14 of whom came from Glasgow or its vicinity, the latter having been mobilised by organisers sent from the city.

The leaders of Chartism at its peak in Glasgow came mostly from the lower middle class or the artisan stratum of the working class. James Moir, a Gallowgate tea dealer, was very influential, along with George Ross, who owned a shoe shop, and W.C. Pattison, secretary of the local steam engine makers union.[45] Moir and Ross had been prominent in the Political Union in the early 1830s. As a rule, and as might be anticipated from such leaders, Glasgow Chartism was of the highly moderate variety. The concept of a Chartist general strike won little approval among local leaders, and the reaction to the Newport rising was that violence, and even its threat, should be eschewed by the movement. Instead, petitioning of Parliament was held to be the main medium by which the Chartist programme would be implemented.[46] Hence, great emphasis was placed on efforts to raise the intellectual and moral level of the working class so that they would appreciate fully the case for the Charter. Many of the city's Chartists helped to establish educational schemes to fund Chartist churches (there was a large congregation in Bridgeton) and to spread co-operative stores as part of this constitutional strategy.[47]

The work of propaganda was particularly well developed in Glasgow, where the *Chartist Circular* had a circulation of over 20,000, and the *Scottish Patriot* also had a large readership.[48] These journals were on the whole less than effusive in the estimation of Feargus O'Connor's leadership of the national Chartist movement. O'Connor's contempt for the Glasgow 'Saints', as he defensively termed them, and the latter's reputation of the extreme views advocated by O'Connor and Harney, led to a bitter squabble in 1841-42 which resulted in a split among city Chartists.[49] The moderates, led by Pattison, seceded to join forces with Joseph Sturge's Complete Suffrage Association, which aimed to forge closer relations between middle- and working-class radicals. The O'Connorites had thus seized control of Glasgow Chartism, but although Moir and Ross remained active in the movement, its peak had been passed. The industrial depression of 1841-42 brought no extra boost, as the spectacle of internal feuding appears to have disheartened many former supporters. Chartism in Glasgow after 1842 was very much a depleted force, and efforts to resuscitate it were unsuccessful, until 1848. In that year a renewal of activity did take place, climaxing in a violent incident when troops fired on a crowd in the East End, shooting 6 people. This episode, although it remained in the consciousness of local people for many years, did not stimulate massive feelings of indignation, as would undoubtedly have occurred in Chartism's heyday.[50] Many of those engaged in Chartist agitation in 1848 seem to have been Irish, and were often young, relatively unskilled workers. These were two categories which had not been so central to the earlier phase of Chartism.[51]

While occasional flickerings of Chartism were to be encountered at points after 1848, the movement in Glasgow more or less was defunct after that year.[52] The aftermath affirmed the general character of Chartism in Glasgow. Many ex-Chartists found themselves quite able to work with middle-class radicals, notably on support for European nationalist movements, which were the focus of political interest among reformers in the 1850s and early 1860s. Louis Blanc, Kossuth, Mazzini and Karl Blind all spoke in Glasgow on the topic of political liberty in their respective countries; meetings to uphold Polish and Danish independence were held; and the despotic governments of Russia, France and Austria-Hungary were regularly denounced.[53] Italian independence was especially popular, with over 250 volunteers from the city going to join Garibaldi.[54] James Moir was much engaged in these causes, as was another ex-Chartist, John MacAdam, who became the foremost advocate of the Italian cause in the city.[55] Middle-class reformers also participated in these campaigns. Walter Buchanan, Whig M.P. for Glasgow from 1857 to 1868, chaired several such meetings, and the Garibaldi Aid Fund attracted hefty subscriptions from the mercantile class with one donor, W.G. Langdon, contributing £200.[56] In the 1857 election, Moir used his influence with reformers to help return to parliament Robert Dalglish, a wealthy manufacturer of an old Whig family, but with radical leanings.[57] Moir himself became a town councillor in the 1850s, eventually being made a magistrate. Perhaps his enduring legacy in municipal affairs was to secure by direct action the right of Glaswegians to walk on the grass in Kelvingrove Park.

III: Scottish Reform League

After the collapse of Chartism in 1848, working-class reform movements for nearly twenty years were sporadic and short-lived in Glasgow. Branches were formed in the city in 1852 and 1858 to support the parliamentary reform agitations of respectively, Hume and Bright, but these quickly foundered in the face of widespread apathy, as did a similar move in 1862 sponsored by the newly-formed Trades Council.[58] This discontinuity in the radical struggle for working-class enfranchisement makes the success of the Scottish National Reform League all the more remarkable. This was founded on 17 September 1866, absorbing the Glasgow Reform Union, which in its brief life had shown the first signs of a revival of political interest among the working classes by drawing an audience of 2,000 at its inaugural conference.[59] The response to the setting up of the Reform League was instantaneous and impressive. Exactly one month after its formation, it convened the largest demonstration seen in Glasgow since the era of the first Reform Bill. Some 40,000 supporters marched through the city centre on 16 October 1866, disrupting all business and closing the bridges and thoroughfares for three hours. At Glasgow Green the crowds listened to orations from John Bright, Ernest Jones, Edmund Beales and others, who spoke from six platforms to 'one vast heaving sea'.[60] Within four months, the Scottish National Reform League claimed 6,354 members, most of whom were in Glasgow, organised in some 50 branches.[61]

The Scottish Reform League was universally agreed to be efficiently managed, and in June 1868 the London-based Executive Council of the whole British movement passed a resolution warmly praising the achievements of the Scots.[62] The mainspring of the organisational performance of the Scottish body was the secretary, George Jackson, a journeyman jeweller who, although only in his mid-twenties, possessed outstanding administrative abilities as well as a highly sophisticated aptitude for political manoeuvring. It was these attributes, rather than his somewhat lacklustre powers of oratory, which placed Jackson at the forefront of Glasgow working-class political circles until his early death in 1885.[63] Jackson's art at political machinations was well illustrated by the manner whereby the League was able to earmark one of the Glasgow parliamentary seats for its chosen nominee in the 1868 general election. Because the city was awarded an additional seat to its existing two in the redistribution scheme accompanying the Second Reform Act, it was possible for the League to make a bid for a share in the return of representatives without disturbing the interests of the sitting M.P.s. Serious efforts were made by Jackson to bring forward as candidate someone of national renown closely associated with the franchise reform movement. When no person of that stature could be secured, a local manufacturer, George Anderson, was selected at a Reform League conference held in July 1868 and attended by two hundred delegates.[64]

With considerable skill the League now simultaneously placated the sitting M.P.s while making Anderson the inevitable and sole extra Liberal candidate in the field. Having chosen their man well in advance of the dissolution, and then establishing his credibility as a potential M.P. by holding a spread of election meetings in August and September, the League had effectively staked its claim to a share in the representation of the city. It thereby outflanked other groups such as the temperance movement, who found themselves unable to act once the contest proper began after the dissolution of Parliament in October.[65] The Reform League insisted on a united front being forged by three Liberal candidates (Anderson and the two sitting Members, Robert Dalglish and William Graham). Dalglish and Graham, on the other hand, were eager to work with the League, which, through its organisational channels of trades and workshop delegates, had a ready-made electoral machine which they, with their older style of organisation based on the politics of personal influence, could not hope to emulate. The involvement of the League was the more appreciated because the city's electorate had been expanded by the Second Reform Act from around 18,000 to over 47,000, and the vast preponderance of the new voters were the very working men whom the League claimed to represent.

The upshot was a combination of forces which proved insurmountable both to the Conservative challenge and to any prospective Liberal break-away group, and indeed the 1868 election resulted in a decisive victory for all three men. Anderson retained his seat until he resigned in 1885 to become the Governor of the Australian Mint. His replacement could not be regarded as in any way the nominee of working-class Liberals, who as-cribed this to manipulation by the middle-class caucus. Jackson promptly took steps to ensure the Liberal working men would in future have con-trol over at least one candidate's nomination. He himself was selected as candidate for Central seat, one of the city's seven constituencies created by the new redistribution legislation. Unfortunately, Jackson died before the general election of 1885, and in his stead a middle-class Radical, who had come second in the nomination contest, was picked.

The acceptance of an electoral compact between middle- and working-class Liberals in Glasgow in the period between the Second and Third Reform Acts was made possible because the latter class shared many of the ideological tenets and policy positions of the former. Beyond suffrage reform and the ballot, the Scottish Reform League's programme embraced disestablishment of the Church of Ireland, a policy advocated by Gladstone; educational reform, the concern of a broad swathe of middle-class opinion; and a revision of the laws governing relations between capital and labour. Although the last topic might be the source of a breach, middle-class Liberals were reassured by the squabble over this issue which flared up between the League and the Glasgow committee formed to repeal the Master and Servant Act. The Repeal Committee decided in 1868 to invite the Conservative M.P., Lord Elcho, to a dinner in the city, in order to convey their gratitude for his work on behalf of their cause. For consorting with a political opponent of Liberalism, the Repeal body was bitterly criticised by the League.[66] In addition, the grounds advanced by the League for extending the franchise were not revolutionary, but rather old-fashioned in tone. The prevailing references were to the lost rights once held by Anglo-Saxons, to Magna Charta and to the principle of no taxation without representation.[67] Stress was placed on the progress made by the working classes in the preceeding 20 or 30 years, and also to their self-discipline, as shown in the great peaceful demonstration of 1866. Thus the winning of the vote was seen as a badge of full citizenship and the end of political serfdom, and not as the prelude to any profound economic and social changes.

Instead the central concerns of working-class Liberalism in Glasgow were close to those of both the older Whig and the newer Radical elements of middle-class Liberalism. 'These are some of the red-letter days in our calendar', Jackson informed a working-class audience in 1868, itemising Catholic and Jewish emancipation, the First Reform Act, the repeal of taxes on food and knowledge and the disestablishment of the Irish Church.[68] This was virtually an identical list of the central pillars of Liberalism as those enunciated by the arch-Whig Graham in his speech at the 1868 hustings. On the other side, shared support for disestablishment in England and Wales, and opposition to the Contagious Diseases Acts, drew middle-class evangelical Dissenting radicals into a sense of similar goals to those working-class Liberals.[69] The decision to choose Anderson

as candidate by the Reform League stemmed not from a sense of deference, but was made because he shared the interest of working men in
educational provision and in stopping the arrestment of wages. When the
League selection conference learned that Anderson had written pamphlets
on those two issues, the veteran Chartist, George Ross, rose to observe
that 'in that case there could not be a better candidate for the working
class (Cheers)'.[70]

Since working-class Liberals were firmly positioned within the framework of the existing Liberal party, both by virtue of having Anderson as
M.P. and of possessing common ideology, attempts by disaffected working-
class radicals to disturb the *status quo* were rendered doubly difficult. In
the 1874 election campaign, the working-class Criminal Law Amendment
Act Repeal Committee wished to put up a candidate, but a meeting of the
city's trade delegates rejected this proposal, opting instead to try to maintain the existing position of Anderson running with two non-working-class
candidates as the sole Liberals in the field.[71]

Although the Trades Council asserted its intention in 1876 to field
a candidate of its own choosing, orthodox working-class Liberalism con-
solidated its position at that very point. In place of the defunct Reform
League, Jackson and his allies formed the Glasgow Liberal Working Men's
Electoral Union (GLWEU). The GLWEU did not envisage its role as advancing distinctly working-class issues, or to promote working-class candidates. Its main function was to convert working men to the Liberal
Party, and to stimulate an interest in the great principles of Liberalism.[72]
The preferred heroes of the GLWEU were Bright and Gladstone, not the
newer, more radical figures of Dilke and Chamberlain, and it remained
steadfastly loyal to Gladstone's second administration, whereas discontent was rife among middle-class radicals.[73] After the abject collapse of
a bid by the Trades Council to promote a labour candidate in 1885, the
Council concluded that 'it would not be unfair to infer that a mistake has
been made in thinking that there was any great desire among the working
classes to send one of their own class to Parliament'.[74]

Much of the foregoing suggests that mid-Victorian working-class Liberalism was cravenly subservient to the prevailing values of middle-class
Liberalism, preferring collaboration to confrontation. The fact that almost
all of the leaders of working-class Liberalism in Glasgow were 'aristocrats
of Labour' (out of the 15 members of the GLWEU Executive, 4 were printers and 6 were building craftsmen) seems to reinforce this view. It is sometimes claimed that this elite of the working class, because of the benefits
they reaped from the existing economic and social system, were disinclined
to favour more radical political doctrines, while their commanding position

within the working-class structure enabled them to stifle any potentially more militant tendencies among the less privileged sections of the labour forces.[75] However, there is evidence of a sense of independence from and suspicion of middle-class Liberals in the history of the GLWEU. The reasons for setting up the Workingmen's Electoral Union were the distrust felt by these men at the aims and conduct of the Glasgow middle-class Liberal caucus. When the latter founded the Glasgow Liberal Association in 1878, the GLWEU withdrew from it at the very start, because they saw the new Association as a front for middle-class radicals to dominate Liberal politics in the city. A particularly bitter argument arose in 1881 over a move executed by the Liberal Association to exclude the GLWEU from having any representation on the newly formed Scottish Liberal Association. However, successful lobbying by the GLWEU got his ploy reversed by the national leaders of Scottish Liberalism.[76] In an earlier, equally fractious episode, a veteran working-class Liberal observed to loud applause that 'at no time since the passing of the last Reform Act has the breach in the Liberal party been wider than since the Glasgow Liberal Association came into existence'.[77] Furthermore, it was frequently the politically involved working-class elite who wished to move in a more radical direction, but were held back by the complete allegiance to orthodox Liberalism shown by the rank and file working-class voters. Thus the candidature of George Jackson as an Advanced Liberal in the 1869 municipal elections for the heavily working-class Bridgeton ward resulted in his clear defeat. Jackson lost to a Tory cotton master, not because of deference to a large employer of labour, but rather, it appears, because of dislike at Jackson's aggressively class-based campaign and because of his injection of party labels into local government elections.[78] Again, in 1873, the Trades Council and working-class educational reformers (many of whom were the leaders of the Reform League) made thorough preparations to contest the first School Board elections, advocating a national, non-sectarian schooling system. Yet this alliance fared poorly at the poll, with Jackson coming thirty-first out of thirty-eight candidates, and only one of their slate winning a seat on the fifteen man board.[79] The Glasgow School Board was therefore dominated by sectarian religious interests, an event all the more notable because the education franchise was broader than the parliamentary one, and therefore had a more proletarian electorate.

IV: Socialism and the Labour Party

Between 1914 and 1924 Glasgow gained the reputation of being one of the most fervently socialist centres in Britain. The war-time rent strikes; the militant resistance of the Clyde shop stewards movement to government plans to erode trade union rights and powers during the war; the activities of John MacLean; and the election of the I.L.P. 'Clydeside Rebels' to Parliament in 1922 are all part of this pattern. The extent to which these currents were already in train before the First World War among the city's working class must be assessed. Certainly before the 1890s there was very little apparent interest in socialism. There had indeed been a brief Owenite phase in the 1830s, while the tail-end of Chartism produced a spasm of socialist activity, but there was no longevity in either phase, and very little connection between these flickerings.[80] The socialist revival of the early 1880s in Britain seemed likely to be felt in Glasgow, where a very large working-class population lived and worked in conditions which were a standing indictment (to William Morris, at least) of the capitalist system. Moreover, the semi-socialistic arguments put forward by Henry George in favour of land nationalisation were having at that very time a considerable impact on the Radical wing of the Glasgow Liberal Party.[81]

After a meeting in March 1882 addressed by H.M. Hyndman, Henry George and leading local land reformers, a branch of what became the S.D.F. was set up in Glasgow, but by June 1884 it was admitted to be in-active. A reconstitution of the branch was achieved at the end of that year, after public lectures by Hyndman and Morris.[82] Almost at once, however, Morris broke with Hyndman and about half of the Glasgow membership followed the former into the Socialist League. The League contained the abler Glasgow socialists, notably J. Bruce Glasier and James Mavor, but by 1890 or 1891 it had collapsed, despite intensive propaganda efforts, which, as Glasier confessed, attracted audiences only out of curiosity, not out of conviction.[83] The S.D.F. limped along, held together thanks largely to the efforts of W.J. Nairne, a dour, teetotal day labourer of rigid Marxist doctrines, but its impact was very limited, with its main activity being the holding of weekly meetings on Glasgow Green, the 'Speakers' Corner' of Glasgow.[84]

This failure to establish a thriving socialist presence in the city was galling to Glasgow socialists, especially in the light of the vigorous growth experienced in Edinburgh, whose leaders undertook the revitalisation of the Glasgow S.D.F. in 1884.[85] There was, in truth, no great interest among the existing political groupings in Glasgow towards socialism. The Irish nationalists, as discussed below, pursued their own objectives single-mindedly. The demands of land law reformers—a numerous body, because of the large Highland element in the city—received sufficient encourage-ment from prominent city Radical M.P.s like Dr Charles Cameron and

Gilbert Beith to keep the vast majority comfortably within the Liberal fold.[86] While the more extreme Scottish Land Restoration League kept aloof from the Liberal Party, the S.D.F. soured relations by denouncing the League for its faulty economic analysis, as an extended exchange of views in August 1884 between Hyndman and J.M. Cherrie, the League's Glasgow leader, revealed.[87] Orthodox working-class Liberal opinion remained unimpressed. When the GLWEU received a copy of the S.D.F.'s policy statement, it recorded that 'the general impression of the members was that the programme contained elements of too wide and revolutionary a nature'.[88] The extent of the ground still to be gained was emphasised by the attitude of the old secularist Chartist who told Glasier: 'Na, Na, it hasna' come in my day, and it'll no come in yours, and it'll no come at a' if you're going to creck the Liberal Party as you and some of your friends are trying their best to do'.[89]

The social composition of the Socialist League in Glasgow testifies to the early socialist group's inability to build a working-class following. The League, to be sure, had some working-men members, notably a brass finisher called Pollack, besides some Russian Jewish cigarmakers and German glassblowers.[90] But the bulk of the League consisted of middle and lower-middle class men. These included businessmen like the Stevenson and Muirhead brothers; educationalists like Jolly, a school inspector, and MacLaren, an assistant professor of Greek at the University; clerks like Mavor and Glasier; and artists like Pittendrigh MacGillivray, the sculptor, and Craibe Angus, an art dealer.[91] These young men were largely, it seems, attracted to socialism by an aesthetic rejection of capitalism rather than by any economic analysis. Morris's visits to the League in Glasgow in the later 1880s frequently took the shape of literary or artistic discussion circles, not political seminars.[92]

It was not really until the 1890s that a new socialist strand emerged, after the eclipse of the League, and this time it was more clearly appealing to the working classes of the city.[93] Keir Hardie's candidature in the Mid-Lanark by-election of 1888 inspired the creation of the Scottish Labour Party, which some five years later joined the I.L.P. The I.L.P. quite rapidly grew in size, and it was easily the largest socialist organisation in Glasgow before 1914. Hardie was supported in his election fight by both the Glasgow Trades Council and the leaders of the city's Irish Nationalists. While the Irish subsequently backed down from full commitment to the new party, and the Trades Council could not persuade its constituent unions to join the Scottish Labour Party, this was an undoubted fillip to the cause of independent working-class politics in the city. Progress in this direction from the early 1890s until 1914 can be charted. Branches of the I.L.P. were formed in most districts of the city; a Labour Army was created; a women's section was launched; and Socialist Rambling Clubs flourished. By 1913 the Glasgow I.L.P. had one half of the total Scottish membership. The formation in 1899 of the Scottish analogue of the L.R.C., the Scottish Workers' Parliamentary Representative Committee (SWPRC), produced a vigorous response in Glasgow, with committees set up in the more working-class seats. After the SWPRC was absorbed into the Labour Party in 1908, the spread of Labour Party organisation in Glasgow continued. A major stage in consolidating organisation came shortly before the outbreak of war, when the Glasgow City Labour Party was constituted. This city-wide body was designed to co-ordinate propaganda and electoral work by eliminating overlap and supplementing the activities of weaker areas.[94]

In addition to the growth of the Labour Party, and its main socialist affiliate, the I.L.P., the pre-war decade also witnessed something of a recovery among the more Marxist parties. The B.S.P. (the re-titled S.D.F.) expanded under John MacLean's influence, and in particular it won a small but very able number of recruits such as Tom Bell and David Kirkwood among the heavy engineering trades.[95] The more intransigent Socialist Labour Party, a breakaway from the old S.D.F., had only a handful of adherents in Glasgow. However, the intensity of their schooling in Marxism made them powerful advocates of their cause, and as many of them were shop stewards in shipyards and engineering works, they were well-placed to exploit the wartime crisis.[96]

There was, then, much to indicate that socialism, and especially the I.L.P. variety, was advancing in Glasgow. The continuous propaganda work by the I.L.P. elicited envious admiration from the two main parties. The regular winter Sunday evening lectures in cinemas and theatres were always packed; open-air speakers performed the whole year round; much effort was put into factory gate meetings. The Glasgow I.L.P.'s vigour and confidence was reflected in and reinforced by the publication of *The Forward*. Begun in 1906 by a group of young local I.L.P. members under the editorship of Tom Johnston, it settled in after a shaky start to its intended role as a lively and influential journal of socialist opinion.[97] In addition, the influence of the I.L.P. went beyond opinion-forming, as a steady growth in the party's representation on elected authorities indicated. In 1894 two candidates were voted on to the city School Board. A year later the party won its first two seats on the Town Council and its presence was also felt on the Parish Council. Much good work in ameliorating social conditions was achieved by the socialist representative on the various municipal authorities. William Haddow led a successful campaign to induce the School Board to pioneer medical inspection of pupils and also the provision of school meals. On the City Council, an alliance to promote social issues was forged in the 1890s between the I.L.P. and the Irish Nationalists.

The mounting menace of socialism among the Glasgow working class was acknowledged by the managers of the Scottish Liberal Party in a confidential memorandum submitted in February 1908 to the Master of Elibank, the Government Chief Whip. It noted that 'the Socialist and Labour movements are steadily gaining adherents in Scotland', more especially in the West. The Labour Party was said to be picking up voters from the other two parties, as well as winning those who had never voted before. The 'extraordinary enthusiasm' with which Labour carried on its propaganda work was contrasted with the difficulties faced by the Liberals in this department.[98] Unionists shared these views. Bonar Law was assured in 1907 by a Glasgow Tory that Liberal working-men had become virtually extinct in the Clyde shipyards, due to the evangelising undertaken by the socialists.[99]

It must be noted, however, that evidence from within the socialist camp does not always conform to this image of an inexorable advance. Certainly, the experience of the I.L.P. (by far the most vibrant of the socialist bodies) from its inception in the early 1890s was not one of ceaseless expansion, but rather a pattern of advances followed by retreats. Thus by the end of the 1890s, the initial forward impetus seemed to be held in check. Possilpark branch intimated its demise in 1897 as a result of a continuous decline in membership and the apathy prevailing among the remaining comrades. Also in that year, the Glasgow Women's branch decided that it could not afford to reaffiliate to the I.L.P., as its membership had fallen to a mere twenty-nine. In the following year the head of the Glasgow Central branch admitted that despondency and apathy had settled over the I.L.P. in the city. Few of those who joined remained in the party long enough to be effective workers for the cause, and his prognosis for the future of the party was deeply pessimistic, since the supply of new members seemed to have dried up.[100] Some five or six years later, Bruce Glasier, who had joined the I.L.P., lamented the depressingly low level of support the party was getting in Glasgow.[101]

Although some stimulus was given by the feeling of disappointment at the early inertia of the Liberal government, there was still much to be done. In 1908-09, Bridgeton I.L.P. branch contained only a score of members, and at the start of 1910 Keir Hardie's brother George, surveying the previous year's efforts by the I.L.P. in Glasgow, bemoaned the lack of enthusiasm at branch level and the poor quality of organisation. He blamed this state of affairs on five years of internal wrangling and issued a sombre warning: 'The Party must draw itself together. It is ineffective at present'.[102] Two years later a similar review of the past year's work (but not by Hardie) concluded that the former vigour of the I.L.P. was much depleted.[103] In the early 1920s, one of those most intimately involved in the pre-war party confirmed this view: 'The record of the Glasgow I.L.P. Executive from 1906 to 1912 is a struggle against adversity. The party did not seem to make much headway'.[104] As an instance of this, the city party's income in 1911 of £228 was almost identical to that of 1903. In the two years before the war a recovery took place under the guidance of J.A. Allan, 'the socialist millionaire', who acted as chairman of the Glasgow I.L.P. from 1910 to 1913. By 1913 income was up to £696.[105] Membership at this peak phase reached 1,200. Although, as noted, this was one-half of the Scottish total, it was far smaller than the 7,000 members then claimed by Glasgow Unionists. The much-admired propaganda exercises undertaken by the I.L.P. and other socialist bodies had, according to I.L.P. sources, only mixed results. In 1898 the Central Branch drew in only two new members, despite considerable efforts to spread the message.[106] A decade later the Scottish I.L.P. organiser pointed out that despite attracting vast crowds to their indoor Sunday meetings, actual membership of the I.L.P. remained stubbornly well below the numbers attending any one of these lectures.[107]

The advent of the Labour Party did little before 1914 to augment the achievements of the I.L.P. Until 1908 the SWPRC controlled the development of the Labour Party in Scotland, and its efforts were characterised by poor organisation and lack of drive. After receiving a visit in 1903 from the SWPRC Secretary, George Carson, to discuss the prospects of contesting St Rollox constituency, the local branch complained that he had been obstructive and unhelpful in his attitude.[108] The merger of the SWPRC with the Labour Party did not have immediate beneficial consequences. In 1910 only one of the Glasgow constituencies had an L.R.C. affiliated to the national party.[109] Conflict between the party in Scotland and the National Executive over an appropriate organisational structure prevented substantial progress being made north of the border. Thus, as noted, it was only in 1913 that a Glasgow City Labour Party was established, and that body had not accomplished very much before the outbreak of war. The Secretary of the Scottish Labour Party confessed late in 1914 that the Glasgow City Party had not yet settled down, adding that its membership basis was hopelessly complicated.[110]

The electoral performance of the socialist and labour bodies was likewise somewhat uneven in the pre-1914 period. Some gains were indeed notched up at the local elections, but these proved disappointingly hard to translate into parliamentary seats. In the 1890s, Labour candidates stood in several seats. In the 1892 general election only 225 votes were received at St Rollox, while Cunninghame Graham, with 906 (11.9 per cent of the poll), did rather better at Camlachie. It is symptomatic of the faltering advances made by Labour before the First World War that the next general election, in 1895, saw the highest number of such candidates fielded in Glasgow before 1914. Five ran,[111] whereas none stood in 1900, three in 1906 and in January 1910, and two in December 1910. In the run-up to the 1895 election the Scottish Liberals became alarmed at the impact Labour might have in Glasgow, and so in 1894 entered into discussions with the I.L.P. to try to reach some arrangement which would lead to united action. No agreement could be reached, primarily because the I.L.P. was fully committed to opposing the Liberals, but in a sign of their concern at the threat posed by Labour, the Liberals called for Parliament to be petitioned in favour of the Second Ballot.[112] In the event, the outcome of the 1895 general election was satisfactory to the Glasgow Liberals, for only one Labour candidate even reached 10 per cent of the poll.

This was a major reverse for Labour, who had entertained high hopes towards several seats. Thus, Bridgeton had been identified as an attractive proposition, since social conditions in the constituency were very bad, even by Glasgow standards.[113] Getting only 609 votes there was a grave disappointment. In this seat, as in Blackfriars, the Labour vote in 1895 was well below that obtained by land reformers in 1885. In Bridgeton the figures for 1885 and 1895 were, respectively 948 (12.1%) and 609 (9.4%), while in Blackfriars they were 1,156 (14.4%) and 448 (7.1%). So poor were the Glasgow results in 1895 for Labour that three of these seats were not again contested before 1914. The failure to run any candidates at all in the 1900 election may be attributed to a reaction to the 1895 results, and also to the deterioration in the I.L.P.'s strength, as already discussed.

In the 1906 general election, Labour certainly made an identifiable advance in Glasgow, where George Barnes won Blackfriars for the party against both Unionist and Liberal opposition. Barnes' victory seems to have in good measure come because the Irish Nationalists, who had voted Unionist in 1900 as a protest against the Liberal candidate who was felt to be lukewarm on Home Rule, switched to Barnes, who was an enthusiastic Home Ruler.[114] Elsewhere, progress remained patchy. No suitable candidate could be found for St Rollox, while Tradeston and Bridgeton, seats with a solid working-class vote, were left unfought. Labour's best prospects came in Camlachie and Govan, where the party polled 2,568

(30.0%) and 4,212 (29.0%) respectively. Yet the two elections in 1910 indicated the limitations under which the party operated. In January 1910, Labour's vote in Camlachie held to its 1906 benchmark, getting 2,443 (28.9%). But in the December contest, almost 40 per cent of that vote was transferred to the Liberals, in an effort to prevent the Unionist carrying the seat, leaving Labour with 1,539 (18.12%). In Govan, where about one-sixth of Labour's 1906 vote was lost in January 1910, no candidate was put forward in the later 1910 election.

Labour showed little evidence of gaining ground in the 1910-14 phase. By-elections were held in these years at Govan, St Rollox and Tradeston, but Labour, despite the difficulties of the Liberal government, did not fight any. Tradeston, where Labour had cherished very warm hopes in the early 1900s, was pronounced by the party's National Agent not to be worth fighting as there was no organisation and little propaganda work had been done recently in the constituency. St Rollox was similarly not contested because of defective local organisation. The same seems to have applied to Govan, where the absence of a Labour challenge is the more striking as that was the only extra seat to be won by Labour in Glasgow in the 1918 election. Although there was brave talk in 1914 of fighting three or four Glasgow seats in addition to Blackfriars at the next election, this may have been less confident expansion than a bid to persuade the Liberals to arrive at some form of electoral pact. MacCallum Scott was asked by some leading city socialists in that year to consider striking a bargain whereby he would not be opposed by Labour in Bridgeton if Camlachie was abandoned by the Liberals, leaving Labour to fight the Unionists.[115] Such an offer, initiated by Labour, hardly betokens optimism on that party's side.

One reason for the relative failure of Labour before 1914 seems to have been that socialist ideas did not seem to have penetrated very far into the bulk of the Glasgow working class; though they were undoubtedly making some inroads. John Paton, who was involved in both the Bridgeton and Springburn I.L.P. branches in the pre-war decade, found that most of his fellow members were either clerical workers or highly-skilled craftsmen, with very little interest being shown by the rest of the working classes.[116] Indeed, many Labour candidates seemed anxious to minimise the socialist content of their message. George Barnes was always unhappy at the extreme doctrines and violent language adopted by the city members of the I.L.P. In the January 1910 election he rejected an offer from Bruce Glasier, one of the I.L.P.'s finest speakers, to come and speak on Barnes' behalf in Blackfriars.[117] Barnes, the Secretary of the Engineers' Union, felt that the main ingredient in his appeal to the voters was the presence in the constituency of many members of his union.[118]

This approach seems also to have been taken by J. O'Connor Kessack, who fought Camlachie, Labour's brightest hope, twice in 1910. In 1907 Kessack had criticised the Labour Party for not being sufficiently socialist, contending that the I.L.P. and the S.D.F. were very close in both their analysis of and solutions to 'the capitalist wilderness'.[119] In 1910 Kessack responded at the I.L.P Annual Conference to a speech attacking the party's tendency to subordinate socialism to other matters. 'At one time', Kessack explained,

> he used to deliver speeches like unto those . . . but it was not until he dropped them that he was taken any notice of. Some people seemed to complain that if a Labour Member candidate did not get on a platform and talk about the 'class war', 'wage slavery' and the 'bourgeoisie', he was guilty of subordinating the interests of socialism. In his campaign at Camlachie, he never spoke without driving home his whole cause, and he never had occasion to use any of these shibboleths.[120]

Again, at Govan where the by-election arose in 1911, the I.L.P. concluded that a candidate nominated by them would not be likely to win, but better fortune would certainly attend a trade union nominee standing for Labour.[121]

It may be asked how far these difficulties encountered by Labour were caused, as some have argued in studies of other areas, by a revival of the Liberal Party's strength among the working-class voters, especially by the party's championing of social welfare reforms.[122] There is no detailed evidence on the extent of working-class participation in Liberal Party affairs in the city in the pre-war decade. But there are indications, notably in the 1908-14 era, that Glasgow Liberalism was assuming a more progressive stance, as social reform legislation was warmly approved of by the Glasgow Liberal Council. The controversial 1909 Budget was hailed as a 'fair and equitable' solution to the dilemma of financing social reform and simultaneously maintaining the defence of the Empire. By 1912 the Council was even keener on social reform. Legislation to impose minimum wages in the coal industry was applauded, while the National Insurance Acts, the bugaboo of the middle class, were hailed as a major step forward. Speakers at the Council repeatedly urged the government to press on with further measures of social reform, as the fringe of these problems had only been touched.[123]

The type of candidate being brought forward by the Liberals for Glasgow seats also underwent a significant change at this time. The best instance of this new Liberal emerging after 1906 was Alexander MacCallum Scott, who sat for Bridgeton from December 1910. Scott began his parliamentary career by resolving to immerse himself in issues of specific relevance to the position of the Scottish working class. After a few months of further reflection and research, he determined to advocate a sweeping programme of constructive social reform founded on the general principle of the Minimum Standard, which would be applied to wages, health, housing and the poor laws.[124] In this respect Scott was abreast of the most advanced thinking on social reform, and other Glasgow M.P.s, whom he found himself close to on such matters included D.T. Holmes, who won Govan in 1911, and J.D. White, M.P. for Tradeston. At one point it was considered introducing the leading New Liberal thinker, Joe Chiozza Money, as Liberal candidate for Camlachie in 1910. The prospect of Money standing threw the I.L.P. into a panic, for they believed this would render the seat unwinnable.[125]

Scott's efforts to maintain and develop his constituency organisation also reveals the overall grassroots strength of the Liberal Party in a very pronounced working-class seat. In December 1910 he found a virtually moribund association, and he had difficulty finding local party workers who were willing to deliver leaflets or to canvas. By the spring of 1913 Scott felt pleased that he had now managed to have his local Liberal Association actively working the constituency.[126] Although he remained uneasily aware that Labour ran their affairs with greater energy, it was reassuring for him to feel that his party had certainly not abandoned organisational effort in Bridgeton.[127] Open air meetings were held by the Young Liberals; a Woman's Section was begun; and the fight was taken to the socialist enemy in 1914 with a decision to emulate the Labour Party by holding factory-gate meetings.[128]

It would seem that while the Labour Party and the ideals of socialism were making some advances before 1914, the collapse of the working-class support for the Liberal Party had not yet occurred. Several recent works have suggested that the evidence from other parts of Britain indicates that the Liberal Party had rediscovered its sense of purpose and was making a very effective appeal to working-class voters by embracing social reform. The electoral evidence from Glasgow also tends to confirm another related argument that in the 1910 elections the advance of Labour had been contained, and in the by-elections between 1910 and 1914 give little evidence of a renewed Labour advance.[129] As the post-war organiser of the I.L.P. in Scotland reflected, there were few portents before 1914 that Labour, even in Glasgow, was poised on the brink of a major electoral expansion.[130]

V: Working-Class Conservative Movements

The working-man Tory was regarded in Glasgow as a mythical creature by most Liberals, and even those sympathetic to Conservatism were at times sceptical. In 1872 a humorous pro-Tory weekly described the contribution of the city's Working Men's Conservative Association to a procession celebrating Disraeli's visit to Glasgow as a procession of 'the Members of the Association (eleven in number) marching in Indian file'.[131] Yet there is tangible evidence of a persisting tradition of organised working-class conservatism for much of the period between the First Reform Act and the First World War.

In 1837 the Glasgow Conservative Operatives' Association was formed after working men sent an invitation to Sir Robert Peel to attend a public dinner organised by them on the occasion of his installation as Rector of Glasgow University. Such was the success of the dinner and the interest in conservatism it aroused that a permanent organisation was set up which lasted until 1843, when conservatism in Glasgow collapsed generally. In 1869 the Glasgow Workingmen's Conservative Association was established. It described its own beginnings thus: 'This Association owes its origins to an advertisement inserted in the Newspapers of 1868 by Mr Cadman, a working man, convening his fellow workmen for the purposes of forming among them a Conservative Association'.[132] On the eve of the World War there was a further burst of activity. A Democratic Unionist Association was formed in the city after the January 1910 elections, partly to tap the politically underutilised younger Tories, but also because 'workingmen were in many cases somewhat disheartened through the lack of sufficient encouragement'.[133] A Scottish Labour Federation was started in Glasgow in 1913 by Conservatives to counter socialist propaganda among the working classes and to advocate a non-socialist but pro-labour social policy.[134]

Impressive though this record might appear, two arguments could be adduced to argue that these manifestations of working-class Toryism exaggerate its true extent. Firstly, the degree of support given to these bodies needs to be established, as the creation of paper bodies was a well-practised device to enhance political credibility. Secondly, the extent to which support for these organisations was in reality drawn from the working classes of the city needs to be examined. In particular the inclusion of terms like 'working men' could easily be a move designed to appeal to the ideals of Tory Democracy, without really conveying the social composition of these associations. The Operatives' Association attracted 2,000 signatories to their requisition sent to Peel, and 270 members attended the first Annual General Meeting. Membership did fall off, so that only twenty-four were present at the Annual General Meeting in 1843, the year in which the

Association was wound up. But this decline was due to external factors, discussed below, and did not indicate internal inadequacies. The Association was actively engaged in canvassing and registration work on behalf of the party, and it held frequent meetings and dinners at which conservative principles were expounded. In 1840 a Reading Room was opened, but administrative and financial problems prevented it from flourishing as intended. A committee, usually numbering up to thirty, ran the Association. A system of district superintendents was introduced in 1840, to build up links in the various localities of the city. This was presumably a sign that the Association was too large for the central committee to keep in contact with all the adherents. While it can therefore be deduced that the Association was fairly active and sizeable, the working-class credentials of the members are less easily ascertained. The committee in 1837 comprised 2 wrights, 4 cloth lappers, 7 printers, 3 warehousemen and 1 shopman, fringemaker and sawyer apiece. There were four individuals whose occupation was uncertain. Again, both in 1839 and 1840 annual meetings were stated—by a favourable source—to have been attended almost exclusively by working men.[135]

The assertion that the Working Men's Conservative Association was formed in 1869 at the instance of a working man has already been referred to. However, within a very few years, the 'Working Men' part of the title was dropped, and it was now called the 'Glasgow Conservative Association'. This does not in itself prove that its social basis was not in practice working-class: the decision to amend the title came in response to a request from Disraeli that all such bodies should do so. Nevertheless, the background to the foundation of the Association was that during the general election of 1868 several middle-class Tories floated the idea of launching a Conservative Operatives' Association similar to one recently established in Preston.[136] As some 3,000 working men were claimed to have voted in the Glasgow contest for a Tory candidate who was regarded as fairly ineffective, there did seem to be a potential working-class support worth recruiting. The William Cadman credited with instigating the formation of the Association was almost certainly a leather merchant, living in the 1870s in Park Place, perhaps the most select residential area of the city. Although one or two of those who spoke at the inaugural meetings were indeed working men (notably William Russell, a shoemaker and veteran of the 1830s Operatives' Association), the proceedings were dominated by solid bourgeois Tories like J.A. Campbell and A.K. Murray.[137] The Conservatives in the 1874 general election did return their first Glasgow M.P. since the First Reform Act, but this reflected more on the disunity of the Liberals than on an upsurge of support by the new working-class electors for the Conservatives. Nonetheless, there was a solid working-class presence in the Glasgow Conservative Party, as an analysis indicates that between 20 per cent and 45 per cent of the different candidates' election committees in the 1874 and 1880 elections were working-class.[138]

Yet in the aftermath of the 1880 general election, which represented a setback for the Conservatives in Glasgow, the response was to try to expand the working-class component. In November 1880 the Association's president observed: 'One thing he had noticed during the past few years was that the Conservative Association—and he regretted it bitterly—from previous circumstance has not been sufficiently *en rapport* with the great masses of working men'.[139] A rekindling of the working-class Conservative spirit was already in progress at that point. It had begun in the eastern part of the city, and its local leader emphasised that it was predominantly working men who were behind the resurgence. An East End District Association was formed to build up political influence in the area, and the idea quickly spread to other parts of the city. Besides the usual duties of canvassing and registration work, District Associations engaged in a wide range of activities. A regular supply of speakers on political topics was laid on; annual soirées were held; an annual summer trip attracted up to 300 members and their families; reading rooms were opened; and leisure facilities such as draughts were provided to boost attendance at these rooms.[140] That there was indeed a large working-class element behind this grass-roots Conservative organisation is suggested by the complaint made in 1889 by the east-end Camlachie constituency association that its membership was almost entirely composed of working men. It bewailed the reluctance of the middle classes to come forward and participate in the Association's work.[141]

The Democratic Unionist Association of 1910 was largely based on the heavily working-class areas of Bridgeton and Partick, and it claimed to have 500 members within a year of its inception. The *Glasgow Herald* felt that the Association constituted an important bid to woo back those working-class Tories uneasy in the Unionist Party's commitment to tariff reform and its resistance to social reform.[142] The anti-socialist trade union movement of the same era claimed to have 3,000 members late in 1913 and predicted a rise to 5,000 in a fairly short time.[143]

The grounds which attracted a goodly proportion of working men to conservatism in nineteenth century Britain are sometimes stated to have been the ideas of Tory Democracy. In Glasgow this formed only a very small portion of the party's appeal to that class. In the 1830s, when in England Tory Radicals led the campaign for stiffer Factory Acts, the issue raised no great interest among the Glasgow Conservatives' Association, and in 1839 it went so far as to stress the 'hopeless futility' of looking to political means to improve social conditions.[144] Moreover, the leading factory reformer in the vicinity was Sir John Maxwell of Pollock, a Liberal M.P.[145] In the later nineteenth century no stronger concern for social reform is detectable among either working- or middle-class Conservatives. Of the former James MacManus' speech to Salisbury on his visit to Glasgow in 1884 is typical. MacManus explained that Disraeli's influence on the working class (of which MacManus was a member) derived from his foreign policy at Berlin and from his defence of ecclesiastical establishments. MacManus did not allude to the social reform legislation of Disraeli's 1874-80 administration as a factor.[146] For the position of the local Tory leadership the election addresses of the five candidates who stood in the general elections of 1868, 1874 and 1880 are instructive. Three did not refer to social reform; one made a passing comment. Only the sole successful candidate, Alexander Whitelaw, gave an explicit and extended acknowledgement of the issue, promising to work for 'the solution of Social and Sanitary questions involving the Improvement of the Habits, Homes and Happiness of the People of this Country'.[147] Once in the Commons, however, Whitelaw's performance was less impressive. He spoke on five occasions during his period as an M.P. Only in one speech, when seconding the motion on the Queen's Speech in 1875, did he mention social reform, and even then it came low in priority in the sequence of issues he touched on.[148]

On labour matters Glasgow middle-class Toryism was deeply unsympathetic to any favourable treatment of unions. Leading Tories included several members of the great Baird dynasty of ironmasters, whose industrial record was notoriously poor.[149] As discussed above, the Tory M.P. for East Lothian, Lord Elcho, was given a dinner by Glasgow Trade Unionists, and the main Glasgow working-class newspaper used the occasion to contrast Elcho's support for trade union rights with the indifference shown by the local business community.[150] Lord Randolph Churchill's Tory Democracy was not widely supported in Glasgow in the mid-1880s, as he himself complained. An east-end Conservative activist warned the party against bringing forward candidates from the Churchill wing to fight Glasgow seats, insisting that what was wanted was a thorough-going Conservative.[151] By 1910, however, a desire to stress the party's sympathy for social reform and the rights of the working man had been a key theme of both the Democratic Unionist Association and the Scottish Labour Federation. This reorientation may well have followed from working-class hostility to tariff reform, the campaign for which in Glasgow angled almost exclusively towards industrial and commercial men.

Protection was at no time electorally appealing to the working classes of a city whose basic industries (first cotton, then shipbuilding and heavy engineering) stood to benefit from tariffs. Most of the city's Tories in the 1830s were robust free traders, and the Conservative Operatives' Association studiously avoided any declaration of support for protection. The fair trade movement of the 1880s had little impact on working men, as the Glasgow Conservative paper admitted that attendance at one such meeting was 'not numerous'. More headway, however, was recorded among businessmen.[152] Among working men, as correspondents acknowledged to Bonar Law in 1911 and 1912, tariff reform was generally held to have been rejected.[153]

In many areas of Britain imperialist fervour and jingo sentiment did play a part in mobilising working-class Conservatives. However, at the time of the great jingo outburst of 1877-78, Glasgow Tories were notably quiet, and only 3,000 signed a petition in 1878 which supported Disraeli's handling of the Eastern question.[154] Even in the 1900 general election, when the Unionists won the seven Glasgow seats, there were many who felt that this sweeping victory was not wholly due to imperialist sentiment among the working class. The *Times'* correspondent found Glaswegians had been 'notoriously less excited than most other large communities' by the Boer War, an interpretation which Campbell-Bannerman also adhered to.[155]

The issue which above all was stressed as the central factor binding working-class voters to the Conservative cause for almost all of the post-1832 period was religion, and in particular support for the established protestant churches of Britain. The Operatives' Association proclaimed in its constitution that, 'a prominent object of the Association shall be, to defend the interests of the Ecclesiastical and Educational Establishments of Scotland as an integral part of the Constitution'; and the address to Peel concluded on the same note: 'Sir, we love the Church of Scotland, for all it has suffered and all it has done, to provide the poor with religious instruction and to afford their children a Bible Education in its Parish Schools'.[156] The addresses delivered to the Association were often on politico-religious topics, and the disintegration of the Association was caused by the rift in the Church of Scotland between the Moderates and the evangelical Non-Intrusionists. The Operatives' Association voted to support the latter, and when the Disruption of 1843 led to the formation of the Free Church, the Association was in the process of being wound up, as many Non-Intrusionists felt betrayed by Peel's refusal to act to keep the Church of Scotland united.[157]

The Working Men's Conservative Association of the 1860s owed much of its early impetus to similar religious factors. Support of the endowed territorial Church was a principal tenet of the Association, enshrined in its objects as second only to upholding the prerogative of the Crown. In 1872 five of the seven lectures given to members were on the theme of the maintenance of protestantism among the national institutions.[158] At this time the religious impulse behind working-class conservatism was heightened not just by the mounting Radical campaign for disestablishment, but also by the emergence of the issue of religious instruction in state schools. The 1872 Education Act set up a national system of popularly elected school boards with full management powers. This meant that the Established Church would lose the control over the staffing and curriculum it had enjoyed in the parochial schools. Moreover, it seemed likely that in Glasgow, where the Church of Scotland was relatively weak, the school boards could well be controlled by non-Established Church influences. In the first elections for the School Board, however, the Use and Wont Party (representing those who wished to retain the existing form of religious instruction in the new schools) won six of the fifteen places, while the Dissenting churches only won three seats. Nearly all the lay leaders of the Use and Wont Party were Conservatives, two of them, Whitelaw and J.A. Campbell, later sitting as Tory M.P.s, and the Conservative Association threw itself wholeheartedly into the education controversy on the Use and Wont side.[159] The theme of maintaining religious instruction in schools formed the foremost theme of Whitelaw's successful parliamentary election campaign in 1874, which reflected the realisation that the working class responded to this topic. Much of the credit for marshalling and disciplining this Tory working-class school board vote was claimed by a secret society, 'the Knoxites', who operated in the east end.[160] It is quite probable that this political machine was available to Conservatives at parliamentary contests, for the Knoxites were composed of Orangemen and sympathisers, and the Tories had exceptionally close ties with Orangeism, through which in the post-Second Reform Act they recruited much of their working-class support.

There had been Orange Lodges in Glasgow in the 1830s, but these had all been proscribed in 1836, so that their suppression predated the flowering of working-class Toryism in the decade.[161] The Orange movement revived in Glasgow in the 1860s, and it grew remarkably in the following decades, so that the city had a disproportionately large share of the non-Irish Orange membership. A report in 1878 remarked that: 'At the present moment the numerical strength of the brotherhood in this country (i.e. Britain, excluding Ireland) is 90,000. There are altogether 600 lodges in England and Scotland in full operation. . . . In Glasgow alone there are a hundred lodges and a membership of from 14 up to 15,000'. A listing in 1913-14 shows Glasgow still dominated the Scottish scene, with 107 lodges out of a total of 400.[162] Concomitant with this growth went a greater involvement in politics: for instance, one Glasgow lodge called itself the 'Beaconsfield Purple Guards'. The leader of the Scottish Orangemen told a Glasgow demonstration shortly after the 1874 election: 'They had returned to a Conservative member for Glasgow. . . . Every sound Orangeman was a Conservative; if there were any Radicals in their ranks they were as rare as black swans.'[163] The politicisation of the Order was a reaction to what was perceived to be a mounting threat to the protestant religious settlement of 1689. This threat began in the 1860s, and the agitation to disestablish the church if Ireland provoked counter-demonstrations in the city by local Orangemen. The debate over religious instruction in schools stirred the order, and it co-operated wholeheartedly with the Conservatives in publicising the Use and Wont cause.[164] The Orange candidate, Harry Alfred Long, topped the first School Board poll, with 4,000 more individuals voting for him than anyone else, and Long remained at the top of the poll in each of the next four triennial elections.

The most obvious case of the Orange Order's part in Glasgow politics came in the 1880 general election. Then the Order was able to bring forward its preferred choice, Sir James Bain, in the face of the patent reluctance of middle-class Tories to accept him. Bain, a wealthy ironmaster, was first publicly mooted as a possible Tory candidate at the 17th Annual Orange soirée in 1878, and on polling day a press notice appeared under signature of the chief officials of the Glasgow district lodges, urging all their members to vote for the other Conservative candidate, in addition to casting their vote for Bain.[165] The first choice Conservative candidate for Glasgow withdrew to fight elsewhere after Bain's emergence, and it was not until a fortnight before voting that a second candidate, William Pearce, could be found. Bain lacked the support of official Glasgow conservatism; 14 of the 18 vice-presidents of the Conservative Association backed Pearce, 2 Bain and 1 both. Of those who became vice-presidents in the next twenty years, 10 were for Pearce, 2 for Bain and 3 for both. More detailed study of the social bases of the committees of the two candidates suggests that Bain, the Orange choice, enjoyed greater working-class support. Forty-five per cent of Bain's committee belonged to the working class, only twenty-two per cent of Pearce's.[166] The recrudescence of working-class participation in Glasgow conservatism after the 1880 election was heavily associated with an increased Orange presence. Thus, in October 1881 the Glasgow-based Orange Institute of Scotland convened a meeting 'to endeavour to consolidate the parties belonging to the Conservative interest and to bring them together in a firm and compact body in spite of all opposition'.[167] The Orange Order was given a place on the executive of the Conservative Association, thus making explicit the ties between the two bodies. This process of integration seemed complete on the occasion of Salisbury's visit to the city in 1884, when he was presented with an address from the Grand Orange Lodge of Scotland immediately after one from the Glasgow Conservative Association, and ahead of any other Conservative society.[168]

The growth of Orangeism in the mid-Victorian period was not simply a reaction to the Irish immigration which was such a feature of Glasgow's population expansion in the nineteenth century. The greatest volume of Irish influx occurred in the decade of the Irish Famine, some twenty years prior to the rise of the Orange movement. One factor was the sizeable Ulster protestant element to be found in Glasgow. In the years 1876-81, 83.2 per cent of the Irish immigrants to Scotland came from Ulster, with the four most protestant Ulster counties providing 58.7 per cent of the total inflow.[169] Here would be a clear source of Orange ideas and attitudes in Glasgow. Some of the Orange feeling may well also have derived from the return of Clydeside shipyard workers from Belfast, whither they had been imported in the late 1850s by William Harland in order to train native Ulster labour in the skills of iron ship construction. Belfast shipyard workers were perhaps the most ardently Orange sector of the city, and in Glasgow, the Partick shipyards were also staunchly Orange.[170]

There was in addition an upswelling of popular protestantism in Glasgow in the 1860s and 1870s, as the promulgation of the Syllabus of Errors and the Doctrine of Infallibility stirred fears for the civil and religious liberty of the British protestants. These worries were heightened by the restoration in 1878 of the Catholic hierarchy in Scotland.[171] To counter these trends, several organisations were formed, of which Harry Alfred Long's Glasgow Working Men's Evangelical Association was specifically designed to recruit the working class of the east end of the city. It was members of this body, which was formed in 1870, who suggested creating the Knoxites, whose semi-clandestine electoral operations have been noted.[172] Long was the foremost popular orator of this working-class Orange Tory tradition in the last quarter of the century. He was one of the most regular speakers at Orange meetings. In the 1874 election he was summoned by acclamation to address an east-end audience on behalf of the Conservative candidates, and his endorsement of Bain in 1880 was crucial to the latter's credibility with working-class Tories.[173] Shortly after the 1880 election, Long was made a vice-president of the city Conservative Association, and thereafter he was a frequent speaker at meetings of the party, especially in working-class districts.

The role of Orangeism as a factor in mobilising working-class votes for the Tories remained significant down to the start of the First World War. As late as 1906, the Unionist M.P. for Partick drew attention to the importance for his party's prospects there of the large working-class Orange presence. John Paton wryly recalled taking part in a march in 1908 or 1909 organised by the Bridgeton I.L.P. which was confronted by some Partick Orangemen. Whereas the socialists were mainly white collar workers, the Orangemen were nearly all shipyard workers.[174]

VI: The Irish

Throughout the nineteenth century the Irish Catholic portion of the population of Glasgow constituted a separate community within the city's social system, segregated by a whole bundle of distinguishing characteristics— race, accent, religion, occupations, residence and politics.[175] At the same time their attempts to gain an influence in public affairs in Glasgow commensurate with their size as the second biggest Irish contingent in Britain outside London were handicapped by the very factors which fashioned their social isolation and solidarity. The famine of the 1840s markedly accelerated the already steady volume of immigration into Glasgow from Ireland, and the later part of the century there were perhaps 80-100,000 Irish Catholics in Glasgow, forming roughly one quarter to one fifth of the total population.[176]

Despite this size, the political impact of the Irish was very slight, for several reasons. Firstly, the Catholic clergy were generally hostile to political activity by their congregations. Thus they opposed efforts by the Irish Home Rulers to turn the centenary celebration of Daniel O'Connell's birth from a tribute to his work on behalf of Catholic emancipation into a commemoration of his championing of the cause of Irish Nationalism.[177] The vigorous clerical criticism in the pre-war decade of John Wheatley for trying to recruit his fellow Irish Catholics to socialism was only one of the more outstanding examples of this attitude.[178] Another obvious impediment to their full weight being felt in politics was the position occupied by Irish Catholics in the social structure of Glasgow. It seems likely that, as in Greenock, they tended to be found predominantly in unskilled jobs, and experienced a low incidence of upward occupational mobility.[179]

Their concentration in certain residential quarters, notably Bridgegate, Cowcaddens, Gorbals and Maryhill, served to reinforce their isolation. This weakness was emphasised by their inability to get a representative elected to the city council. Although several determined bids were made—particularly in the early 1870s—no success came until John Ferguson, the Irish Nationalist leader in the city, won a ward in 1893. The first Catholic magistrate in Glasgow since the Reformation was Patrick O'Hare, who was made a baillie in 1903. By 1883 the Jewish community, numbering 300, had produced a councillor. This was a decade before the Irish Catholics, 100,000 strong, achieved the same breakthrough.

The 1870s did, however, mark a watershed in the political power of Irish Nationalism in Glasgow. Hitherto, with only a few hundred voters and no permanent organisation, their effusions of political feeling had never been long-lasting. The Second Reform Act, which increased greatly (the precise number is discussed below) the size of the Irish electorate, gave a stimulus to political action. Another boost was the success of Catholics getting 3 candidates placed on the 15-man School Board in the first election, held in 1873. Inspired by Ferguson, these signs of political cohesion were linked to the renascence of Irish Nationalist movement under Butt and Parnell. The Glasgow branch of Butt's Home Government Association was launched in 1871, when Butt himself delivered an address on Home Rule. In the ensuing decades the Nationalist movement in Glasgow proved very active and important. A regular stream of nationally-known figures came to speak in the city, and there was a wide range of local meetings and social events.[180]

Thus the coherence and political awareness of the Irish was promoted. But measuring the extent of the Irish vote was a further vital stage in deciding how to act in Glasgow politics. Enthused with their triumph in the 1873 School Board elections, the Irish Catholics put up a candidate in the 1874 parliamentary election. While around 9,500 voted for the Catholics in the 1873 contest, half that figure—4,444—voted in the general election in the next year. The reasons for this discrepancy lay in the different qualifications required, with payment of the rates essential for the parliamentary franchise, but not so for the school board one. Moreover, as a very mobile sector of the city's population, moving frequently in pursuit of employment, the Irish often failed to meet the twelve month residential qualifications required before getting on the parliamentary roll.[181] Despite strenuous efforts to build up the Irish vote, economic and social factors dictated against any large increase. In the 1900s well-informed authorities put the total Irish vote in Glasgow at little more than 10 or 12,000, out of a total electorate of 80,000.[182]

The Irish were thus in a dilemma as to how to exercise political influence in Glasgow. With the heavy Liberal preponderance before 1886, they could not perform a balanced voting block between the two main parties. Running a candidate in 1874 to represent the Irish and Catholic demands had no decisive impact on the result, even though the Liberals did not lose one seat. In the 1880 election the Liberal candidates simply ignored the calls from the Irish Nationalists for pledges of support for their cause, and the results were still a convincing victory for the Liberal Party. Again in 1885, in conformity with national instructions, the Irish Nationalist vote went solidly to the Tories (including prominent Orange sympathisers), yet the Liberals carried all the seven Glasgow city seats. The consequence of these interventions was to reinforce the isolation of the Irish, for rank and file Liberals were infuriated at these tactics. There was not a great measure of sympathy for the Irish cause among working-class Liberals. In 1882 a motion proposed at the Liberal Workmen's Electoral Union condemning the policy of coercion in Ireland could find no seconder.[183]

Ironically, the Liberal schism of 1886 only served to sharpen the difficulties of the Irish. On the one hand, their voting and organisational power was now badly needed by the depleted Gladstonians. At Blackfriars in the 1886 election, 'the members of the William O'Brien branch of the Irish National League worked like tigers, and we have been informed that nearly three hundred Irishmen sacrificed their days' earnings and volunteered their services to Mr Provand's committee'.[184] Nevertheless, by being tied too closely to one party, the Glasgow Irish Nationalists ran the risk of losing their scope for independent action. There was always the worry that Irish Home Rule might be abandoned by the Liberals as an electoral liability. Many of the leading Scottish Liberals—most of all Lord Rosebery—were at best lukewarm advocates of the issue, and on Gladstone's retirement, which seemed imminent, a reappraisal of the Liberals' Irish commitment was probable.

The Irish accordingly tried to demonstrate to the Liberals that their electoral support was not to be relied upon as automatically forthcoming. This strategy forms part of the background to the support given by Ferguson to Keir Hardie's candidature at Mid-Lanark in 1888, and the Irish interest in the creation of the Scottish Labour Party.[185] This encouraged the decision of independent Labour or socialist candidates to fight Glasgow seats. At Camlachie, Cunninghame Graham was confident of doing well, given Irish support. In 1890-01 this all came to a stop as the aftermath of the Parnell divorce crisis pushed the Irish Nationalists back to total backing for Gladstonian Liberals, out of gratitude for the latter's espousal of Home Rule. Graham fulminated impotently: 'The Parnellite split has I fear dished the labour movement in Scotland. All the fools are united on Gladstone'.[186] Indeed, as discussed earlier, Labour polled badly in the Glasgow seats in the elections of 1892 and 1895. A few years later, however, the Irish had become somewhat estranged from the Liberals, and in the 1900 general election much of the blame for the rout of Liberal candidates in Glasgow was ascribed by Liberal managers to the defection of the Irish.[187] Certainly Bonar Law's surprise victory at Blackfriars against Provand was seen as the product in good part of Irish anger that Provand, the man they had worked for so strenuously in 1886, now proved to be a very tepid exponent of the Irish Home Rule cause.[188] Joint meetings of Irish and socialists in the city to protest against the government's handling of the Boer War emphasised the drift of the former away from the Liberals and the Irish-socialist alliance on the city council, 'the Stalwarts', added to this trend.[189]

Yet by the 1906 elections the Irish had again reversed direction, as indicated by Ferguson's membership of the executive of the Glasgow Liberal Council. In only two of the seven city seats were the Irish instructed to vote Labour rather than Liberal, and efforts to induce Michael Davitt, the most socialistic of the Irish leaders, to visit Glasgow on Labour's behalf were rejected as contrary to the best interests of Irish Nationalists.[190] The two 1900 elections confirmed the continuing Irish attachment to the Liberals, not to Labour. In the January election they were even instructed to switch their votes at Camlachie. Here in 1906 they had been urged to go for Labour, now they should go for the Liberal, because he had a better chance of winning.[191] At St Rollox in 1912, in what was to be the last by-election in the city prior to war, the Scottish organiser of the Irish Nationalists worked assiduously to ensure that the 1,800 Irish votes in the constituency went to the Liberal.[192] Labour made no bid to fight this highly working-class seat, judging its hopes to be very slender.

Thus, right down to the very outbreak of war, the Irish lobby remained concerned with their own issue, which led them to pursue a course of action independent from the emerging Labour movement. Admittedly there were indicators of a change in process. Wheatley's sterling evangelistic efforts have been noted, and there was also the involvement of Patrick Dollan in the I.L.P., and especially in the columns of *The Forward*. But these were pointers to the future, not much more. Most of the Irish electors remained loyal to their national, not their class, identity. Efforts to reverse the instructions at Camlachie in January 1910 to change from voting Labour to Liberal were easily seen off by the Irish National League's local officials, and commentators accepted that the vast bulk of the Irish vote did go to the Liberal.[193]

The Glasgow socialists, seeing their previous links with the Irish exposed as merely an alliance of expediency of the latter's part, shifted in the immediate pre-1914 period to a critical stance. Thus in 1911 *The Forward* denounced Irish Nationalist politicians in Scotland as 'publicans, slum property owners, model lodging-house keepers and provision merchants', and called on all socialists and Labour people to fight against the Irish National League.[194] On the other hand, the Liberals were under no illusions about the reasons why they were receiving the support of the Irish. Some Liberals wished to have Ferguson expelled from the party's Council Executive after the Irish had helped Labour against Liberal candidates in two seats in the 1906 elections.[195] As the new progressive Liberals increasingly regarded social reform politics as affording the best way forward for the party, sympathy for and commitment to the Irish cause seemed to be peripheral to the future of Liberalism.

VII: Conclusion

On the whole, working-class politics in Glasgow for most of this period worked relatively amicably in tandem with middle-class political currents. This is not to say the former were incorporated or subordinated by bourgeois values. There was always a sense of sturdy independence and a wariness of being condescended to by the middle class, and this gave a tension to relations between the two classes, especially in Liberal and Radical movements. The fragmentation of the city's working class, and in particular the persistence of ethnic and sectarian loyalties, meant that working-class unity and solidarity was difficult to achieve and still more to maintain. Here the First World War and the post-1918 developments, particularly in Ireland, paved the way for the fusing of that powerful working-class solidarity and class-consciousness which were to be the prevailing feature of Glasgow politics in the next phase.

Notes

1. K. Logue, *Popular Disturbances in Scotland, 1780-1815* (Edinburgh, 1979), pp. 155-60.
2. H. Cockburn, *Memorials of His Time* (Edinburgh, 1856), p. 80.
3. H.W. Meikle, *Scotland and the French Revolution* (Glasgow, 1912), pp. 70-1.
4. Logue, *Popular Disturbances*, pp. 133ff.
5. *Ibid.*, pp. 148-9.
6. Meikle, *Scotland and French Revolution*, p. 186.
7. *Ibid.*, Apps. A and B.

8. *Ibid.*, p. 137.
9. *Ibid.*, pp. 146-7.
10. P. MacKenzie, *Old Reminiscences of Glasgow and the West of Scotland* (Glasgow, 1890), I, pp. 27-8.
11. N. Murray, *The Scottish Handloom Weavers, 1790-1850* (Edinburgh, 1978), pp. 41-2, 50, 209.
12. Meikle, *Scotland and French Revolution*, pp. 92-3.
13. Murray, *Handloom Weavers*, pp. 213-4.
14. *Ibid.*, p. 214; also the very valuable thesis by J.D. Brims, 'The Scottish Democratic Movement in the Age of the French Revolution' (Ph.D., Edinburgh, 1983).
15. Murray, *Handloom Weavers*, p. 214; Brims, 'Scottish Democratic Movement', pp. 15-8.
16. Meikle, *Scotland and French Revolution*, pp. 139-41.
17. *Ibid.*, pp. 164-5.
18. *Ibid.*, pp. 186-8.
19. Murray, *Handloom Weavers*, pp. 40-2, 211-2.
20. P.B. Ellis and S. MacA'Ghobhainn, *The Scottish Insurrection of 1820* (London, 1970), pp. 75-6, cf. Brims, 'Scottish Democratic Movements', pp. 206-9.
21. Murray, *Handloom Weavers*, pp. 214-5.
22. W.M. Roach, 'Alexander Richmond and the Radical Reform Movements in Glasgow, 1816-17', *Scottish Historical Review* (1972), pp. 1-2, Meikle, *Scotland and French Revolution*, pp. 221-4.
23. J. Smith, ed., *Life and Recollections of James Turner of Thrushgrove* (Glasgow, 1854), especially pp. 25-8.
24. Murray, *Handloom Weavers*, pp. 216-7; Roach, 'Richmond', pp. 2-3.
25. Roach, 'Richmond', pp. 3-14 for a full account.
26. Murray, *Handloom Weavers*, p. 220.
27. Ellis and MacA'Ghobhainn, *Scottish Insurrection, passim*, for a recent narrative.
28. *Ibid.*, pp. 292-300.
29. *The Lord Provosts of Glasgow From 1833 to 1902* (Glasgow, 1902), pp. 15-9.
30. There is a copy between pp. 96-7 of Ellis and MacA'Ghobhainn, *Scottish Insurrection*.
31. Ellis and MacA'Ghobhainn, *Scottish Insurrection*, pp. 141-2; cf. W. Roach, 'Radical Reform Movements in Scotland from 1815 to 1830' (Ph.D. Thesis, Glasgow, 1970), pp. 193-200. This is a very useful piece of work.
32. Ellis and MacA'Ghobhainn, *Scottish Insurrection*, between pp. 96-7.
33. For an opposing view, *ibid.*, pp. 132-3; but see Roach, 'Radical Movements', pp. 200-8, 244-6, whom I follow here.
34. J. Fife (ed.), *Autobiography of John MacAdam (1803-83), with Selected Letters* (Edinburgh, 1980), p. 6.
35. *Ibid.*, pp. 5-7.
36. *Ibid.*, pp. 4-5. For this generally, F. Montgomery, 'Glasgow and the Struggle for Parliamentary Reform, 1830-32', *Scottish Historical Review* (1982), pp. 130-45.
37. Montgomery, 'Glasgow and Reform', pp. 143-5.

38. H. Cockburn, *Journal of Henry Cockburn* (Edinburgh, 1874), I, pp. 18-9.

39. J. Cannon, *Parliamentary Reform, 1640-1832* (London, 1972), p. 227.

40. *The Durham Festival, Glasgow, Wednesday 29th Ocotber 1834* (n.p., n.d.).

41. *The Glasgow Election* (n.p., n.d.).

42. W. H. Fraser, 'The Glasgow Cotton Spinners, 1837', in J. Butt and J.T. Ward, *Scottish Themes* (Edinburgh, 1973), pp. 80-97.

43. *List of Tories, Churchmen and Chartists who united at the Late Glasgow Election and Voted for James Campbell and George Mills* (n.p., n.d.); G. Crawford to Lord W. Bentinck, 20 July 1837; G. Mills to Bentinck, 10 January 1838, Portland MSS., Nottingham University Library, Pw Jg 82, 258.

44. A. Wilson, *The Chartist Movement in Scotland* (Manchester, 1970), pp. 43-51.

45. A. Wilson, 'Chartism in Glasgow', in A. Briggs, ed., *Chartist Studies* (London, 1959), pp. 263-6.

46. Wilson, *Chartist Movement*, pp. 81-7, 103-5, 118-9.

47. *Ibid.*, pp. 126-45.

48. Wilson, 'Chartism in Glasgow', pp. 267-72.

49. Wilson, *Chartist Movement*, pp. 167-79.

50. J. Campbell, *Recollection of Radical Times Descriptive of the Last Hour of Baird and Hardie and the Riots in Glasgow, 1848* (Glasgow, 1880), pp. 20-32; W. Freer, *My Life and Memories* (Glasgow, 1929), pp. 15-6.

51. Wilson, *Chartist Movement*, pp. 216-27.

52. The last embers are reported in *Glasgow Sentinel*, 31 January 1852, 17 March 1855; *North British Daily Mail*, 3 April 1856. Also L.C. Wright, *Scottish Chartism* (Edinburgh, 1953), pp. 202-6.

53. e.g. *Glasgow Sunday Post*, 14 June, 18 October 1851; *Glasgow Herald*, 26 January, 21 November 1853, 26 January 1855, 9 and 11 September 1857, 17 February 1860, 18 October 1861; *Glasgow Sentinel*, 8 July 1854, 6 and 13 October 1860, 11 April 1863; Freer, *My Life*, p. 125.

54. For Italian meetings: *Glasgow Sentinel*, 17 December 1859, 12 May 1860, 21 April, 4 May 1864; *Glasgow Herald*, 26 July, 15 August 1861, 4 July 1866; *North British Daily Mail*, 31 January 1861, 8 March 1863, 20 December 1867.

55. Fife, *MacAdam*, pp. 16ff.

56. *Glasgow Herald*, 26 November 1860; *North British Daily Mail*, 23 January 1861.

57. R. Dalglish to J. Moir, 2 April 1857, 11 April 1859, Moir MSS., Mitchell Library, Glasgow.

58. *Glasgow Sentinel*, 28 February 1852; *North British Daily Mail*, 28 October 1852; *Glasgow Herald*, 10 and 26 November 1858; *North British Daily Mail*, 14 September 1859, 6 May 1862.

59. cf. G. Howell to G. Newton, 27 November 1865, 24 February 1866, Howell MSS., Bishopsgate Institute, London.

60. Scottish National Reform League, *Great Reform Demonstration at Glasgow: Tuesday 16 October 1866* (Glasgow, 1866).

61. *Glasgow Herald, North British Daily Mail*, 30 January 1867, 17 September 1867.

62. G. Howell to G. Jackson, 26 June 1868, Howell MSS.

63. *Glasgow Herald*, 31 August 1885 for a full obituary.
64. 'Programme of Business for Electoral Conference, Trades Hall, Glasgow, 7th July 1868', Moir MSS.; *Glasgow Evening Post*, 8 July 1868.
65. *Glasgow Herald*, 2 October, 6 and 13 November 1868.
66. W.H. Fraser, 'Trade Unions, Reform and the Election of 1868 in Scotland', *Scottish Historical Review* (1971), pp. 143-51.
67. Scottish National Reform League, *Address by the Executive Council to the People of Scotland* (Glasgow, 1866).
68. *First Ward Municipal Election. Advanced Labour and Working Class Interest, Mr. George Jackson's Address to the Electors in the First Ward 1st October 1869* (n.p., n.d.).
69. Glasgow and West of Scotland Branch of the Scottish National Association for the Abolition of the State Regulation of Vice, *Annual Report*, 1879, p. 7.
70. *Glasgow Herald*, 8 July 1868.
71. *Glasgow Herald*, 30 January 1874.
72. *North British Daily Mail*, 3 July, 16 October 1876.
73. A.J. Hunter to W.E. Gladstone, 31 March 1884, W.E. Gladstone MSS., B. L. Add. Ms. 44, 485, f. 318; *Glasgow Herald*, 26 February 1881.
74. Glasgow United Trades Council, *Annual Report*, 1884-5, pp. 8-9.
75. R. Gray, *The Aristocracy of Labour in Britain, 1850-1914* (London, 1981), *passim*.
76. Scottish Liberal Association, Minute Book, 5 January 1882, Edinburgh University Library; *Glasgow Herald*, 21 January 1882.
77. *Glasgow Herald*, 4 October 1879.
78. *Glasgow Sentinel*, 6 November 1869.
79. *Ibid.*, 12,13,20,28 March 1873.
80. e.g. *Glasgow Sentinel*, 26 October 1850.
81. J.B. Glasier, *William Morris and the Early Days of the Socialist Movement* (London, 1921), pp. 98-9; J. Mavor, *My Windows on the Street of the World* (London, 1923), I, pp. 173-7.
82. *Glasgow News*, 21 March 1882; *Justice*, 31 May, 28 June 1884; Glasier, *Morris*, p. 28; *Glasgow News*, 2 December 1884.
83. Glasier, *Morris*, pp. 61, 72-4, 84-8, 98, 108-10; cf. J. Brown to J.B. Glasier, 5 November 1890, Glasier MSS., Liverpool University Library, I. 1. 1890/4.
84. Glasier, *Morris*, p. 33.
85. *Justice*, 31 May 1884.
86. G. Beith, *The Crofter Question and Church Endowments in the Highlands, Viewed Socially and Politically* (Glasgow, 1885).
87. *Justice*, August 1884 *passim*, and 1 November 1884, for this controversy.
88. *North British Daily Mail*, 28 May 1881; *Glasgow Herald*, 29 April 1882.
89. Glasier, *Morris*, pp. 27-8.
90. *Ibid.*, pp. 40-1, 67-8, 72-4; Mavor, *My Windows*, I, p. 177.
91. Glasier, *Morris*, pp. 38-9, 61, 87-8, 98-101; Mavor, *My Windows*, I, pp. 176-8.
92. J. Mavor, 'Labour and Politics in England', *Political Science Quarterly* 10 (1895), p. 503; also, 'Militant Socialism: the Movement in Glasgow, A Retrospective Glance', 25 January 1918, *Glasgow Herald*. This was possibly written by Mavor.

93. 'Militant Socialism', *Glasgow Herald*, 25 January 1918.

94. Labour Party MSS., London, NEC Minutes, 15 July 1913.

95. T. Bell, *Pioneering Days* (London, 1941); D. Kirkwood, *My Life of Revolt* (London, 1936).

96. J. Hinton, *The First Shop Stewards Movement* (London, 1973), pp. 121-5.

97. T. Johnston, *Memories* (London, 1952), pp. 32-3.

98. 'Confidential Memorandum on the Socialist and Labour Movements in Scotland', endorsed 'February 1908', Elibank MSS., National Library of Scotland MS. 8801 ff. 145-51.

99. F.C. Gardiner to A. Bonar Law, 21 November 1907, Bonar Law MSS., House of Lords Record Office, BL 18/3/47.

100. M. Guthrie to T. Mann, 15 and 22 February 1897; M. Bruce to Mann, 1 April 1897; J. MacDonald to Mann, 18 June 1898; Johnson MSS., British Library of Political and Economic Science, 1897/4, 5, 13, 1898/91.

101. J.B. Glasier to E. Glasier Foster, 24 November 1905, Glasier MSS., I. 1. 1905/20.

102. *Forward*, 1 January 1910; J. Paton, *Proletarian Pilgrimage* (London, 1935), p. 166.

103. *Forward*, 30 December 1911.

104. (W.M. Haddow), *Socialism in Scotland: Its Rise and Progress* (Glasgow, n.d.), p. 49.

105. *Ibid.*, pp. 50-1.

106. J. MacDonald to T. Mann, 18 June 1898, Johnson MSS., 1898/61.

107. J. Duncan to 'Mabel', 12 November 1907, Duncan MSS., National Library of Scotland, Acc. 5490/1, ff. 24-6; also J. Hill to J.S. Middleton, 16 November 1907, Labour Party MSS., LP/GC/20/182.

108. J. Kelly to J. Ramsay MacDonald, 22 April 1903, Labour Party MSS., LRC/8/340.

109. Labour Party MSS., NEC Minutes, 13 April 1910. Camlachie was affiliated.

110. *Forward*, 12 July 1913; B. Shaw to J.S. Middleton, 5 and 10 July 1914, Labour Party MSS., LP/SAC/14/8, 10.

111. This includes Govan, then a Lanarkshire seat, but in many respects Govan was part of the city, as its incorporation into Glasgow in 1911 recognised.

112. Scottish Liberal Association Minute Books, 4 April, 11 May, 14 June 1894.

113. A. Hunter to J.K. Hardie, 20 November 1895, Johnson MSS., 1895/158.

114. A. Bonar Law to J. Chamberlain, 19 January 1906, Joseph Chamberlain MSS., Birmingham University Library, JC 21/2/16.

115. A.M. Scott Diary, 25 April 1914, Scott MSS., Glasgow University Library, MS. 1465/5.

116. Paton, *Proletarian Pilgrimage*, pp. 172, 199-200.

117. G. Barnes to J.B. Glasier, 21 December 1909, and endorsed by Glasier, Glasier MSS., I. 1. 1909/5.

118. G. Barnes, *Workshop to War Cabinet* (London, n.d.), pp. 60-3.

119. J. O'Connor Kessack, *The Capitalist Wilderness and the Way Out* (Glasgow, 1907).

120. I.L.P. *18th Annual Conference* (1910), p. 70.

121. J.S. Taylor to F. Johnson, 2 & 7 December 1911, Johnson MSS., 1911/331, 336.
122. e.g. P.F. Clarke, *Lancashire and the New Liberalism* (London, 1971); H.V. Emy, *Liberals, Radicals and Social Politics, 1892-1914* (London, 1972).
123. *Glasgow Herald*, 8 July 1909, 6 April 1912.
124. Scott Diary, 16 May, 13 August 1911, 10 July 1914, Scott MSS., MS. 1465/2, 5.
125. W. Stewart to J.K. Hardie, 30 November 1908, Johnson MSS., 1908/493.
126. Scott Diary, 5 March, 19 and 30 April 1911; 14 April 1913, Scott MSS., MS. 1465/2, 4.
127. Scott to R. Cumming, 2 July, 30 September 1912, *ibid.*, MS. 1465/181-2, 189.
128. Scott Diary, 19 August 1911, 1 July, 1 October, 25 September 1913, 19 January 1914, *ibid.*, MS. 1465/2-5.
129. N. Blewett, *The Peers, the Parties and the People* (London, 1972); Emy, *Liberals, Radicals:* Clark, *Lancashire and the New Liberalism.*
130. J. Paton, *Left Turn!* (London, 1936), pp. 141-2.
131. *The Baillie*, 4 December 1872, also 8 January 1873.
132. Glasgow Workingmen's Conservative Assoc., *1st Annual Report* (1869).
133. *Glasgow Herald*, 3 February 1911, 6 May 1910.
134. G. Younger to A. Bonar Law, 9 October 1913, Bonar Law MSS., BL 30/3/12.
135. Based on Glasgow Conservative Operatives' Association Minute Books, Scottish Conservative and Unionist Association MSS.; J.T. Ward, 'Some Aspects of Working Class Conservatism in the Nineteenth Century', Butt & Ward, *Scottish Themes*, pp. 141-59.
136. *Glasgow Herald*, 21 October, 5 November 1868.
137. *Ibid.*, 21 January 1869.
138. For an explanation of the terminology and methodology used, see I.G.C. Hutchison, 'Politics and Society in Mid-Victorian Glasgow' (Ph.D. Thesis, Edinburgh University, 1974), pp. 391-2, 589-90.
139. *Glasgow News*, 10 November 1880.
140. *Ibid.*, 8 and 10 October 1880, 27 January 1883, 27 February 1884; Glasgow Conservative Association, *12th Annual Report, 19th Annual Report* (1880-7).
141. Glasgow Conservative Association, *21st Annual Report* (1889).
142. *Glasgow Herald*, 3 February, also 31 January 1911.
143. G. Younger to A. Bonar Law, 9 October 1913, Bonar Law MSS., BL 30/3/12.
144. Glasgow Conservative Operatives' Association. *2nd Annual Report* (1839).
145. J.T. Ward, 'The Factory Reform Movement in Scotland', *Scottish Historical Review* (1962), pp. 100-23.
146. *Glasgow News*, 4 October 1884; for more of the same, *ibid.*, 16 December 1881.
147. *Glasgow Herald*, 28 January 1874.
148. Hansard, *Parliamentary Debates*, 3rd Series, vol. CCXXIII, cols. 46-53.
149. A.B. Campbell, *The Lanarkshire Miners. A Social History of Their Trade Unions, 1775-1874* (Edinburgh, 1979), *passim.*

150. *Glasgow Sentinel,* 2 and 30 May 1868.
151. *Glasgow News,* 14 December 1882.
152. *Ibid.,* 16 August 1884.
153. K. Oliver to A. Bonar Law, 17 November 1911, G. Younger to Law, 6 November 1912, Bonar Law MSS., BL 24/3/49, 27/4/7.
154. Glasgow Conservative Association, *9th, 10th Annual Reports* (1877-8).
155. *The Times,* 26 October 1900; H. Campbell-Bannerman to H. Gladstone, 22 October 1900, Campbell-Bannerman MSS., BL Add. MS. 41216, ff. 27-8.
156. Glasgow Conservative Operatives' Association Minute Book, 10 February 1837, 23 December 1836.
157. *Ibid.,* 10 March 1842, 8 March, 30 May 1843.
158. Glasgow Workingmen's Conservative Assoc., *4th Annual Report* (1872).
159. *Ibid.*
160. *Reasons for Organising a Protestant Confraternity to be called 'The Knoxites'* (n.p. n.d.).
161. H. Senior, *Orangeism in Ireland and Britain, 1795-1836* (Dublin, 1966), for this phase.
162. *Glasgow News,* 13 July 1878, 5 January 1875; *The Scottish Orangeman's Historical Directory, 1913-14* (n.p., n.d.).
163. *Glasgow Herald,* 13 July 1874.
164. *Ibid.,* 6 November 1868, 12 December 1871; Glasgow Workingmen's Conservative Association, *3rd Annual Report* (1871).
165. *Glasgow News,* 9 November 1878, 2 April 1880.
166. Hutchison, 'Politics and Society', p. 391.
167. *Glasgow News,* 27 October, also 29 March 1881.
168. *Glasgow News,* 1-4 October 1884. The Knoxites took part in the street processions in Salisbury's honour.
169. E.G. Ravenstein, 'The Laws of Migration', *Journal of the Royal Statistical Society* (1885), p. 178.
170. *North British Daily Mail,* 12 July 1869, cf. 9 August 1875.
171. e.g. J.C. Gibson, *The Diary of Sir Michael Connel* (Glasgow, 1895), p. 169 (14 February 1877).
172. Glasgow Working Men's Evangelistic Assoc., *12th Annual Report* (1881).
173. *Glasgow News,* 31 January, 2 February 1874.
174. J.P. Smith to Mrs Smith, 26 January (1890), Smith of Jordanhill MSS., Strathclyde Regional Archives Office, TD1/227; Paton, *Proletarian Pilgrimage,* p. 172.
175. J.E. Handley, *The Irish in Modern Scotland* (Cork, 1947); W.M. Walker, 'Irish Immigrants in Scotland: Their Priests, Politics and Parochial Life', *Historical Journal* 15 (1972), pp. 649-67, although about Dundee, has implications for Glasgow.
176. See R. Howie, *Churches and the Churchless in Scotland* (Glasgow, 1893), p. xxvii.
177. *Glasgow Herald,* 7 and 9 August, 7 October 1875; *Glasgow News,* 24 August, 3 September 1875; *North British Daily Mail,* 20 August 1875.
178. See Paton, *Proletarian Pilgrimage,* pp. 186-7, 200-11 for Roman Catholics in the I.L.P.

179. R. Lobban, 'The Irish Community in Nineteenth Century Greenock', *Irish Geography* 6 (1969-71), pp. 270-81.
180. *Glasgow Herald,* 15 November 1871, 18 September 1872, 30 April 1873, 1 August 1876.
181. J.F. McCaffrey, 'The Irish Vote in Late Nineteenth Century Glasgow: A Preliminary Survey', *Innes Review* (1970), pp. 30-7.
182. *Glasgow Observer,* 20 January 1906.
183. *Glasgow Herald,* 29 April 1882.
184. *Glasgow Observer,* 3 and 10 July 1886.
185. J.G. Kellas, 'The Mid-Lanark By-Election (1888) and the Scottish Labour Party (1888-94)', *Parliamentary Affairs* 18 (1964-5), pp. 318-29.
186. R.B. Cunninghame Graham to J. Burns, 15 December 1890, Burns MSS., B.L. Add. MS. 46284, ff. 71-2.
187. R.C. Munro Ferguson to H. Campbell-Bannerman, (24 October 1900), Campbell-Bannerman MSS., B.L. Add. MS. 41222, ff. 330-3.
188. *Glasgow Observer,* 13 January 1906; A. Bonar to J. Chamberlain, 19 January 1906, J. Chamberlain MSS., JC 21/2/16.
189. D. Lowe to J.K. Hardie, 26 February 1890, Johnson MSS., 1890/70.
190. *Glasgow Observer,* 6, 13, 20 January 1906; J.S. Middleton to G.N. Barnes, 6 January 1906 (copy), Labour Party MSS., LRC/30/272.
191. *Glasgow Observer,* 15 January 1910.
192. *Glasgow Herald,* 27 February 1912.
193. *Glasgow Observer,* 1, 15, 22 January 1910.
194. *Forward,* 25 March 1911, also 29 January 1910.
195. *Glasgow Herald,* 5 April 1906.

Chapter Six

POPULAR CULTURE IN GLASGOW

Elspeth King

I: Introduction

The study of popular culture in Scotland is still the preserve of the anti-
quarian rather than the social historian, a frivolous frill seen in terms of
amusements, sports and pastimes and ignored in favour of subjects with
more apparent seriousness. This is as true for the popular culture of the
middle and upper classes as it is for that of the working classes. While
there are some excellent studies on individual aspects of the subject, leisure
activity, if considered at all in general terms, comes as an afterthought.

Seminal studies, such as the work of Kellow Chesney and Gareth
Stedman Jones on working-class culture in London,[1] and the detailed pioneering study of popular literature and music halls in the north of England
done by Martha Vicinus,[2] are still awaited for Glasgow. Even though ballads, broadsheets and pieces of ephemeral literature survive in significant
quantities for Glasgow, and although David Murray who collected it made
a plea for the study of 'the vulgar literature of Scotland' fully sixty years
ago,[3] there have been no recent publications in this field. Similarly, while
theatre and music hall history have received a great deal of attention elsewhere, we still lack even a basic study in Glasgow.[4] Although there has
been stage and media interest in the careers of performers such as Harry
Lauder, Will Fyfe and Dave Willis, this interest does not pre-date the
advent of recorded sound, and is rarely analytical. No one has attempted
to examine the penny theatres of Glasgow, as Paul Sheridan has done for
Victorian London.[5]

It is odd that the development of the different branches of the leisure
industry has failed to attract the attention of the industrial and economic
historians. The leisure industry can be examined like any other industry.
Its physical structures —its theatres, halls, stadiums, circuses and rinks—

have been as impressive and as enduring as any of the other industrial buildings and monuments in Glasgow which have been so meticulously studied. The money which is generated must have equalled that of other industries, and indirectly, it must have touched every industry by affecting the quality of life and hence the capabilities of those working in them. In turn it was shaped by industrial developments, and the transition from a rural to an industrial society is as clearly marked in leisure activity in Glasgow as it is elsewhere.

Part of the reason that the leisure industry in Glasgow has been over-looked may have something to do with the fact that the actor-managers and the theatre, music hall and circus owners were never held in the same high regard as the entrepreneurs in other fields. Although they may have been both adored and reviled as John Henry Alexander (1796-1851), man-ager of the Theatre Royal, was by his audiences, they were in an essen-tially dubious business, and Alexander spent a great deal of his time in the courts either defending himself or raising actions against others. He achieved equality with his peers only in the Glasgow Necropolis, where his tombstone, Saltire-shaped because of his nationalism and with prosce-nium, last curtain, and life-sized weepers, rivals that of its neighbours in grandeur and size.

In the period before the Great War, the leisure industry offered better and more flexible employment prospects and freedom from persecution to those interested in pursuing a political career. Several ILP councillors in Glasgow were for example picture house owners, and a few like George Singleton ('Mr. Cosmo') were highly successful businessmen and involved in labour politics. However, none of these men could be classified as either captains of industry or labour leaders, and their lives have attracted no at-tention. Within this group only John S. Clarke (1885-1959), the lion tamer and one-time ILP MP for Maryhill, has won the attention of biographers.[6] Others, like the eccentric A.E. Pickard, were far too idiosyncratic to be considered as part of the business or the political community. Pickard came to Glasgow in the early years of the century 'because he heard that there was money to be made' and advanced his career as a shows and cinema owner with outrageous publicity stunts which included issuing riv-ets as ammunition to his potentially disgruntled vaudeville audiences and standing for election to parliament as an 'independent millionaire'.[7]

Whatever the reason, many aspects of popular culture have been regarded as issues of little importance, and the lack of detailed studies upon which to build makes it difficult to come to any enduring conclusions at this point in time. In this contribution I therefore intend to look only at certain aspects of working-class culture in the period 1750-1914 and suggest areas of further research which will in time give a clearer picture of developments in this field. This contribution should be looked upon as a very tentative essay to open up the subject, and, hopefully, researchers in the field of social, economic and political history will be interested enough to give greater consideration to the forces affecting leisure activity.

II: The Culture of the Streets

One factor which is common to the entire period 1750-1914, and which is almost outwith the understanding of the present generation, is the amount of leisure time which was spent in the streets. When housing was uncomfortable or overcrowded, promenading in the streets became a pleasurable pastime. A writer in 1901 describes Sauchiehall Street thus:

> ...the street of youth and evening promenade. Here comes every night the young persons who have spent the day cooped in shops or warehouses, or offices, and who find sitting at home in dreary lodgings an intolerable torture. On Saturday they come in all the greater number—'the crood brings the crood'. They have no other place in which to spend spare time. . . . The lighted street demands no admission money, and so they come in droves. The girls, one hears, come from the South Side—from Paisley Road—because Paisley Road at night is a promenade for the dwellers in Govan.[8]

Promenading was not the preserve of the working classes; another observer of the period writes with contempt of the 'mashers', the young, middle-class men of fashion who haunted Sauchiehall Street.[9] In some streets such as Saltmarket and Argyle Street, working people predominated, and the activity of the streets is commemorated in many penny song sheets. A 'highly humorous song, nightly sung with rapturous applause in the Glasgow Saloon' in 1853 tells us that,

> In Saltmarket Street on a Saturday night
> Half the people of Glasgow (or very near)
> 'Twixt six and twelve are walking there
> All other streets are deserted quite
> For Saltmarket Street on a Saturday night

The same author in 1865 produced a similar song about Argyle Street on a Sunday night, listing the different tradespeople who included 'niffers, drivers, giggers, bellers, weavers, shavers and haircutters'.[10] Although different streets were in fashion at different times, the practice continued, and in 1914 the young working people living in the west end of the city went on 'the pad', which was a walk in Sauchiehall, Buchanan and Argyle Streets. ('Up Sauchie, doon Buckie, alang Argyle').[11]

Although all ages of people took to the streets, evidence indicates that the practice was of particular importance to young people doing their courting. In a song of 1855 called 'Glasgow Courtship' ('sung with rapturous and deafening shouts of applause by Mr. Charles Watson, the inimitable comic singer of the Shakespeare Saloon') we learn that,

> They're all Courting, court, court, courting
> They're all courting in Glasgow town
> They're all courtin as through the streets your walking
> In High Street, Saltmarket, Argyle Street and all
> And another place too, they meet, to pass away the time
> Round the river side, till the clock strikes nine
> Then the lads they take their lasses home
> For they must not keep them out too long
> Hence, they all come to the Poet's Box to buy his last song.[12]

Promenading remained popular not only because it cost nothing, but because there were few alternative attractions. Even when holiday-makers went 'doon the watter' to the Clyde coastal resorts, the highlight of an evening in Rothesay or Dunoon was the promenade to the pier to meet the incoming steamers. Cartoonists were quick to notice that the promenade was unaffected even by torrential rain.[13]

Notwithstanding the harmlessness of such activity, like other working-class amusements, it earned the censure of concerned clergymen and moralists. One conference on public morals in 1913 for example, dismayed at the amount of Sabbath breaking in Scottish cities, called upon the police and Salvation Army 'to unite in endeavouring to deal with evils attendant upon street promenading'.[14]

By contrast, the comparatively frequent public processions organised by trades, political, friendly society, temperance and religious groups were considered to be morally uplifting and educative. These occasions were demonstrations of solidarity, strength and respectability for their causes, as well as providing an opportunity for pageantry, colour and ceremony on the streets. The largest and most flamboyant demonstrations in Glasgow in the 19th century were those held prior to the passing of the various Reform Bills. Many descriptive broadsheets of them have survived, and such demonstrations must have provided a colourful diversion and considerable free entertainment for the working classes.

Even a generation later, the Reform Bill processions were remembered as 'the greatest free show ever seen in Glasgow'.[15] The processions were usually carefully planned in advance, with details of the order in which the trades would march, a description of their banners, and the objects which each section would carry issued to interested printers. The routes often varied, but all of the larger demonstrations began and ended on Glasgow

Green, the city's common grazing, washing and playground, and political arena.

Each trade tried to keep their achievements to the fore. In the procession of 8 September 1831 in honour of William IV's coronation, the band from Marshall's Panorama, one of the chief places of amusement in the town at that time, marched with those from the printing trade. Marshall had 'a splendid banner of dark blue silk, with a superb crown on it, and the following words in gold letters "Panorama of Calcutta, Algiers, Sydney and the late French Revolution"'.[16]

The Reform League procession of October 1866 was organised on a massive scale, taking over two hours to leave the Green and forming 'a living girdle round the central parts of the city'. As usual, the carters led off the procession, followed by the Forresters 'who with their green sashes, splendid banners and profuse display of evergreens, attracted general admiration'. The *Glasgow Herald* gave a detailed report:

> Flags were flying in all directions and men were mustering in every quiet street, covered with medals, rosettes of all colours, aprons and silk sashes, and attended by instrument bands . . . I saw stalwart stonemasons and bricklayers, plasterers and slaters, plumbers and painters by the hundred, wearing sashes aprons and rosettes and bearing splendid banners, miniature houses and monster chimney stalks. Blacksmiths, joiners, ship carpenters and cabinetmakers were also there, carrying model ships, model machinery, anvils, vices, chests of drawers, wardrobes, pulpits, tester beds, sections of ship fittings and other articles of similar description. Then came coal miners, iron miners, engineers, bottle blowers, cotton spinners, coopers, brassfounders, bakers, pipemakers, printers, tobacco spinners, tailors, shoemakers, potters and so on. . . .
>
> But the letter press printers, the lithographic ditto, the pipemakers and the nail makers took the shine out of the representative models displayed by the other trades. They had large lorries or wagons where their trades were carried on as the procession moved along and people by the way had the opportunity of seeing the work done and of getting printed bills, pictures, tobacco pipes or horse nails, hot from the hammer, the hand and the printing machine.[17]

On 6 October 1883 the foundation stone of the new municipal buildings in George Square was laid, after a similar trades procession, which gave the Liberal Party and the various trades an opportunity to practise for what was to be the biggest demonstration of the century—the Reform Bill Demonstration of 4 September 1884. Trade virtually ceased in Glasgow on that day, for most of the workers seemed to want to participate in the demonstration. It was similar to the 1866 procession but even more spectacular, and included some of the material which had been carried in the earlier demonstrations. The Upholsterers for example,

> carried with them a sofa which had its place in the Reform Demonstration

of 1832, and a profusion of models of couches, sofas, easy chairs, ottomans
richly upholstered and a half tester bed with rich hangings, and bearing
the inscription 'The Death Bed of the House of Lords'. A large furniture
van, tastefully decorated and drawn by four greys was fitted up with an
upholstery workshop with men at work in different departments.

Many other trades employed the same device: the tinplate workers went
into the procession building a ship's water tank, and the Glenboig Union
Fireclay Company's heather-decked lorry had firebrick makers, retort builders, and sewage-pipe makers at work.[18]

While the demonstrations of 1832, 1866 and 1884 were exceptional
by their size, those of the various friendly and temperance societies were
more frequent and could be equally colourful. Although the entire area
of the foundation and growth of the friendly societies in Glasgow needs
detailed study, it is obvious that the high membership of such bodies
cannot be attributed to the need for life and sickness insurance alone.
Some organisations, such as the Independent Order of Good Templars
and the Orange Order had no insurance provisions.

In a rapidly changing society, where work could be dull and bru-
tally hard, the opportunity of belonging to an ostensibly ancient order
(Forresters, Gardeners, Oddfellows, Shepherds, Rechabites, Templars, Hi-
bernians) provided an anchor in the past and the chance to dress up and
parade in colourful clothing. Many working people chose to spend their
leisure hours in Forresters' Courts, Druid Lodges and Rechabite Tents.
The professed antiquity of these organisations which were mostly favoured
by the working classes offered a welcome stability, ritual and colour which
was otherwise absent. Glasgow sustained over half a dozen firms of regalia
makers to meet the demand at its height, and while belonging to a friendly
society was never an option open to the poorest classes—membership and
regalia were not cheap—the banners and regalia when paraded on the
streets provided a shared experience of pageantry.[19]

An additional source of free entertainment to be had in the streets in
the two decades prior to the Great War was the weekly Barrows Market,
situated originally in East Clyde Street and subsequently moved to its
present site in Calton. 'The Barras' has since become an indispensable
Glasgow institution. Its origins are rooted in poverty, with people who
could find no other work attempting to make a living by selling second
hand goods from a cart. Their wits sharpened by the need to sell, there
was always a strong entertainment element in the market. An oral study
of the Barrows of the 1920s and 30s has revealed the tactics used—sham
fights between barrow boys to draw a crowd, exaggerated descriptions of
the powers of the goods (particularly the medicinal and herbal remedies)
and every second vendor a pirate or a smuggler.[20] There is no evidence

to suggest that it was much different in the early years, and numerous newspaper articles testify to its entertainment value.[21]

III: Popular Literature

Prior to the repeal of the Stamp Tax in 1855 which put paid to the tax on knowledge and paved the way for penny newspapers, the popular literature of Glasgow, in the form of cheaply printed news and broadsheets, poetry and chap books, was very much part of the culture of the streets and street entertainment as it was elsewhere. The primary function of the 'penny dreadful' in the eighteenth century was to satisfy the thirst for news of murders, disasters, melancholy accidents and last confessions, topics of great interest, if judged by the number of broadsheets on these subjects which survive.

Printed regularly were sheets such as 'A full and particular account of the proceedings of the Circuit Court of Justiciary opened at Glasgow on Tuesday 10th April, 1792. . . with an account of the sentences of the different criminals'.[22] Others, for isolated crimes, were packed full of detail, such as the 'Account of a bloody and barbarous murder committed on the body of James Gray, weaver, at the foot of Clyde Street Calton 27th February 1798 by a corporal and a number of recruits belonging to the Royals',[23] or the 'Account of the apprehending of James Plunket who along with George Davidson made their escape from Glasgow jail on the night of the 11th October last when under sentence of death, and the manner he was detected, in stealing silk stockings from a shop in Trongate. . . 25th November, 1791'.[24] Gruesome stories relating to burials or body-snatching were also popular, such as the 'Wonderful account of a woman who was buried alive, and who broke open the coffin while they were laying her in the grave. . . Glasgow 1821'[25] or the 'Horrible seizure of Dead Bodies 8th December, 1826' when imported Irish corpses were found packed in barrels on the Broomielaw.[26]

Many broadsheets were produced purely for entertainment, to be sold in the streets. The 'Wonderful effects of the Bridgegate three bawbee whisky on fish wives, bowl wives, fruit sellers, butcher caddies, speech cryers, ballad singers, knife grinders, fortune sellers, shoe tye sellers, herring dealers, pudding cleaners and especially the city orator, Jamie Blue'[27] are of this nature. Others, like the 'Lament for the destruction of the Holy Land in Candleriggs March 1823' (a brothel) and the 'Complete list of all the Sporting Ladies who are to be in Glasgow during the Fair, with the Names, Characters and where they are to be found, together with an account of their different Prices'[28] are more prurient in nature.

A number of ballad criers and hawkers made a precarious living from retailing such literature. Only a tiny minority of them such as Dougal Graham (1724-1799) were able to write it. Most relied on the printers and stationers to produce it, and some, like the above mentioned Jamie Blue (James McIndoe, d.1837), although dubbed 'the city orator', were totally illiterate and had to rely on memory when crying ballads. Fortunately, one of the most successful of them, William Cameron (d.1851) alias 'Hawkie' was literate enough to leave an autobiography and a first-hand account of crying broadsheets.[29]

Hawkie describes how he arrived in Glasgow one Saturday night in 1818 almost destitute with only three pence. He bought a dozen ballads at two pence, and began crying them. He found that he had a talent for selling, and kept returning to the printer for further supplies. By the time the printing shop shut at 8 pm, he had made six shillings.

Itinerant ballad criers and 'flying stationers' were always attracted to Glasgow when a public execution was imminent, as a lot of money could be made from a population wanting news or a souvenir of the gruesome event. When the execution of a man named Robertson, who was under sentence of death for housebreaking and theft, was to take place on 7 April 1819, the town was swamped by criers. Hawkie and Jamie Blue were crying a tract entitled 'A Reprieve from the Punishment of Death', as it was considered likely that Robertson would be reprieved. Others were crying different stories, and causing such a commotion that fifty of them, including Jamie Blue were rounded up and jailed until the execution was over. Hawkie escaped to Paisley.[30]

There were perhaps about a dozen stationers and printers in Glasgow in the mid-nineteenth century who were writing and publishing broadsides and ballads, to feed the ballad vendors, street performers and the singers in the free-and-easies.[31] Among the most flamboyant were Matthew Leitch (d.1852) and his son William Munzie Leitch (d.1910) who ran a small shop known as the Poet's Box, 'the Grand Temple of the Muse! the boast and pride of Millions! The Attraction of Cities! The Glory of Nations! and the Luminary of the World! No. 6 St. Andrew's Lane, off Gallowgate Street, and first street from the Cross, right hand side'. Several hundred of their printed sheets survive, and as each is dated, the collection is a rich source for social historians.

W.M. Leitch's repertoire seems to have covered every subject— 'ancient and modern Ballads of England, Ireland and Scotland; Amatory, Bacchanalian, Jewish, Masonic, Military, Naval and Sporting Songs; Comic and Sentimental Songs of every kind; Medleys, Madrigals and Pastorals;

Duets, Trios, Glees and Choruses'. According to a list of 1854, he also had a fair line in Orange songs—'The Poet has also got the Battle of the Boyne, 2 versions the Orange Banner; The Priest and the Lady or Transubstantiation Exposed; Rennisons's Grand Orange Chair; Pollokshaws Heroes; The Shipwreck of Religion by Popery; Protestant Soup; Daniel O'Connell in Purgatory; Old Father Dan, and a host of others'.

Leitch supplemented his income by selling 'many a nic-nack bargain— such as laces 1d. a dozen, soap 1d. a cake, ink 1d. a bottle; Braces 1d. a pair, Bell's matches one farthing a box. The Poet's Blacking is rich with Glittering grandeur—to be had only in the Box for one halfpenny a packet. Raffle Tickets printed by the Poet for 1s. a hundred' as well as doing a variety of other printing jobs. David Murray visited the Poet's Box as a university student in the period 1857-1865 to commission songs for rectorial candidates, at a cost of 2s. 6d. a time.[32] Leitch was obliging, and would do a number of things for the right payment; he attempted to strangle Outram's nascent *Evening Times* in 1878 by advertising large quantities of waste copies of it, to destroy the faith of its paying advertisers.[33]

Leitch was however very generous towards different groups of workers on strike. In 1851 he supported the struggle of the clothlappers or calendarmen for a ten-hour day, by publishing a song in the third week of their strike.

> The clothlappers agreed to strike
> To work from six to six, you see
> A nobler or a juster cause
> To be required there could not be

To this was added the invitation that 'Any clothlapper who may be gifted with the muse, will be kindly dealt with by calling at the Poet's Box. .

The Poet's Yankee Press is at all times ready to put up a good thing'. As the strike dragged on, he was offered 'The Calendarmen of Glasgow's Song on Liberty' written by union members. 'The Poet at once hands it over to his Yankee Press, and that little honourable machine will do its duty by throwing off as many copies as will supply the wants of the Clothlappers. The Poet would advise the Committee and every member of the Calendarmen Society to circulate this song far and near. Let them send it to Paisley, Manchester, London and America. Ay, and every place they know a calendar is set up. Let them all see for what reason they are out on strike.'

In May 1857 the shoemakers received similar support with a song.

> Come all you gallant shoemakers wherever you may be
> I pray you give attention and listen unto me
> In the year of fifty seven boys, when springtime it came round
> We vowed to raise our wages in famous Glasgow town

A vote was then taken, likewise a show of hands
All by our loyal chairman, who waited our commands
The committee did smile in glee, and master's men did frown
For all the men were ready there in famous Glasgow town
Oh! If that our employers had only heard the cheers
It should have broke their hears my boys and caused them
to shed tears
To think that we would all unite whom they thought to down
But the journeymen are all true flints in famous Glasgow town.

Surprisingly few trade union songs and broadsheets have survived for Glasgow, which is probably due more to the predilections of the later collectors than a reflection on the original production, although ephemeral literature survives for the 1820 Rising and different weavers', cotton spinners' and miners' strikes. Operatives seem to have turned their hands to verse too, the best known example in this case being the weaver Alexander Rodger (b.1784) who became a local celebrity on account of his poetry and his involvement with various radical newspapers including *The Spirit of the Union* and the *Reformer's Gazette*.[34]

James Lindsay Junior, a stationer, printer and bookseller similar to Leitch, but operating on a much larger scale with three different premises in the city between the years 1848 and 1909, published some political songs. In the depression of 1853, for example, he published 'Scotland's Stagnation, or Where is all the Money gone?' which had this chorus:

Tens of thousands out of work, what will the country come to?
I cannot think says every one, where all the trade is gone to
I wonder where the trade has gone says Jack to Jenny Harding
Laddies used to spend half a crown, but now can't spend a farthing
The flesher cannot sell his fat, the miller's bags are dusty
The baker says his penny rolls are getting stale and musty
The chimney sweeps are all discharged, the barbers and the tailors
12,000 snobs are out of work, and a million navigators.[35]

It is unfortunate that so little is known about the social status and political leanings of the various ballad publishers. David Murray notes that William Love, who kept a 'Stall of Science' similar to the Poet's Box was one of the early socialists in Glasgow, and married a daughter of Alexander Campbell (1796-1870) the great pioneer of co-operation.[36] Little of Love's works seems to have survived however.

The ballad and broadside writers and publishers were crucially important in the study of leisure activities because they touched every facet of the subject, providing detailed information about pastimes which because of their transitory or illicit nature, were not reported elsewhere. 'Senex' for example describes ritualised street battles among different groups of adult men using stones, which were apparently popular in the summer evenings at the beginning of the nineteenth century.[37] It is evident from ballads such as 'Barrowfield Brig' (second issue of 10,000 copies since 14 April 1855) and the 'Battle o' Ruglen' (1874) which describe similar mêlées, that brawls of this nature and stories about them were periodically popular.[38]

The broadsides are the chief source for the early history of boxing. This sport seems to have been viewed with revulsion and disgust by all who wrote about it, from the broadside writers of the early 19th century to John S. Clarke, who in 1929 wanted to keep it out of the Kelvin Hall. Bare-fist fighting was undoubtedly brutal; the match between Glasgow boxers Brown and Paton fought on Eaglesham Moor on 4 February 1825 went 44 rounds and was attended by 'pugilists, dogfighters, cock fighters, dandy bakers and loungers . . . highly pleased with the beastly scene they had been witnessing'.[39]

Such matches were the occasion of extensive betting. The writer describing the match between Scotch Robinson and Yorkshire Robinson on 1 December 1829 claimed that 'Since the battle was first talked of, all the tap rooms in Glasgow and even better places of resort have been familiar with their names . . . The colonists of Bridgegate, those bowers of innocence and ease never closed an eye on Monday night, or if they did, it was only to think on the great battle. Wagers of all sorts and sizes from one pound to ten . . . flew round at the usual places of resort'. In the morning 'Those who had to pad the hoof were off early, and chaises, noddies, carts etc. were occasionally departing till 10'clock, all filled with amateurs and professionals of every description'.[40] On this occasion, the fight took place 'half way between Edinburgh and Glasgow' out of reach of authority. There was no fixed place for these great prize fights, which might take place 'in a field near Dunoon', 'in a field near Falkirk' or at some other equally remote place for fear of reprisals.

Pugilism had a bad reputation. John Henry Alexander tried to destroy his rival's reputation as a theatre manager by accusing him of having held pugilistic exhibitions and cock fights in his hall; in the 1820s and 30s a theatre manager could apparently stoop no lower. Many publicans however, ran sparring matches and kept cock and rat pits in their back courts.[41]

One of the men who helped to rescue the reputation of boxing as a sport at a later date in Glasgow was Charles Donaldson, sports writer with the *Evening Times* who in 1901 purchased the Coffin public house in Whitevale Street. The house was so named because of its size, six customers forming a crowd. Donaldson enlarged and improved the premises, turning it into a shrine to boxing, with portraits on the wall of all the known champions from James Figg (1693-1754) onwards. The Coffin became a mecca for boxers visiting the city, and Donaldson counted among his famous visitors world champion Jack Johnson who with his wife (wearing £20,000 of diamonds) came to the Coffin and danced the tango.[42] This was in 1915, by which time boxing had a large and respectable following. Although the last bare-fist fight is recorded as having taken place in 1889, boxers had been fighting with gloves under the Marquis of Queensberry rules since 1867, and the sport became a means whereby talented working-class men could escape from their environment.

IV: The Struggle of the Penny Theatres

What opportunities did the working classes have for theatre going and what was the quality of the theatrical productions in Glasgow? From 1825 until the passing of the Theatre Regulation Act in 1843, which removed the monopoly of the major or patented theatres, allowing the minor theatres to present drama, the Glasgow theatrical scene was racked with disputes, acrimony, legal actions, personal vendettas and commercial competition of a sometimes quite spectacular nature. Disputes of this type were going on in every town in Britain which had a theatre licensed under the Act of 1737. Such theatres, often known as Theatres Royal by virtue of their letters patent from the Lord Chamberlain, had a practical monopoly on performing drama. 'Drama' had a very narrow interpretation and showmen with their travelling booths were relentlessly persecuted, particularly if they seemed to be making money. The actions of the patent holders were mercilessly satirised; one theatrical magazine under the title of 'War against Wombwell and the Monkies' printed a spoof letter from John Henry Alexander to the menagerie owner, claiming

> that if a Lion do ROAR, that ROARING
> is part of the *legitimate* drama, as performed
> by myself in Dunlop Street, and if the said roar
> is responded to by the Bengal Tiger. . . it
> shall be held as DIALOGUE, and you, the
> proprietor, liable to prosecution. . . the chattering
> parrots and parroquets. . . must also be held as
> an *infringement* of MY *patent*, as also that of the
> *pantomimic* action of your infernal
> monkies. . . .[43]

John Henry Alexander's theatrical career in Glasgow began in 1825 when having failed to get the lease of the Caledonian Theatre which went to his rival Seymour, he rented the cellar and set up a rival illegal theatre. On the opening night Seymour staged 'Macbeth', while Alexander in the cellar below staged a rollicking drama adapted from Scott's 'Fair Maid of Perth'. Thus, during the dagger scene above, a noisy battle scene was enacted below, with clashing of swords, banging of drums, and shouts of soldiery accompanied by clouds of 'blue fire' which seeped through to ruin the performance above. This competition ensured that both theatres had full audiences, coming to enjoy the competition between the two theatres, rather than the respective plays.[44]

Seymour was not the best of theatre managers however. He had a bad reputation for failing to pay his actors on time, and when this happened once too often, the entire cast of his production of *Aladdin* went on strike in the middle of the play. Seymour hastily went round the boxes in the interval recruiting volunteers to take their place. This effort resulted in chaos as the actors joined the audience and shouted for their pay.[45]

When, after the burning of his Queen Street Theatre in 1829, Seymour left Glasgow and his unpaid debts, Alexander purchased the letters patent and hence the monopoly of the 'legitimate drama' in the city. This monopoly he guarded jealously through the law courts and with a war of words issued against his opponents, some of whom had been his employees. When some dared to address the Lord Provost and town council on the subject of free trade theatre for the amusement of 'the labouring man and his wife and little family dressed out in the best clothes' who preferred 'productions full of sound and fury, broad sword combats, pistol shooting, doses of blue fire, poisoned cups and daggers, pugilistic exhibitions and suppings full of horror', Alexander issued a scathing twelve page pamphlet against the 'free trade polyartists'.[46]

There was no shortage of opponents to the theatrical monopoly in Glasgow in this lengthy literary war. Magazines such as *The Pepperbox* seem to have been produced with the sole aim of criticising Alexander or satirising his attitudes. When Alexander had the penny showman David Prince Miller imprisoned in 1842, Miller published his own story in twelve parts, recounting in detail how he and the other showmen had been persecuted.[47]

Miller won a great deal of public sympathy for the cause of the penny theatre showmen, and the popularity and success of their shows posed a very real economic threat to Alexander and the legitimate theatre. Showmen like Miller came to Glasgow at the time of the Fair and the New Year holidays with their portable canvas-roofed wooden booths. These were often quite sophisticated internally, with stage, pit and gallery and some could seat between 1,000 and 2,000 people. Miller had come to Glasgow first in 1839, and returned for the Fair of 1840 with his greatly-improved 'Sans Pareil Pavilion'. According to the evidence given in the Court of

Justiciary during his prosecution, the Sans Pareil seated between 1,000 and 1,200 people, and Miller held at least two or three performances per day at only a penny admission. The result was that 'every idle young man and woman who could beg, borrow or steal this small piece of currency' visited the theatre. Theatres such as his

> held out from their cheapness, great inducement to the lower orders to attend them, and are calculated, from the mode in which they are carried on, to do anything rather than promote the moral welfare of the community.[48]

The prosecution of John Henry Anderson (1814-1901), the magician and 'Wizard of the North' tells a similar story. His booth of 1841 could accommodate 800-1,000 persons, had stage, side wings, orchestra, boxes, pit and gallery, and drew away the audiences from the Theatre Royal, according to Alexander's own admission.

> The performances, it may be added, are not less detrimental to public morals. . . and the extreme cheapness of them (. . . being not more than one penny) serving to draw large numbers of the young into a vortex of temptation.[49]

Usually, when a showman was prosecuted by a patent holder for performing drama, the showman did his best to change the act into a different type of performance, often substituting an animal or equestrian act for the sake of peace. Miller made no such pretence and made a stand for penny performances for the working classes. Shakespeare was a speciality:

> We performed Richard the Third twenty seven times in seven hours. Indeed, it was our boast to the crowd that we excelled in our art, for at any theatre in the Kingdom it would occupy fully two hours and a half. . . whereas we could perform it in twenty minutes.

There is no doubt that public sympathy in Glasgow was on the side of the prosecuted showmen, who milked it for all they could. When two other showmen, Mumford and Dupain, were cited to appear in court in 1842, Dupain came straight from his wife's funeral in his mourning clothes, the crape streamers from his hat almost sweeping the floor, knelt at Alexander's feet, tore open his shirt and asked Alexander to stab him to the heart.[50]

The Theatre Regulation Act of 1843 put paid to such theatricals, and the penny theatres were allowed to flourish. Miller built the Adelphi in Jail Square and had it licensed in 1843, while John Henry Anderson built the lavish City Theatre nearby in 1845, accommodating 5,000 people and flying a flag proclaiming 'Alexander defeated. The Wizard Triumphant'.

It should not be imagined however that Alexander's Theatre Royal catered only for the middle classes. As the evidence of the various prosecutions show, Alexander and the showmen were fighting for the same au-

diences and were often staging the same plays. The Gods of the Theatre
Royal was largely patronised by the working classes and the 65 people who
were tragically killed on a Saturday night in July 1849, due to a false fire
alarm and panic, were 'young lads and girls of the poorer class attracted
by the low prices'.[51]

Nonetheless, it was the wooden penny theatres of the Saltmarket/Jail
Square area which had the reputation of being unsafe and unsavoury.
They were in general terms not held in high regard except by those who
patronised them. In September 1845, 60,000 people signed a petition to
get rid of the theatre and booths as an encroachment on the Green.[52]
In November 1845 Anderson's City Theatre was destroyed by fire, almost
taking its neighbours with it. In November 1848 Miller's Adelphi was
burned to the ground.[53] The less permanent structures were discouraged,
and in 1870 Glasgow Town Council decided that the site of the shows be
moved from Saltmarket and Glasgow Green east to Vinegarhill.

Those among the middle classes who lived and worked in the neigh-
bourhood rejoiced at the move. J.F.S. Gordon, the minister of the Episcopal Chapel situated next to the Queen's Theatre in Greendyke Street,
recalled that

> Penny Theatres, half darkened, were crammed every half hour from 10 till
> 10, with unkept Hizzies, with whom every filthy Joke and Liberty taken—
> while coarse Puns and Waggery from the Stage fortified the Depravity
> which was being carried out. Shameless, pimple-skinned Jades displayed
> themselves half nude, and capered and kicked up behind and before—ran
> upon their toes and stood and spinned upon one leg; Limmers that, when
> freed of their Rouge and Make up, as Burns said 'would spean a Foal'.
> . . every Philanthropist cannot but exult in the final annihilation of the
> Shows at the Glasgow Fair, and laud *Sic transit gloria mundi*.[54]

Apart from the commercial theatres there was a certain amount of independent working-class interest in theatrical performances. Mackintosh,
who worked as a theatre props man and who wrote under the pseudonym
'Old Stager', describes the numerous 'spouting clubs' which were common
in Glasgow in the 1820s. These amateur dramatic societies staged their
own plays, and in the production of Hamlet performed by Mackintosh's
club in the 1820s, the cast was headed by William McCulloch, a weaver
from Stevenson Street, Calton, who was reckoned to be the best actor and
familiar with all the chief stage parts. It also included Alexander Eadie,
a bookbinder, John Ferguson, a letterpress printer, J. Russell, a plasterer,
Alex Burnet, 'a dandy little bootmaker who gradually declined into a
grimy, black thumbed cobbler' and D. McDonald, a typefounder. Their
hall in London Street was in the loft of an old tan works and accessible by
a wooden ladder-type stair, and the audience and players were sometimes

trapped when the roughs from the Saltmarket removed the ladder and threw it into the nearby Molendinar Burn.[55]

V: The Glasgow Fair

The Glasgow Fair has always been the chief date in the city's leisure calendar. The time of the Fair, in mid-July at the feast of Sts. Peter and Paul, was established in mediaeval times, and has been adhered to ever since. In origin it was a trade fair, and before it was moved from the Stockwell Gate to the Saltmarket at the High Court, it was noted as being quite rural in character, similar to the 'Tryst of Falkirk'. After the re-siting of the Cattle Market at Graham Square and the removal of the livestock, the Fair, sited in front of the High Court from 1820, became quite urban and directed towards entertainment purposes only, 'chiefly got up for the budding Beauties of our Spinning and Weaving factories and for their admiring swains of the Engineering Shop or Print Work'.[56] The word used most often by commentators of the period when describing it is 'Saturnalian'.

The other great time of celebration was the New Year. This holiday originated in the fifteenth century when the twenty day Yule or St Mungo's fair was established for the period prior to 13 January, the Feast of St Mungo.[57] By the mid-nineteenth century it had been reduced to a day or two celebrated in blind drunkenness by those who could afford it, or anticipated with fear and apprehension by those in the 'submerged tenth' who could not afford to give up their sweated labour for the holiday period. Other occasions such as the King's Birthday, celebrated in the eighteenth and early-nineteenth centuries by a military parade on the Green, a bonfire at the Cross and sometimes a riot thereafter,[58] or Empire Day, established in the late-nineteenth century, were more transitory.

The Fair attracted travelling showmen, circuses and freak shows from all over Britain with a wonderful variety of acts, which alone could fill a book. There was always a tendency for commentators to be sentimental about the Fair—the writer in the *Glasgow Herald* in 1840 expressed the regret that the Fair was not so good as it had been in the old days. The Giantess in 1840 was 'not so noble, and coarser spoken' and the usual Punch and Judy was absent.[59]

Even in the 1820s, showmen came from far and wide to attend the Fair. The juggler Patrick Feeney (1800-1883) who was never absent from the Glasgow Fair, recalled seeing in the 1820s Pollito's wild beasts, Antony Powell's Circus, Ord's Circus, Kit Newsome's Circus, and the Cardonis, an Italian family who specialised in juggling and who brought the first Punch and Judy show to Glasgow.[60] Above all, however, were the freak shows.

The freak and side shows were a constant feature not only of the Fair, but at every other time of the year as well. To make a living from such shows, the proprietors had to travel the length and breadth of Europe exhibiting wherever they could get a paying audience. Consequently, different showmen found their way to Glasgow at odd times. Robert Reid (1773-1865) left a detailed and absorbing account of the shows which he personally witnessed, in the period 1783-1800, as well as mentioning earlier shows which had had an impact. He took a delight in seeing the various learned pigs, dogs and horses, in comparing the Irish Giants, stroking the heads of the two-headed calf and meeting the armless lady from Newfoundland, who could sew and cut watch-papers using her toes. He felt revulsion at the 'three-monstrous craws' who were exhibited for their terrible deformities, and some sorrow for the polar bear chained beside its tin bath and roaring in distress.

In Reid's time there was no fixed exhibition venue. The showmen hired a room in a public house, coffee house or auction room, and for performances the various dancing halls used by the middle classes, such as Fraser's in King Street, or the hall above Weigh House. Admission was usually a shilling, which was very expensive, but often a double pricing system was advertised, servants and tradespeople being admitted for sixpence. Such shows were always a big attraction, and there is no doubt that working-class people patronised them as much as the 'ladies and gentlemen' did, although Reid's story about the country wife from Pollokshaws paying her admission money then killing the main performer in the flea circus of 1763 sounds apocryphal.[61]

Many of these shows were run by crooks or people down in their luck. David Prince Miller, who became a travelling showman in the 1830s, describes how he impersonated a Black Giantess, wearing a fantastic costume of feathers and beads. He was discovered when the male customers demanded kisses and the make up came off, but the joke was taken in good part by all concerned.[62]

Another, less amusing show with which he travelled was the 'Pig Faced Lady'; the unfortunate creature was a bear with its face shaved and strapped in a sitting position. His favourite show however was 'Bosjesman', a group of 'savages' from Africa. He persuaded their owner to exhibit them at the Glasgow Fair of 1846 for a penny admission. The owner objected to the low price, but Miller knew the ways of the Glasgow Fair; 96,000 persons visited the show in thirteen days. The hardened

Glasgow audience was highly sceptical—some thought that the Bosjes-mans were Irishmen, or sweeps or Paisley weavers dressed up, and the broadside writers had a field day making up stories to that effect.

Miller, who had again fallen on hard times through the loss of his Adelphi Theatre by fire in 1848, had to try to build his career from scratch and started again at the Glasgow Fair as a conjurer. He was deeply embarrassed but grateful for the support and sympathy which he received:

> . . . however I might astonish the unsophisticated at a country fair, the Glasgow 'chappee's' are not so easily deceived, for they have seen so much of the same sort of thing these last ten years that I question if there is a lad above ten years of age who has accustomed himself to witness the conjuring exhibitions, but what is himself an amateur . . . I am also perfectly aware that if any other person had attempted the same exhibition in Glasgow that he and his show would probably soon have found their way into the Clyde, which winds its way by the side of the fairground.[63]

The proliferation of the penny theatres at the time of the Fair has been mentioned already. It was on account of the siting of the Fair at the foot of the Saltmarket that this street and its surrounding district became for a generation the permanent entertainment centre for Glasgow's working classes. The Saltmarket was the home of the singing saloons or free-and-easies, the fore-runners of the modern music hall, and from time to time these saloons would attain a transitory reputation for the quality of their performances. Among others, the Shakespeare, the Oddfellows and the Sir Walter Scott flourished in the 1840s and 50s.

The free-and-easy was a room in a public house, with a platform and piano at one end. The proceedings were conducted by a chairman, who could also sing and perform until the volunteers came forward. Some of these saloons, like the one described by 'Shadow' were 'beautifully fitted up, finely painted and brilliantly illuminated'.[64] Admission was usually the price of a drink, and the customers sat on long wooden benches at tables. While halls like the Shakespeare had star performers, the majority of the others relied on voluntary vocal contributions.

The quality and content of material used in these halls can be judged from the large number of set pieces and songs printed by stationers such as Leitch to promote the performer, the saloon or both. Leitch seems to have had a good relationship with the singers from the Shakespeare and the Oddfellows saloons. The preface to 'Happy Go Lucky' issued in January 1855 is typical of many:

> The Poet feels great pleasure in being able to lay before the public another of Mr. Charles Watson's splendid productions. Mr. Watson's peculiar and original style of singing this song is certainly almost without parallel. The *furor* which he has created in this city since he came is certainly

no less than what he justly merits, and no more than what an intelligent public justly owe. All who have not heard Mr. Watson ought to go immediately to the Shakespeare Saloon, as they will certainly get a great treat. 'Happy Go Lucky' is one of Mr. W's own productions, and cannot be too highly prized. Copies of it can only be had in the Poet's Box.[65]

Walter Freer, manager of Glasgow Corporation Halls from 1890, was familiar with the old singing saloons of the Saltmarket in his youth. Later, he looked back in amazement at how well these 'extraordinarily crude and rowdy entertainment parlours' were patronised. He describes how Hughie Leggat, a singer in the Britannia Music Hall in Trongate when booed off the stage for boring an audience with the same old song would cunningly switch to 'The Puirhoose'. This was a song and recitation number which contained a highly colourful and comical description of the poorhouse, the singer playing the part of a pauper, and it never failed to win an audience. 'This sort of stuff was received with shrieks of laughter and vociferous applause. Perhaps it was because we were all wretchedly poor ourselves and felt a certain comfort in knowing that some folks were even not so well off as we were.'[66]

An equally big hit in the Britannia Music Hall in Trongate at that time was N.C. Bostock's 'Coal Jock':

> I can whustle, I can sing
> I can dance the Heilan' fling
> I can hump awa' a basket or a poke
> I can drink a pint o' yill
> Frae that tae half a gill
> An' that's aboot the size o' Coal Jock.

One of W.F. Frame's popular early numbers was 'The Pawn Shop in Bleezes', while the last proprietor of the Shakespeare Saloon had a smash hit song of the same genre, entitled 'The Lovely Flea'.[67] Thus, all of the un-welcome aspects of working-class life—fleas, pawnshops, the poorhouse—were wrung for a laugh. Drink was almost universally celebrated for most of these songs were written for performance in the free-and-easy in the company of drink, and were always better appreciated after the audience had had a good drink.

Although licensing legislation and the temperance movement got rid of the free-and-easies by 1900, such establishments were still flourishing in the early 1870s. An investigator from the *North British Daily Mail*, writing articles on 'The Dark Side of Glasgow', discovered 19 such estab-lishments within a five minute walk of Glasgow Cross. Those which he visited had mainly young males aged between 16 and 22 in their audience, although some places had a scattering of women. The songs sung were mainly sentimental— 'Annie Laurie', 'Maggie May', 'Mother, kiss me in my dreams' and the like, interspersed with the occasional clog dance. In one establishment the song being sung was so indecent that the investigator was compelled to leave, and in other establishments, when fighting was about to break out, the landlord had always to threaten to screw down the gas to restore order. The investigator reckoned that there would be twice as many as the 19 places he had discovered on his casual visit, and that each of them held between 100 and 150 persons at a time.

Other investigators working for the *North British Daily Mail* also looked at the shebeens and brothels, estimating that in the old city centre district (King Street, Goosedubbs, Bridgegate, Princes Street, Gallowgate, High Street, and Trongate from King Street to Saltmarket) there were 200 brothels and some 150 shebeens. The latter were divided between 'respectable' shebeens (where only the licensing law was broken), disreputable shebeens which were used as a base for criminal fraternity, and 'wee shebeens' 'on the stair head, where a drunken old hag in a greasy mutch with trembling hands pours out from her black bottle a compound of whisky and methylated spirits, a glass of which being swigged off in the dark and the money paid, the recipient staggers down the stairs and out again to the streets'. These do not seem to have been much different from the establishments visited by 'Shadow' in 1858, except for the complex system of scouts and lookouts employed 1871 to warn against the police.

Yet another investigation revealed for the *North British Daily Mail* a surprising factor:

> Glasgow literally swarms with cheap, low dancing places, where the youths of both sexes among the lower ranks of society meet regularly once or twice a week to dance, drink and enjoy themselves . . . these dancing parties are got up on the club system. A number of lads in a factory or mill club together to hire a room from ninepence to one and sixpence a night, if possible in a public house, if not in any building where a room can be had cheaply. They meet . . . every Friday and each brings a partner or partners with them. The music is, if possible, for economic reasons supplied by themselves, there being generally one or two in the society able to play the violin, or failing that the flute or whistle. I have even known cases where a jews harp or trump was the only instrument, and one in which a rustic Orpheus discoursed dance music with his lips alone.

The investigator attended several of these dances. The first he visited was held in a long, dark, low-roofed room in the Gorbals lit by eight candles, and there were a dozen couples dancing. At another venue, the walls were decked out in greenery, and the shoemaking and tailoring apprentices were dancing reels, quadrilles, polkas, petronellas, The Floors o' Edinburgh and Torriburn Lassies with the shop girls, dressed in their best clothes. A stock of drink was always laid in, with soft drinks for the girls, and the investigator was astonished by the decorum with which these dances were run and the good conduct and friendliness of the dancers. He came to the conclusion that 'cheap dancing clubs are among the most common means of enjoyment which obtain with the poorer classes' and 'that in four out of six cases, there was nothing to give the most fastidious of persons any cause for complaint'.[68]

It is strange that in view of the obvious demand for dance halls, these were not organised in Glasgow on a commercial basis until after the Great War. The Glasgow photographer John Urie, looking back to the 1830s, recalled that during the Fair there was to be seen from nearly every window in the Saltmarket a notice to the effect that 'penny reels' might be had within. 'This meant that for this humble sum a dance might be engaged in, and the householders in the main thoroughfare made a good deal of money by allowing the lads and lasses who paid their pennies to dance to the music of a wheezy concertina or a squeaky fiddle.'[69]

VI: Cleaning up the Amusements

When the Glasgow Fair and its shows were moved from Glasgow Green, Jail Square and the foot of Saltmarket to a site at Vinegarhill in 1870, J.F.S. Gordon, the minister of St Andrews-by-the-Green Episcopal Church heaved a sigh of relief. For 25 years he had remonstrated against the

> woeful scenes of Drunkenness, Immorality, Thefts, Fights and general Mischief. . . the deafening Shoutings and Clangour which issued from the manifold Comedians, Tragedians, Clowns, Drums, Brazen Trumpets and all kinds of music rendered the whole Scene a shocking Babel. Jugglers, Thimble riggers, Card-sharpers and all the Tramps in the three Kingdoms looked forward to the Glasgow Fair.

The last public hanging in front of the Jail took place in 1865, and Gordon rejoiced that 'the Public Hangings and the Shows have been almost simultaneously Gibbeted'.[70]

The removal of the Fair from the entertainment centre it had nourished for fifty years was part of the grand urban renewal programme initiated by the City Improvement Trust Act of 1866, designed to rid the inner city of its pestilent slums. After the wholesale demolition and by the time the last new City Improvement Trust tenement was built in Saltmarket in 1894, none of the old free-and-easies had survived. The Glasgow Corporation resolution of 1890 to allow no licensed premises on Corporation property ensured that none of the old establishments could come back to re-infest the new buildings.

The free-and-easies had always given great cause for concern. Both Walter Freer, the manager of the Corporation Halls, and W.F. Frame, the music hall artist who became an international star, testified to the powerful attractions of the free-and-easies, for both had frequented them as boys, drawn by the music and the happy atmosphere. That both of them spent all of their adult lives working in the cause of temperance exemplifies the cultural change which the different forces of temperance opinion had wrought in the city between the 1840s and the end of the century.

Temperance principles were first introduced into Glasgow in 1829, and a strong radical temperance movement grew and developed, taking on many different forms and branching out in many different directions. It was embraced by Chartists, Co-operators, Liberals and Socialists wholeheartedly. Many labour leaders, including Keir Hardie, Willie Gallacher and David Kirkwood got their first political education in a Good Templar Lodge which on principle taught working men how to conduct meetings and take minutes. By 1890, when the resolution that no more licensed premises would be allowed on Corporation property was passed, temperance councillors and temperance opinion predominated in the city.

From the beginning the temperance elements worked on the counter-attraction principle. The free-and-easies and their drinking songs were popular, so a mass of temperance songs were written and printed in the same fashion. Some, such as 'The Drunkard's Raggit Wean' and 'Whisky's Awa' were real tear-jerkers, and others, such as 'The Wild Rover' so successful that a later generation could re-adopt them as drinking songs.

Tee-total concerts, similar to the free-and-easies, but replacing the drink with tea and pastry, were organised on a wide scale. These were commonly known as 'the bursts' from the practice of blowing up and bursting the pastry bags by way of applause.[71] The most successful of these concerts were the City Hall Saturday evening concerts, run by the Glasgow Abstainers' Union from 1854 to 1914 without a break. The professed aim of the concerts was to 'counteract the pernicious influence of the drinking and singing saloons, and to afford amusement to those who had been wont to seek it amidst scenes of vice and dissipation'.[72] These concerts quickly became an institution in the city, and people like Freer and Frame, who had been attracted to the drinking halls, were won over. The Abstainers' Union encouraged and provided musical training; they picked up Helen Kirk, singing on a street corner in 1858, and gave her two years training before launching her on their platforms as a star.[73] From the first they set out to bring the best musical performers to Glasgow, and they regularly hired opera stars of international fame, as well as the best performers from the British music halls.

The Abstainers' Union employed the professionals. Amateur talent found its outlets on the stages of the Good Templars Harmonic Asociation, the musical organisation which sprang from Good Templary in 1872. While the Abstainers' Union filled the City Halls, the Good Templars ran their concerts from the Bridgeton Temperance Institute in James Street, the Albion Hall in College Street and the Wellington Palace in Gorbals, on successive evenings entertaining some 4,000 at a time. Although they too hired well-known names, they ran regular competitions and As-You-Please sessions to discover new talent, and it was generally acknowledged that their concerts were the best launching platforms for a musical or stage career. Harry Lauder started his career in a Good Templars Saturday night competition, although he was disqualified for copying W.F. Frame's act when original material only was the rule.[74] In addition to these formal concerts, many informal entertainment sessions were held by different Templar Lodges and other temperance organisations on a weekly basis and from time to time new organisations, such as the Glasgow Temperance Crusaders (established 1910)[75] were spawned, adding variety to the available entertainments.

Some of the old theatre buildings on the edge of Glasgow Green survived, but were given over to other purposes. Parry's theatre, next to the Episcopal church in Greendyke Street, was bought over as a centre for mission work in 1860, and it was from here that W.M. Miller, a working man, started choral singing for the working classes, introducing the tonic sol-fa to Glasgow. Walter Freer, who attended the classes, later described how the hall was packed to capacity with boys and girls who had done a heavy day's work, and who next morning would go to work singing in parts before their 6 am start.[76]

Again, as part of the cleaning-up process, Mumford's Theatre was taken over as a clothes market, and the second hand clothing trade—Paddy's Market—was municipalised by the opening of an additional covered clothes market in Greendyke Street, controlled by Glasgow Corporation, in 1875.[77] Until then trading in rags had been done in the street, in the open, and usually in the Bridgegate area where Paddy's Market was a recognisable entity.

Another development which was very important at this time was the establishment of the Glasgow United Evangelistic Association, following on the great Moody and Sankey revival of 1874, when an evangelical tent of theatre proportions was erected on Glasgow Green. From this the Tent Hall in nearby Steel Street, Saltmarket was built, the informal headquarters of a loose network of mission halls which looked after the needs of the poor and provided free Christian-orientated entertainments in the form of tea meetings, lantern lectures, Pleasant Sunday Afternoons and Fresh Air Fortnights.

Interest in choral singing was sharpened by the formation of the Glasgow Choral Union, which from 1862 held concerts in the Cathedral. The presence of musical instruments in a Presbyterian church was always a source of criticism, and a contemporary observer commented on the

> infant organ near
> Wi' soun' sae dep and hollow
> The thin end o' the wedge they say
> For Popery to follow.[78]

The presence of an organ during the service was anathema in most Glasgow Presbyterian churches until the mid-1870s. Freer describes how Ira D. Sankey outwitted the Session of Trinity Free Church, playing an organ, singing at the top of his voice, and breaking down their resistance.[79] The importance attached to music and singing by Moody and Sankey coloured the evangelical revival and gave the mission halls the edge over the established churches as far as the working classes were concerned. Beautiful singing combined with colourful lantern slides, whether on its own or as part of a burst, was an irresistable attraction, and in the two decades before the Great War, this kind of entertainment in the mission halls, at the Band of Hope, in the temperance societies and finally in the churches, became firmly established as an important facet of popular culture in Glasgow. This was true regardless of political attachment: after a lifetime's devotion to the cause of communism, Willie Gallacher could still remember with fondness the favourite temperance/evangelical lecture of his childhood, 'Buy your own cherries'. These moral stories were rarely delivered without some hymns and choruses by way of re-inforcement, and often, it was the singing which was the attraction for the audience.[80]

Naturally, it was not only religious bodies who were interested in singing. The various socialist choirs came out of this veritable tidal wave of choral singing—the Toynbee (established 1901), the Orpheus Choir (1906), the William Morris Choir, the various Clarion Choirs, the U.C.B.S. Excelsior Glee Party—and all of them shared the City Hall and Good Templar platforms. Some historians, looking at the world famous Orpheus Choir in isolation and believing its creator's contention that there was no choral tradition in Glasgow before the Orpheus, have dismissed it as an alien cultural form imposed from above and extraneous to working-class experience.[81] Technical elitism and cultural elitism should not be confused however; Hugh S. Roberton because of his high standards and discipline took the Orpheus into a class on its own. Nevertheless, the Orpheus was no oddity. It came from the mainstream of the popular culture of its time.

After the demise of the old penny theatres of the Saltmarket, a crop of new theatres and music halls was built elsewhere to meet the public demand. Some were deliberately built in the suburbs to serve the local population—the Gaiety was built at Anderston Cross, the Globe in Calton (1874), the Princess's in Gorbals (1878), and the Prince of Wales in Cowcaddens (1867). Others, such as the Royalty (Sauchiehall Street, 1879), the Princes Theatre Royal (West Nile Street, 1863), and the Gaiety (Sauchiehall Street, 1874, and later renamed the Empire) were city centre investments, aimed at the monied classes. These were later supplemented by even more splendid theatrical palaces in the early twentieth century— the Savoy (Hope Street, 1911), the Pavilion (Renfield Street, 1904), the King's (Bath Street, 1904), the Alhambra (Wellington Street, 1910), the Palace (Gorbals, 1904), the Olympia (Bridgeton Cross, 1911), and the Metropole (St George's Road, 1913).

Only two new theatres were built in the old centre of entertainment, and these were the Scotia Music Hall (Stockwell Street, 1863) and the Star Music Hall (Watson Street, off Gallowgate, 1872). Both of these in their programmes and presentation stressed their respectability, and it was the quest of the latter for respectability and popularity that led to the proprietor being bought out and having his theatre shut down. The Star suffered terrible publicity, when on 1 November 1884 there was a false fire alarm and 14 were killed in the ensuing panic, with 18 others injured.[82] Rechristened the 'New Star Theatre of Varieties for the Working Classes' the stigma seems to have remained, for in November 1892 it was opened again as the People's Palace. When the manager offered shares for sale, he was taken over by a consortium of Liberal councillors, no doubt worried by the confusion which might arise between the music hall and their own municipally funded People's Palace museum and art gallery, scheduled to open on Glasgow Green in 1898.[83]

For the entire period of its short life (1892-1897) the People's Palace music hall, like the Star and New Star before it, claimed to be a family hall of eminent respectability. No alcoholic liquors were served, and the management claimed that it was the only hall in Glasgow where no charge was made for pass out checks or transfer checks, where standing in the passages was strictly prohibited, which had ladies and gentlemen's lavatories on every floor, and where there was no extra charge for special engagements. 'The comfort and convenience of patrons is studied in a manner that is not even attempted in the higher-priced halls', claimed the programme. From time to time a portrait of Mrs Ormiston Chant of the Social Purity League who was fighting to clean up promiscuousness at the Empire Theatre in London, was featured on the programme, with the assurance that 'The People's Palace in Glasgow is where you can take your family!'.[84]

Although the free-and-easies had been eliminated by demolition and counter-attraction, and although the theatre operated in more sophisticated surroundings, some of the older amusements did not change. The freak shows, if anything, became more numerous with lobster clawed ladies, elephant men, giants and humans and animals with all manner of deformities. These were regularly exhibited in Trongate and Argyle Street in the waxworks there—the Wonderland, run by Herbert Crouch at 137 Argyle Street, Fell's Waxworks at 101 Trongate, Macleod's at 151 Trongate and Pickard's Panopticon at 115 Trongate, incorporating the Old Britannia Music Hall. There was no outcry or protest against this. Even the radical newspaper *Forward*, which could raise socialist objections to zoos, took an illustrated advertisement from Pickard for the Bear Woman, 'the most curious freak on earth'.[85] The last of the waxworks with its freak shows died out only in the 1940s.

Nevertheless, time and the development of the railways and river traffic brought greater choice to the working classes of Glasgow in the matter of their recreation at the time of the Fair. By 1820 day trips to Loch Lomond were possible. By 1844 the competition between steamers on Loch Lomond was such that it was possible to sail from Balloch to the head of the loch and back for sixpence steerage.

During the Glasgow Fair of 1850 an enterprising company offered a single-day excursion to Ireland and back. During the 1851 Fair, David Hutcheson & Co ran cheap excursions 'in order to afford the operative classes and others an opportunity of viewing the Western Highlands and Islands' with a three-day sail priced at 10 shillings or 12 shillings and sixpence for a married couple.[86]

The great goal of the Glasgow artisan on holiday, however, was the resorts 'doon the watter' at Rothesay, Dunoon and Millport. Rothesay was changed from a sleepy backwater into a bustling holiday resort, and the effect of the steamer and the holiday trade can be seen in the development of Rothesay's harbour to accommodate it from 1824 onwards.[87] Although many of the steamers carried day trippers, even by 1833, visitors could find accommodation in half of the 600 houses in Rothesay.[88]

By the time the Glasgow Fair was moved in 1870, going for a sail 'doon the watter' was so much a part of the working-class holiday experience that only the very poorest would spend the entire Fair period in Glasgow. Even so, the various mission halls and temperance organisations were active in organising day trips by train or steamer, and some of the well-established bodies had Clyde coast holiday or convalescent homes of their own to which deserving cases could be sent. The annual exodus 'doon the watter' was so much the custom that in the years prior to 1914, even the Glasgow suffragettes moved to Dunoon and Rothesay for July and August to conduct their campaigns.

The custom of going on steam boat trips became associated so much with heavy drinking that to describe a Glasgow man as 'steamboats' or 'steaming' was to denote his state of intoxication. The temperance reformers inevitably launched their counter-attraction, and the tee-total paddle steamer the 'Ivanhoe' began her long career in 1880. The venture was highly successful and according to a contemporary commentator, 'the running of the Ivanhoe was the most practical and effective temperance service ever preached'. Her evening and moonlight cruises, free from drunkenness and rowdyism, were particularly successful, and on one occasion the company paid a pyrotechnist to mount a fireworks display on the shores of the Gareloch. The 'Ivanhoe' shared the spectacle with ten other steamers, and an estimated 10,000 individuals saw the show. Firework displays were thereafter adopted in Dunoon and Rothesay as annual events.[89]

One might have expected, given the Glasgow taste for dancing and theatricals, to have seen the development of a resort on the Clyde coast with facilities similar to those in English resorts. By 1878 for example, Blackpool Winter Gardens with its Indian Lounge and Italian Gardens boasted the magnificent Empress Ballroom, the floor of which was laid on 2,000 springs and which was reputedly the largest dance floor in the world. In 1894 Blackpool Tower with its Roof Garden, Oriental Lounge, circus, menagerie and even bigger ballroom, opened in competition with the Winter Gardens. With its additional piers, shows and circuses, Blackpool was the premier resort for the working classes of the north west of England.

This kind of intensive capital development could not and did not happen in Scotland, for the wealthy classes, merchants and industrialists had discovered the Clyde coast, staked a claim and built their holiday mansions fully fifty years before the steamers brought the working classes to this scenic paradise. There were many vested interests who wanted to see as little tourist development as possible. When Rothesay needed a tramway, the Marquis of Bute objected that 'Bute was no place for tramways'.[90]

The Rothesay Winter Gardens were not built until 1928. When the first Sunday steamer called at Garelochhead in July 1853, Sir James Colquhoun of Luss, owner of the piers and Lord Lieutenant of the County, had the piers barricaded and a number of police backed by 20 of his own men ready to do battle.[91] In Rothesay and Dunoon even the water pumps were padlocked on a Saturday night in preparation for the Sabbath day and the great unwashed from Glasgow were expected to promenade, un-refreshed, as they did at home.

The history of the resorts 'doon the watter' still await the attention of the social historian, however, and a full analysis is long overdue.

VII: The Nature of Music Halls

The content and nature of the music halls of London and the north of England have been examined and analysed by several historians, and the beer-and-Britannia Toryism of the acts which left working-class audiences content with their lot, devoid of political ambition or the desire for change, have been the subject of comment.

From the eighteenth century onwards there was considerable exchange and sharing of travelling shows, panoramas and entertainments which moved around Britain from town to town in search of new audiences. It was therefore no new phenomenon when the top music hall artists from England came to the Glasgow halls to perform on a regular basis, bringing their jingoism, Toryism, and aristocratic mateyness and leaving behind them in the streets 'that most pathetic of Glasgow sounds, an English music hall song given with a local accent'.[92] There was, however, no visible Glasgow equivalent of the Lion Comique, the swaggering Champagne Charlies and Burlington Berties, who populated the English stage. The escapist stereotype developed in urban Glasgow by Frame, the boot and soor milk boy and apprentice engineer, was the 'Bonnie Hieland Laddie', resplendent in kilt and toorie, accompanied by pipes and dispensing in-comprehensible pawky patter and springs of heather indiscriminately. This gross caricature was further developed and refined by a visit to the USA, where he took the Carnegie Hall by storm in 1898, and was subsequently copied by Lauder and others.[93]

The image of the Scotch Comic has been much more damaging and politically negative than the Lion Comique. The whole debate on 'Scotch Myths', 'the residue of fatigued romanticism and home-grown caricature which blossomed in the period before the First World War' was opened up by Barbara and Murray Grigor's exhibition and film of that name in 1981, and is still current. The Grigors examined the phenomenon mainly through the imagery of postcards, whisky and shortbread labels and tartanalia.[94] The stereotype in the music halls was developed from the same source—the novels of Sir Walter Scott.

In a recent assessment of Sir Walter Scott's influence on nineteenth century art, it was estimated that his works were used as a source of inspiration and depicted by artists more than those of any other writer, excepting Shakespeare.[95] A cursory reading of theatre bills and programmes for nineteenth century Glasgow suggests that the same was true for theatre and music hall, although such programmes need studying in detail. 'Rob Roy' was frequently played as a pantomime, and it is probably from such adaptations that the Scotch Comic stereotype of the 1880s and 90s was developed.

Another equally bizarre stereotype which at times seems to have dominated in the Glasgow music halls was the Negro Minstrel. At the Fair of 1850, the Sir Walter Scott Saloon in Saltmarket had as its attraction 'a *rara columba* in the person of a female Ethiopian Serenader, whose performances are worth witnessing as much for their intrinsic merit as their novelty'.[96] By the 1860s, however, the blacked-up Negro Minstrel had a regular slot on most music programmes. The African Opera Troup who appeared at the City Hall singing 'refined negro music' on 22 and 29 December 1860 had a fairly typical repertoire:

> A little log hut in old Virginny
> There was a darkey came from Guinea
> Old massa kick him very little
> Give him plenty of work and whittle
> Old massa Jim was a clever old body
> Every day he drinks his toddy
> And when de sun sinks in de ribber
> He stops de work to rest dis nigger.[97]

By the 1890s there was scarcely a popular concert held without such a performance. During the twenty-ninth season of concerts held by the Good Templars Harmonic Association in 1898-9, only two of the 32 concerts did not have Negro Minstrels. The acts included J.A. Wilson, the Black Oracle, Great Negro Comedian, Dick Andrews, the Happy Darkie (Brother to the Dandy-coloured coon) an eccentric Negro comedian and Dancer J.H. Hegarty (The Black Star) Eccentric Negro Commedian Selection Whistler of the World, Tom Berrick, the Black Tit Bit, Paul Langtry, the Black Beauty and Incomparable Negroistic Entertainer, Polly Heath, Coon Songstress and Excelsior All-Round Dancer, Dan Leeson the Great Negro Comedian and Pedestal Dancer and James Hewson, Famous Electric Musical Negro Comedian.[98] It was perhaps not surprising when in 1914 a real black man appeared on an east-end variety stage singing 'Mammy, Are there any Little Angels Black like Me?' he was booed off.[99]

One type of act which recurs in Glasgow music hall programmes again and again is that of the military spectacle. Often, particularly in the years prior to the Great War, it was used as the finale of a pantomime. When local people were recruited for the parts, it no doubt filled the hall. In May 1893 for example, the People's Palace music hall had on its programme 'The Gathering of the Clans Spectacle. Charming Scottish Military Spectacle in which 50 Girls of Glasgow will take part'. In October 1895 the same hall presented 'A New and Original Naval Spectacular Sketch, Rule Britannia. Careful selection of the best Glasgow Girls to be obtained who will appear as Sailors, Slaves, Marines etc'. The formula evidently worked. A month later 'The Grand Juvenile Spectacle, China and Japan, in which will appear 100 children of Glasgow' was being staged.

The People's Palace music hall boasted a programme of at least 15 acts per night. The acts during the second week of January 1893 included a boy tenor, a vocal comedian, a solo clogist, a reel and jig dancer, a humorist, pianist, polyphonist and ventriloquist and the obligatory dramatic sketch. The latter, entitled 'A Docker's Wife' is summarised in the programme:

> Incidents—meeting of the Dock Hands near the Docks—the Resolve to Strike against Oppression and Unfair Wages—the Docker's Home—Poverty versus Wealth—a desperate struggle to keep body and soul together—Abduction of the Docker's Wife—Mass Meeting—The Resolve to Strike in a Righteous Cause—A Fair Day's Wage for a Fair Day's Work—Meeting of Masters and Men—the Workmen's wrongs made right—Rescue of the Docker's Wife and Burning of the Tyrant's Mansion—Happy Denouement.[100]

The working-class patrons of the music halls and theatres in Glasgow evidently enjoyed and expected contemporary and local references to current events and to themselves, preferably in a winning light. This is particularly noticeable in the pantomime scripts of the Royal Princess's theatre in Gorbals, where the scriptwriters had it down to a fine art. In the 1880 'Babes in the Wood' pantomime for example, the opening scene is on the banks of the Clyde where Vulcan is berating the shipbuilders for building Cunarders, paddle steamers and ships of trade and pleasure, and is trying to bribe them to fill the holds of the Czar of Russia's yacht, the 'Livadia' (then on the stocks at Fairfield's) with nitroglycerine to destroy it and implicate the nihilists. Local references are numerous, and here and there specific allusions are slipped in.

A character describes the improvements in the city:

> Oh! The improvements man, would make you stare
> The Railway Stations y'nce sae sma' and mean
> Are noo as grand as ony tae be seen
> St. Enoch, Queen Street and the Central too
> Surpassed by none, are equalled but by few.
> Sir Rupert Graball: Have Dubbs' workmen now been made content?

The Cratur: Oh aye, their seven and a half per cent
            They've got. Their masters could nae fight
            Besides, they kent quite well the men were right![101]

The cheering of the employees of Dubb's south side locomotive works and Fairfields Govan shipyard can be well imagined.

In most of the Princess's pantomime scripts between 1880 and 1914, the villains are clearly identified as capitalists, usually squires by the name of Sir Campsie Hill or Sir Ibrox Hill who want to unfairly raise the rent. Sometimes there are Glasgow fly men, like Wankey Fum in the Robinson Crusoe pantomime of 1897 who has made himself King of the Cannibals and has thrust civilisation on them in the form of a pawnshop, a prison and a poorhouse.[102] The script writers of the period—Fred Locke, Rich Waldon and Harry McKelvie—knew their audience and their expectations intimately. The end-product in this theatre at least was far removed from the middle-class and aristocratic aspirations which were constantly voiced in the London music halls and if the goals won were limited—a reduction in rent, a rise in wages, enough gold to buy a room and kitchen in Govan— they were realistic and had nothing to do with oppressing the Glasgow working man and woman.

VIII: The Coming of the Cinema

The first films were reputedly shown in Glasgow at Christmas 1895 in the Old Barracks Carnival Ground, off Gallowgate. In the early years there was little indication that cinematograph performances would become the new mass working-class entertainment. The films were exhibited by showmen and waxworks proprietors as curiosities and the flickering films did not have the pulling power and enduring qualities of the 'staunin' pictures', as the lantern slide shows were known.

Arthur Hubner, proprietor of the skating palace in Sauchiehall Street was one of the first to realise the possibilities of showing films regularly and began to include films in all his programmes in 1896. In 1897 he also acquired the Britannia Music Hall in Trongate and showed films as part of the programme there. Other music halls followed his example, and short films were included on music hall bills during the entire era of the silent film, although even by 1910 the films in some places were the most important part of the programme, the turns being mere interludes between the films.[103]

Most of the waxworks in Glasgow showed films and an advertisement published by Herbert Crouch in May 1897 shows the state of the art:

Crouch's Wonderland and Cinematograph Theatre, 137 Argyle Street. Perfect and realistic living pictures. Just added—the Corbett Fight, showing every movement during the contest. Worth half a crown to see. If you have seen other cinematographs, and they make your eyes ache, come and see ours and we assure you that you will not only be highly delighted but will recommend it to your friends. Crouch the Leader.[104]

By about 1910 going to the pictures had become an established habit in Glasgow, and in 1911, 57 houses had obtained local licences to show films.

An indication of how popular picture shows had become with the working classes can be seen in the enquiry of the Glasgow Parish Council, conducted privately in 1908 and reported in *Forward* in 1913. Alarmed that picture shows were held in darkness, councillors were sent to investigate the picture houses for themselves. One found that

The audience in all cases is representative of the lower working class and comprises all ages from the unwashed infant in its dirty mother's arms to the elderly. I have also seen a few bookies' runners in those places.

Another discovered that

There is very little to elevate the mind in the whole show and what there is is drowned by the vulgar performances. The admission charge is very low, from 1d to 6d. . . In many instances, girls aged 8 to 12 years had infants in their arms and other younger children under their charge. They were all the poorer working class children, many of them barefoot and ragged. There was a small percentage of women and most of them had infants in their arms, beshawled and bareheaded. The remainder were made up of men of the working class and young lads and lassies.

The parish councillors were most troubled by the reports that attendances and revenues at church Sunday Schools had fallen off, the children preferring to pay their pennies to the picture show rather than the Sunday School collection. For this reason one parish councillor wanted children banned from picture houses altogether, but the only by-law passed was a local one, prohibiting children under 14 from being in a picture house after 9.30 pm, unless accompanied by an adult.[105]

When almost every theatre in Glasgow had on its bills 'Infants in arms Not Admitted' the popularity of the picture houses with young mothers was high. Temperance legislation and moral censure had all but driven women out of public houses in Glasgow, and there were very few places for mothers with young children.

Another source of working-class enjoyment, which was as new as the picture house and which came in for even greater censure was the Italian ice cream parlour. The gaudy ice cream shops with their coloured marbling, painted glass and exotic proprietors must have brought a little colour and excitement into working-class lives in Glasgow in the 1890s. However, the Italians were Catholics, worked hard, and worse still, wanted to trade on Sundays. A municipal conference on Sunday trading held in Glasgow in 1900 roundly condemned the Italians, and delegates talked in terms of 'the traffic' and 'the ice-cream pestilence'.[106]

Such heavy criticism drew sharp comment from contemporary journalists. A writer in the *Bailie* laughed at the idea of entrapment 'where the chill slider has its lair, and the cool Macallum lurks'. 'In the houffs of the slider, the Macallum and the Hot Pea, illicit osculation is not impossible' proclaimed the *Forward*. 'Death to the ice cream shop partition! Working Class cuddle is no more!'

The Italians worked hard at producing new diversions for their customers. One parlour in the Gallowgate in the years before the Great War introduced a large horn gramophone and cylinder records, but this was sabotaged by the young rowdies who frequented the shop. In the reported words of the proprietor, 'Da bad boeys chippa da hoat peas ina da funnel—choadka da Harry Lauder!'. The usual form of harassment however was a Salvation Army band playing outside the shop door.[107]

Some of the Sunday Traders Defence Association literature which survives from this date is printed in both Italian and English. Although the ice cream proprietors should have been the allies of the temperance interests, their Catholicism and desire to work on Sundays alienated them. Their strongest support came from the socialists. 'For some time past, the church-going, starvation-wage-paying-employers of Glasgow have been dictating when the workers of Glasgow will eat ice cream, hot peas and fish suppers, drink lemonade and enter picture shows.' The Independent Labour Party condemned the morality which allowed alcoholic drink for the rich in their clubs on Sundays, while preventing the poor from enjoying an ice cream.[108]

IX: Municipal Provision

With the advent of the urban redevelopment of the 1870s, Glasgow Corporation took a more active part in the provision of leisure opportunities. In a densely populated industrialised city, the acquisition and maintenance of parks was seen as a priority, particularly since working-class opposition to a number of potential encroachments on the old Green had been mobilised repeatedly to drive the message home. Over a generation the opposition to mining coal on the Green, driving a canal and a railway through it, and selling off parts of it had won victory after victory, leaving the park in an unassailable position. The moving of the site of the Fair from the western edge of the Green to Vinegarhill in 1870 was seen by many as an improvement to the park.[109]

Glasgow Green was the everyday playground of the overcrowded city centre:

> It may be regarded as the central park of the city, and on every side it is surrounded with a dense population. The Green is esteemed as peculiarly the birthright and property of the people, and the east-ender watches over it with a jealous care which is almost savage in its manifestations. By uše and wont, rights and privileges have been established on the Green—as sacred in the eyes of their possessors as they are shaky from the legal point of view—and the mere moving of an orator's chair from one side of a railing to another has been known to occasion almost a riot. The Green is the Areopagus of the east-end, although it cannot be said the frequenters of its swards spend their time in hearing what is entirely new. There the fervid Orangeman denounces unweariedly the Pope and all his doings, and nightly he goes over, point by point, against his Romanist antagonist, the whole argument of the well-thumbed 'Hammersmith Discussion'; there the blatant atheist with ease bowls over the enthusiastic but simple-minded soldier of the Salvation Army; there the fiery radical pours withering scorn on the present Government; there the indignant but long-suffering ratepayer—who probably dwells in a municipal lodging-house and who pays no local rates, but who contributes liberally to Her Majesty's excise revenue—denounces the blood-sucking Town Council; there the pure minded teetotaler rails fiercely against the whisky shop; there every faddist, every crank, and every quack finds a stand and an audience. The Green is a marvellous and valuable institution, giving free course and comparatively harmless outlet to sentiment and opinions which otherwise might sometimes attain explosive force. It is a safety valve which should find a place in every great community.[110]

It was the practice of the Glasgow Green orators, as they were known, to set up their platforms on Saturday and Sunday evenings on the Green between the High Court and Nelson's Monument. Socialists such as Harry McShane have testified to the political and educational value of this open air theatre of debate.[111] Peter Walsh, who sold socialist literature there in the 1890s, described it as the 'Glasgow Green University' and pointed out that many Glasgow councillors and Members of Parliament were graduates of it.[112] Although diametrically opposed to the religious orators, the socialists had respect for those like Harry Alfred Long (1826-1905), the Orangeman and 'Glasgow Green Faith Defender', whose powers of oratory attracted massive crowds and earned him a marble portrait bust in the People's Palace. It was Long who ran the Glasgow Working Men's Evangelistic Association from the old Queen's Theatre in Greendyke Street.

All kinds of physical sports were also practised on the Green. Swimming in the Clyde was popular from the 1850s, and diving boards and changing huts were erected at Fleshers' Haugh. Loss of life through the increasing popularity of the sport led to the building of the first municipal baths in nearby Greenhead Street in 1878, and over the next 25 years a further nine were built in different districts of the city.[113] In 1860 an open air gymnasium was erected by way of philanthropic gift,[114] and throughout the summer months, at this period, the regattas organised by the various rowing clubs based on the Green attracted a mass spectator following on an almost weekly basis, with an annual event which lasted three days and brought participants from all over Britain. Football became very popular in the 1880s, and the Fleshers' Haugh area of the Green was laid out with football pitches.[115]

In 1886 Glasgow Corporation managed only three other parks—the West End (Kelvingrove, acquired in 1852), the South Side (Queen's Park, 1857) and Alexandra Park (acquired, 1866). The passing of the Glasgow Public Parks Act in 1878 enabled better management of the parks and empowered the Corporation to acquire additional parks. By 1914 the Parks Department ground amounted to an astonishing 1561 acres (not including the smaller open spaces and cemetaries) tended by 350 employees.

In recognition of the poor climate and short summers, Glasgow Corporation erected winter gardens or conservatories in many of the parks, and had a musical programme which could be staged either out of doors or under glass, as the weather dictated.

All of these parks, serving different parts of the city, had sporting facilities of one kind or another. When a museums policy was developed, it was done as part of the parks network. The first City Museum was established in the eighteenth century Kelvingrove House in Kelvingrove Park in 1870, and all of the others—Camphill House (1895, Queen's Park), The People's Palace (1898, Glasgow Green), Tollcross House (1905, Tollcross Park), Mosesfield House (1905, Springburn Park)—were also situated in the Parks.[116]

It was recognised that the provision of free art galleries and museums would not necessarily make such institutions popular with the working classes. This was the concern which guided those councillors who were involved in the establishment of the People's Palace on Glasgow Green, the museum, gallery, gardens and music hall built specifically for the pleasure and education of the working classes of the east end. Councillor Robert Crawford, who chaired both the Health Committee and the Museums committee, parried the criticism that the working classes did not want museums and galleries by pointing out that it had not been the dirtiest of the population who had petitioned for municipal baths, although they subsequently became the best users of them. Crawford saw public health and municipal art as being 'inextricably linked'.[117] Bailie William Bilsland, the chairman of the special committee which had guided the development of the People's Palace, recognised that most galleries were 'a sealed book to the mass of the population' and sought to run this institution 'on more attractive lines',[118] and it is evident from the many discussions which took place on the subject over the years that the People's Palace on Glasgow Green was to be the first of many, located in different parts of the city. Although the prevailing Sabbatarianism kept the People's Palace closed on a Sunday, during the week it was open from 10 am to 10 pm, to ensure that shift workers got a chance to visit it, and during the first year, it attracted over 770,000 visitors.[119] The People's Palace was loosely modelled on the earlier People's Palace for the east end of London and a considerable amount of municipal pride was invested in it. When the proprietor of the Star Music Hall pre-empted the Corporation and stole the title of their great project for his own establishment, Glasgow's Liberal businessmen bought him out and closed it down at the first opportunity.[120]

It was not unknown for Liberal businessmen to use their personal fortunes for political ends. Walter Freer was first employed as a halls organiser at Christmas 1878, when Lord Provost Sir William Collins feared that there would be outbreaks of rioting because of the City of Glasgow Bank crash. Freer was instructed to 'organise a great municipal treat to circumvent disturbance' and he hired five of the largest halls in the city, entertaining over 8,000 of the crash victims to a substantial tea and concert, with a present of a cake in a fancy box at the end of it. The entire expenses were paid from Sir William Collins' private purse.[121]

While public facilities such as parks and museum buildings often came to Glasgow as a result of private gift, Glasgow councillors, if they felt that a facility could be better run in public hands, had no hesitation in buying it for the city. This was the case when the bankrupt St Andrews Halls were purchased in 1890, and Walter Freer was installed as manager. His appointment was a personal one, and like his employers he was a Liberal and an ardent worker in the cause of temperance. The first thing he did to make the hall popular was to stage Saturday afternoon concerts at a penny and threepence admission. Within a few years he had Corporation Saturday Afternoon Concerts running in ten different city halls, with annual attendances of about 250,000 people.[122]

By 1914 Glasgow Corporation, with Freer's management, was running 22 public halls. The Corporation's musical concerts were but part of the entertainment; the City Hall was let to the Glasgow Abstainers' Union for their Saturday evening concerts on an almost permanent basis and the other halls were let regularly to similar groups for concerts, bursts and PSEs ('Pleasant Saturday Evenings'). This network of cheap, drink-free venues was a radical alternative to what the public houses could offer.

A large part of Glasgow's fine art collection, housed in the Kelvingrove Art Gallery from 1901, came by way of private gift or bequest. Industrialists such as James Reid of the Hydepark Locomotive Works, Adam Teacher, Thomas D. Smellie, James Donald and Archibald McLellan and their heirs and families left substantial collections to the city. The private tastes of these industrialists have guided the acquisitions policy ever since.

In the decades prior to the Great War, Glasgow Corporation always managed their leisure facilities with the disadvantaged labouring classes in mind. When in 1906, Cameron Corbett, MP, presented not only the 220 acre Rouken Glen Park, but also the magnificent Ardgoil Estate at Lochgoilhead to Glasgow Corporation, the Estate was hailed as the great holiday opportunity for the labouring classes. It was then that the Corporation began the practice of chartering a steamer each day of the Fair to take disadvantaged mothers and children 'chosen from among the residents in the more congested parts of the city who otherwise would not be able to afford a day at the coast' on a day trip.[123]

X: The Pursuit of the Outdoors

Every major industrial city has had its outdoor movement and Glasgow was no exception. No number of parks could substitute for the countryside, and always there was a number of people, wage slaves in an urban environment during the week, who felt the need to go out and explore what lay beyond when they could.

The rambling movement was started in 1854 with the publication of Hugh Macdonald's *Rambles around Glasgow*. Macdonald (1817-1860), a calico printer and chartist from Bridgeton, first imparted his knowledge of the countryside in a series of articles in the *Glasgow Evening Citizen*. He provided a stirring commentary not only on the landmarks and historic sites, but on the flora and fauna, and his descriptions were rich in anecdotes of local tales and events. His book went through countless editions, and imitations of it are still in print.

There is no written history of the rambling clubs which Macdonald inspired, but church, temperance and political groups formed their own rambling parties. The non-militant suffragettes and some of the women's guild co-operators favoured the Glasgow Health Culture rambling club, for example.[124] Clubs were sometimes formed on a street basis—about 50 persons from Elcho Street Calton rambled regularly together in the 1920s.

As ramblers were not given to taking minutes and printing programmes, however, it is difficult to assess accurately how popular and widespread the movement was at any given time.[125]

By the end of the 1890s, Glasgow was in the grip of a cycling craze. The cyclists yearbook for 1897 lists 42 cycling clubs in Glasgow, and an additional 3 in Govan and others in Pollokshaws and Thornliebank. In August 1897 the craze reached its peak, when the world championships of the International Cyclists Association were held in Celtic Park, Celtic FC paying the costs of a special cement racing path.[126]

Cycling, like rambling, was a relatively cheap pastime giving the working classes an opportunity to get out into the country. Even so, cycles were in extensive use in the city; the Scotia Music Hall allowed free storage of machines to visiting patrons.[127]

For some sections of the community, cycling became more a way of life than a mode of transport. It fitted in particularly well with socialist philosophy, and there was a league of Clarion Cycling Clubs in Glasgow, based on the organisation and newspaper established by Robert Blatchford in 1891. The Clarion cyclists sold the Clarion newspaper, spread the principles of socialism and enjoyed the companionship of the club.

The Clarion Scouts and Campers were also popular in Glasgow. They had two main summer camps—at Catacol on the Isle of Arran, and at Carbeth to the north of Glasgow. These camps ensured that families got a good healthy summer holiday. The tents usually had wooden floors, and at Carbeth in the beautiful Blane Valley, the sympathetic landowner allowed the campers their own swimming pond and diving board. No canvas is impervious to a wést coast summer, however, and in 1918, after two decades of camping, the first Clarion huts were built at Carbeth.[128]

In spite of heavy opposition from neighbouring landlords, a model holiday camp, which is still in existence, developed, demonstrating the kind of working-class holiday facility which might have developed on the Clyde Coast and the Ardgoil Estate, given the goodwill and right circumstances. Carbeth was the only place in Scotland where Glasgow's working classes were invited to have a real share in the countryside.

XI: Conclusions

Undoubtedly, Glasgow's labouring classes had more choice of and opportunity for their leisure pursuits at the end of the period than they did at the beginning. As one social commentator pointed out, the chief advantage of living in Glasgow in the 1890s was the speed and cheapness with which one could get out of it,[129] and in times of depression, the unemployed always made use of this.

Were there any aspects in which people became worse off? While much research needs to be done, a point of possible consideration is that the Glasgow working classes from the eighteenth to the mid-nineteenth century had more opportunity of enjoying meaningful works of art at first hand. Some of the best artists—Hugh William Williams, Alexander Naysmith, John Knox, William Leighton Leitch, Sam Bough—were earning their living in Glasgow painting panoramas and scenic backdrops for theatres and circuses. For a small sum of money one could visit Knox's panorama of the taking and burning of Moscow for an artistic experience and a lecture in contemporary events with sound and lighting effects.[130] A century later, however, art in Glasgow was the prisoner of the art gallery, limited by the choice of an industrial benefactor and presented out of context without explanation or interpretation. The flickering silent movie could in no way compare with the all-round experience of a panorama.

What were the broad developments in popular culture over the period? One historian looking at the development of the Socialist Sunday Schools, the Clarion movement and other similar bodies, remarks on the development of a 'counter culture' in Glasgow prior to the Great War, and of the ability to go from the cradle to the grave without stepping outside of the socialist movement.[131] To view these developments as the property of any one group of people conducted as part of some kind of underground movements would however be quite wrong. One could, taking into consideration the similar cultural networks set up by the temperance and evangelical societies, make the same kind of claim for their adherents.

Although there are many citable instances of individuals being born into socialist, temperance or evangelical households, growing up in them and availing themselves of the leisure opportunities within them and never having to look outside them, this was not the norm. The important factor was that all of these different social elements were providing a wide range of leisure and cultural opportunities which were not only open to all, but which were offered with the kind of zeal and enthusiasm of which only people who want to reform, save or re-structure their society are capable. What may have been a counter-cultural manifestation in the 1850s, as in the case of the Abstainers' Union concerts, was the dominant culture by 1900. Yet not even the reformist Abstainers' Union was satisfied, and it is this expectation of a better future, the hope of things to come and the burning desire for change which marks Glasgow as being quite different from London or Manchester at this period. James Burn Russell, the Medical Officer of Health for Glasgow from 1871-1904 described his time of office as 'years of intense convictions, burning desires, and remarkable progress in the development of Glasgow towards the possibility of a clean and healthy life for all its citizens'. This incandescence was more than matched by the concern felt for the cultural welfare of the people.

While cultural segregation is always possible, the eclectic nature of the cultural milieu in Glasgow and variety of opportunities available should be borne in mind. James O'Connor Kessack, one of the best and most articulate propagandists of the ILP before the Great War became a socialist almost by accident, when, returning from church one Sunday, Bible under his arm, he stopped out of sympathy to help a socialist speaker who was having a rough time with his street corner oratory.[132]

While temperance bodies held their concerts in the city halls, political groups were equally at home in the music halls on Sundays. The Social Democratic Federation met in the People's Palace while the Clarion were at home in the Pavilion and the ILP in the Lyceum.

While few have attempted to summarise the state of popular culture in Glasgow in the early twentieth century, Sean Damer's assessment of the existence of 'a working class political culture (a partial proletarian hegemony in Gramsci's sense) based on the work of the ILP' and touching a far greater number of people than the membership of the ILP, because of the opportunity of personal and social fulfilment in a wide range of areas,[133] is probably fairly accurate.

Much work needs to be done on specialist areas of popular culture and leisure activities before any enduring conclusions can be drawn. The evolution of the Scotch comic and his bigger brother the Nigger Minstrel in Scottish variety needs to be examined in detail. The development of Glasgow pantomime, its political content and social message needs examination. The appearance of political theatre during the years of agitation for women's suffrage, and its relationship with kailyard dramatics should be studied. The history of local cinema and cine variety is still imperfectly understood. All of these should prove interesting and rewarding fields of research.

Notes

GULSC Glasgow University Library Special Collections
MLG Mitchell Library, Glasgow
SRA Strathclyde Regional Archives
PP People's Palace
   1. Kellow Chesney, *The Victorian Underworld* (1970); Gareth Stedman Jones, *Outcast London: A Study in the Relationship between Classes in Victorian*

Society (1976), and 'Working Class Culture and Working Class Politics in London, 1870-1900. Notes on the re-making of a working class', *Journal of Social History* (1984).

2. Martha Vicinus, *The Industrial Muse* (Croom Helm, London, 1974).

3. David Murray, *Early Burgh Organisation in Scotland* (1924), vol 1., p. 324.

4. But see Marion Hay's, *Glasgow Theatres and Music Halls: A Guide*, Glasgow Room Publications No. 15, Mitchell Library (1980), which is an excellent starting point for any person researching the subject. It is an internal publication, available at the Mitchell Library.

5. Paul Sheridan, *Penny Theatres of Victorian London* (1981).

6. Ray Challinor, *John S. Clarke: Parliamentarian, Poet and Lion Tamer* (1977). See also William Knox, *Scottish Labour Leaders,1918-1939* (1984).

7. For an early biographical sketch of Pickard see *The Eagle*, 11 February 1909. His obituary is in the *Glasgow Herald*, 31 October 1964.

8. J.H. Muir, *Glasgow in 1901* (1901), pp. 185-6.

9. J.A. Hammerton, *Sketches from Glasgow* (1893), pp. 121-2.

10. Poet's Box Collection, Glasgow Room, MLG.

11. Tape recording of Ceclia Russell, pawnbroker's assistant and suffragette (b.1895), 1976.

12. Poet's Box Collection, Glasgow Room, MLG.

13. *Quiz*, 22 July 1881.

14. *Forward*, 22 March 1913.

15. *The Bailie*, 15 April 1908.

16. Broadsheet, PP.

17. *Glasgow Herald*, 17 October 1866.

18. *Ibid.*, 8 September 1884.

19. P.H.J.H. Gordon, *Friendly Societies in England, 1815-1875* (1961), and *Self Help—Voluntary Associations in the 19th Century* (1973) are the standard works for England.

20. Elspeth King, *Barrapatter—An Oral History of Glasgow's Barrows* (1983).

21. See for example 'The Bargain Barrows' in *Glasgow Herald*, 6 March 1908.

22. GULSC, Bh 11-x9.

23. GULSC, Bh 14-x5/6.

24. GULSC, Bh 26-E11.

25. GULSC, Mul-x11/30.

26. GULSC, Bh 14-x5.

27. GULSC, Mul-x11.

28. *Ibid.*

29. See George MacGregor. *The Collected Writings of Dougal Graham, Skellat Bellman of Glasgow* (1883) and John Strathesk, ed., *Hawkie, the Autobiography of a Gangrel* (1888).

30. *Ibid.*, pp. 90-1, 93-100.

31. They include James Lindsay, Jr of King Street, Nelson Street and Trongate (fl. 1848-1909), J. Bristow of 203 Gallowgate (fl. 1850-1856), R. McIntosh of 96 King Street, Calton (fl. 1850-1878), D. Scott of 271 Gallowgate (fl.1840s), Robert Harrison of 29 Jamaica Street (fl.1840s), W. Carse (fl. 1828-1837), Mayne & Co (fl. 1822-1826), John Muir (1826-1844).

32. David Murray, *Early Burgh Organisation*, vol. 1, p. 341.
33. Alexander Sinclair, *Fifty Years of Newspaper Life, 1845-1895* (Glasgow, 1895), pp. 198-207.
34. See *Scotch Poetry Consisting of Songs, Odes, Anthems and Epigrams by Alexander Rodger, an Operative Weaver of Glasgow* (London, 1821), and Alexander Rodger, *Petere Cornclips: A Tale of Real Life with other Poems and Songs* (Glasgow, 1827), and also his *Stray Leaves* (Glasgow, 1842).
35. GULSC, Mu23-yi.
36. Mss. note in volume Mu 23-yi, GULSC.
37. Robert Reid (Senex), *Glasgow Past and Present* (1884), vol. 1, pp. 261-85.
38. Poet's Box Collection, Glasgow Room, MLG.
39. GULSC, Mu 1-x11.
40. GULSC, Bh 14-x5.
41. Rudolph Kenna and Anthony Mooney, *People's Palaces: Victorian and Edwardian Pubs of Scotland* (1983), p. 19. John Urie, *Reminiscences of Eighty Years* (1908), pp. 95-6.
42. Charles Donaldson, *From Figg to Tunney and Who's Who in Sport* (Glasgow, 1928), pp. 79-84.
43. *The Pepperbox*, 1 August 1840.
44. An Old Stager, *Stage Reminiscences, Being Recollections, Chiefly Personal, of Celebrated Theatrical and Musical Performers during the Last Forty Years* (Glasgow, 1866), pp. 87-100. See also Walter Baynham, *The Glasgow Stage* (1892), pp. 114-5.
45. Old Stager, *Stage Reminiscences*, pp. 115-7.
46. John Henry Alexander, *Letter to the Lord Provost, Magistrates, Town Council and Citizens of Glasgow on the Subject of a Pamphlet Addressed to Them by an Individual Styling Himself 'Walter Dennistoun Esq'* (Glasgow, 1835).
47. David Prince Miller, *The Life of Miller the Showman* (Glasgow, April-May, 1842). GULSC. This autobiography was published in Leeds in a complete volume, which is different from the first issue.
48. GULSC, Mu 24-b20. In the Court of Justiciary, 23 December 1841, Answers for John Henry Alexander, Proprietor and Manager of the Theatre Royal.
49. *John Henry Alexander of the Glasgow Theatre Royal versus John Henry Anderson of the Minor Theatre* (Glasgow, 1841), p. 78. See also J.B. Findlay, *Anderson and his Theatre* (Isle of Wight, 1967).
50. Miller, *Life of a Showman* (Leeds, 1849), pp. 111-5.
51. John Urie, *Reminiscences of Eighty Years* (1908), pp. 78-9.
52. *Report by the Town Clerk as to the Common Lands of the City and Royal Burgh of Glasgow, and especially as to Glasgow Green* (1891), p. 18.
53. *Illustrated London News*, November 1845, p. 349 and November 1848, p. 333.
54. J.F.S. Gordon, *Glasghu Facies* (1872), vol. 1., pp. 580-1.
55. Old Stager, *Stage Reminiscences*, pp. 171-7.
56. J.F.S. Gordon, *Glasghu Facies*, vol. 1, pp. 577-9. For a full discussion of the character and literature of the Glasgow Fair, see Murray, *Early Burgh Organisation*, vol. 1, pp. 335-42.

57. Murray, *Early Burgh Organisation*, p. 335. There were highly unpleasant localised customs associated with it until the early nineteenth century, such as the cock shooting which took place at Govan. See 'Senex', *Glasgow Past and Present*, vol. 2, p. 97.

58. The riot during the King's birthday celebrations of 1821 was particularly spectacular. The crowd built a huge bonfire in front of the High Court. The military were brought out and charged the crowd, who in fear rushed to the wooden bridge which collapsed into the Clyde under the weight. See broadsheet, GULSC, Bh 14-x5, and the *Glasgow Courier*, 24 April 1821.

59. *Glasgow Herald*, 16 July 1840.

60. MLG Cuttings Book, *The Dark Side of Glasgow* (1870-1872), pp. 18-9.

61. 'Senex', *Glasgow Past and Present*, vol. III, pp. 313-68. Freak shows remained popular until 1914 and beyond, but from the 1870s, were contained in the various waxworks—Fell's Waxworks, 101 Trongate (1875-1904), Crouch's Wonderland, 137 Argyle Street (1888-1912), Macleod's at 151 Trongate (1874-1906) and Pickard's Panopticaon, also in Trongate (1906-1938). These establishments were a combination of waxworks, freak shows, panoramas, cinematograph, museum, menagerie, picture house and variety theatre. A good surviving example of this type of establishment is the Grevin Museum (1882) in the Boulevard Monmatre, Paris.

62. David Prince Millar, *Life of a Showman, to which is added Managerial Struggles, by David Price Millar, late of the Adelphi Theatre, Glasgow* (Leeds, 1849), pp. 14-5.

63. Millar, *Ibid.*, pp. 141-3.

64. Shadow, *Midnight Scenes and Social Photographs being Sketches of Life in the Streets, Wynds and Dens of the City* (Glasgow, 1858), p. 85.

65. Old Glasgow Street Songs (Formerly Bailie's Library Collection), MLG.

66. Walter Freer, *My Life and Memories* (1929), pp. 34-6. W.F. Frame, *W.F. Frame 'The Man you Know' Tells the Story of His Own Life* (Glasgow, n/d), pp. 13-35.

67. Frame, *W.F. Frame*, pp. 31-42.

68. 'The Dark Side of Glasgow'. Cuttings book of reports on Sheebeens, Brothels, Dancing Halls, Singing Saloons and Baby Farming in Glasgow, printed by the *North British Daily Mail*, 1870-1872, MLG. There is plenty of oral evidence which indicates that dancing was still conducted in this way in the decade before the Great War—PP tape recording of Lizzie Dougan (1880-1982) in 1980, and GN 17/1—evidence of Mary Robertson (b.1900).

69. Urie, *Reminiscences*, pp. 60-1.

70. Gordon, *Glasghu Facies*, vol. 1, pp. 579-81.

71. For a fuller discussion of all aspects of temperance, see Elspeth King, *Scotland Sober and Free—the Temperance Movement, 1829-1979* (1979).

72. *Sixty Years of Work, 1854-1914. The Story of the Glasgow Abstainers' Union* (Glasgow, 1914), pp. 5-7.

73. Freer, *My Life*, pp. 30-1. SRA TD432 15/2, Glasgow Abstainers' Union bound volumes of programmes for Saturday Evening Concerts, 29 December 1860 and 5 January 1861.

74. Freer, *My Life*, p. 42.

75. PP. Glasgow Temperance Crusaders. Pleasant Sunday Evenings. Printed list of speakers and total attendances from 1910-1929.
76. Freer, *My Life*, pp. 78-9.
77. Elspeth King, 'Peter Fyfe, Photographer' in *Cencrastus*, no. 14, (1983), pp. 10-5.
78. *Glasgow Evening Citizen*, 30 September 1867.
79. Freer, *My Life*, pp. 92-4.
80. See Billy Kay, *Odyssey—Voices from Scotland's Recent Past*, II, (1982), pp. 89-99. William Gallacher, *Last Memoirs* (1966).
81. William Knox, *Scottish Labour Leaders, 1918-1939* (1984), pp. 38-40. This depressing assessment of popular culture between the wars is based on an imperfect understanding of what had gone before.
82. *Illustrated London News*, 8 November 1884.
83. Elspeth King, *The People's Palace and Glasgow Green* (1985), pp. 9-18.
84. MLG. People's Palace Music Hall programmes.
85. *Forward*, 19 October 1907.
86. Andrew McQueen, *Echoes of Old Clyde Paddle Wheels* (1924), pp. 38-56.
87. Ian Maclagan, 'Rothesay Harbour, 1752-1975', *Transactions of the Buteshire Natural History Society* 19 (1976), pp. 24-60.
88. R.D. Whyte, 'Rothesay 100 Years Ago', *Transactions of the Buteshire Natural History Society* II (1935), p. 48.
89. Ian C. MacArthur, *The Caledonian Steam Packet Company Limited* (1971), pp. 10-1.
90. Alan Leach, 'Rothesay Tramways. A Brief History, 1882-1936', *Transactions of the Buteshire Natural History Society* 17 (1969), p. 5.
91. McQueen, *Echoes*, pp. 61-7.
92. Muir, *Glasgow in 1901*, p. 194.
93. Frame, *W.F. Frame*, pp. 90-109.
94. Barbara and Murray Grigor, *Scotch Myths—An Explanation of Scotchness* (Exhibition booklet, 1981).
95. Catherine Gordon, *The Lamp of Memory—Scott and the Artist* (1979), pp. ii-iv.
96. MLG pamphlet, *A Guide to the Glasgow Fair* (n/d, c.1850), p. 15.
97. SRA, TD423 15/2, 29 December 1860. Glasgow Abstainers' Union City Hall Saturday Evening Concerts. Bound volumes of programmes.
98. PP Bound Programmes. Good Templars Harmonic Association Concerts. 29th Season, 10 September 1898 to 4 March 1899.
99. PP Tape recording of James Myatt (b.1900) of Gallowgate and the east end.
100. MLG. People's Palace Music Hall programmes.
101. MLG. Royal Princess's Theatre Pantomime Librettos. 'Babes in the Wood or Harlequin Rob Roy'. Written by F.R. Goodyear and Fred Locke (1880), pp. 1-27.
102. *Ibid.*, Robinson Crusoe (1897), p. 43.
103. Scottish Film Council, *Fifty Years at the Pictures* (1947), pp. 1-3. See also Janet McBain, *Pictures Past—Scottish Cinemas Remembered* (1975), pp. 21-4.

104. *Glasgow Amusements and Pastimes* ('delivered free every Monday morning to all places of public resort'), 10 May 1897.
105. *Forward*, 15 March 1913.
106. SRA MP31/13-18. Sunday Trading in Scotland. Municipal Conference held in Glasgow, 23 October 1900.
107. PP tape recording, James Myatt.
108. *Forward*, 15 March 1913.
109. Elspeth King, *The People's Palace*, pp. 27-43.
110. James Paton, 'A People's Palace', Museums Association Annual Report (1898), pp. 50-1.
111. Harry McShane and Joan Smith, *No Mean Fighter* (1978), pp. 12-4, 17, 20-1.
112. P. Walsh, *Glasgow Entertainments during the Last Fifty Years* (c.1930), pp. 11-2.
113. *Municipal Glasgow: Its Evolution and Enterprises* (Glasgow Corporation, 1914), pp. 95-9.
114. SRA, MP 19/721, 19/730, Excerpt from Town Council Minutes, 7 June 1860.
115. P. Walsh, *Glasgow Entertainments*, pp. 9-11.
116. *Municipal Glasgow*, pp. 34-47, 162-84.
117. Robert Crawford, *The People's Palace of the Arts for the City of Glasgow* (Ruskin Society, 1891), pp. 3-8.
118. *Glasgow Herald*, 24 January 1898.
119. James Paton, 'A People's Palace', pp. 55-6, 62.
120. Scottish Record Office, Limited Company Papers for the Glasgow People's Palace Company Limited, Ref. BT 2/2782.
121. Freer, *My Life*, pp. 24-5.
122. *Ibid.*, pp. 87-90.
123. *Municipal Glasgow* (1914), pp. 183-4.
124. PP. Copy negative collection of postcard photographs of Norma Sloan, socialist and member of the Women's Freedom League.
125. There is a great deal of scattered oral information on rambling which needs collecting. It seems to have been a rather unremarkable working-class activity which generated no literature beyond the odd postcard. See however *The Sylvan Rambles—Minutes of First Year's Rambles Published at the Request of the Members* (Glasgow, 1886). This group was limited to 19 persons who during 1885 travelled 353 miles by rail and 87 miles on foot.
126. *The Bike—A Journal for Scottish Cyclists*, 4 August 1897.
127. *Glasgow Amusements and Pastimes*, 10 August 1896.
128. PP and MLG, Lantern slide collections, Glasgow Clarion Scouts.
129. J.A. Hammerton, *Sketches from Glasgow* (1893), pp. 165-6.
130. The whole phenomenon of panorama painting in Scotland needs investigation. It was obviously a major source of employment and income for artists—John Knox (1778-1845) for example produced a panorama annually in Glasgow from 1809-1814. There were four or five semi-permanent panorama buildings—in Saltmarket, the Queen's Rooms, 67 Buchanan Street, the 'large Wooden building adjoining the new theatre' in Queen Street (1805) and the rotunda building in Buchanan Street. One major

panorama building survives in the Netherlands, housing Mesdag's maritime panorama (painted 1881) and complete with sand, marram grass and fishermans' gear. See Ronald de Leeus, John Silleris, Charles Dumas, *The Hague School: Dutch Masters of the 19th Century* (London, 1983), pp. 85-8. I am indebted to my colleague Michael Donnelly for these references.

131. Douglas Allen, 'Culture and the Scottish Labour Movement', *Scottish Labour History Society Journal* (1980), pp. 30-8.
132. 'How I Became a Socialist', *Forward*, 20 July 1907.
133. Sean Damer, 'Review', *History Workshop Journal* 18 (1984), pp. 199-203.

SELECT BIBLIOGRAPHY

Bell, James and James Paton. *Glasgow: Its Municipal Organizatior and Administration* (Glasgow, 1896).

Burnett, J. *A Social History of Housing, 1815-1970* (1980).

Cage, R.A. *The Scottish Poor Law, 1745-1845* (Scottish Academic Press, Edinburgh, 1981).

Cage, R.A. 'The Standard of Living Debate: Glasgow, 1800-1850' *Journal of Economic History* (March, 1983), pp. 175-82.

Chalmers, A.K. *The Health of Glasgow, 1818-1925* (Glasgow, 1930).

Chapman, S.D., ed. *The History of Working-class Housing* (Newton Abbot, 1971).

Checkland, Olive and Margaret Lamb, eds. *Health Care as Socia History: The Glasgow Case* (Aberdeen University Press, 1982).

Checkland, S.G. *The Upas Tree: Glasgow, 1875-1975* (University of Glasgow Press, Glasgow, 1981).

Cunnison, J. and J.B.S. Gilfillan, eds. *The Third Statistical Accoun: of Scotland: Glasgow* (Collins, Glasgow, 1958).

Daunton, M.J. *House and Home in the Victorian City: Working-class Housing, 1850-1914* (1983).

Flinn, M., ed. *Scottish Population History* (Cambridge University Press, 1977).

Gauldie, E. *Cruel Habitations: A History of Working-class Housing, 1780-1918* (1974).

Gibb, Andrew. *Glasgow: The Making of a City* (Croom Helm, Beckenham, 1983).

Gordon, G. and B. Dicks, eds. *Scottish Urban History* (Aberdeen, 1983).

Gourvish, T.R. 'The Cost of Living in Glasgow in the Early Nineteenth Century', *Economic History Review* (February, 1972), pp. 65-80.

Johnston, Thomas. *The History of the Working Classes in Scotland* (Glasgow, Forward Publishing, n.d.).

King, Elspeth. *The People's Palace and Glasgow Green* (1985).

Logue, K. *Popular Disturbances in Scotland, 1780-1815* (Edinburgh, 1979).

Murray, N. *The Scottish Handloom Weavers, 1790-1850* (Edinburgh, 1978).

Russell, J.B. *Public Health Administration in Glasgow* (Glasgow, 1905).

Slaven, A. *The Development of the West of Scotland, 1750-1960* (Routledge & Kegan Paul, London, 1975).

Slaven, A. and D. Aldcroft, eds. *Business, Banking and Urban History* (John Donald, Edinburgh, 1982).

Tarn, N.J. *Working Class Housing in Nineteenth-Century Britain* (1971).

Tarn, J.N. *Five Per Cent Philanthropy. An Account of Housing in Urban Areas Between 1840 and 1914* (1973).

Wilson, A. *The Chartist Movement in Scotland* (Manchester, 1970).

NOTES ON CONTRIBUTORS

John Butt

> Professor, Economic History, Strathclyde University, Glasgow. With J.A. Kinloch, *History of the Scottish Co-operative Wholesale Society* (Glasgow, 1981); *James 'Paraffin' Young, 1811-1863* (Edinburgh, 1983); edited with G. Gordon, *Strathclyde—Changing Horizons* (Edinburgh, 1985).

R.A. Cage

> Senior Lecturer, Economic History, University of New England, Armidale, New South Wales, Australia. *The Scottish Poor Law, 1745-1845* (Edinburgh, 1981); editor, *The Scots Abroad: Labour, Capital, Enterprise, 1750-1914* (Beckenham, 1985).

Elspeth King

> Curator, People's Palace, Glasgow Green. *The Scottish Women's Suffrage Movement* (1978); *Scotland Sober & Free: The Temperance Movement, 1829-1979* (1979); *The People's Palace* (1985).

I.G.C. Hutchison

> Lecturer, History, University of Stirling, Scotland.

INDEX

For Product Safety Concerns and Information please contact our EU
representative GPSR@taylorandfrancis.com
Taylor & Francis Verlag GmbH, Kaufingerstraße 24, 80331 München, Germany

www.ingramcontent.com/pod-product-compliance
Ingram Content Group UK Ltd.
Pitfield, Milton Keynes, MK11 3LW, UK
UKHW021829240425
457818UK00006B/131